The Gardening from Which? Guide to
PESTS AND DISEASES

The Gardening from Which? Guide to
PESTS AND DISEASES

PUBLISHED BY
CONSUMERS' ASSOCIATION AND HODDER & STOUGHTON

Which? Books are commissioned and researched by
The Association for Consumer Research
and published by Consumers' Association
2 Marylebone Road, London NW1 4DX
and Hodder and Stoughton, 47 Bedford Square, London WC1B 3DP

Designed by Linda Blakemore

First edition October 1991

Copyright © 1991 Consumers' Association Ltd

British Library Cataloguing in Publication Data
The Gardening from Which? guide to
pests and diseases
1. Gardens. Pests. Control.
2. Gardens. Diseases. Control
635.049
ISBN 0–340–55000–7

Thanks for choosing this book . . .
If you find it useful, we'd like to hear from you. Even if it
doesn't live up to your expectations or do the job you were
expecting, we'd still like to know. Then we can take your
comments into account when preparing similar titles or,
indeed, the next edition of the book. Address your letter to
the Publishing Manager at Consumers' Association,
FREEPOST, 2 Marylebone Road, London NW1 4DX.
We look forward to hearing from you.

This book was devised and written by the staff of
Gardening from Which? To subscribe
see details on page 137.

Typeset, printed and bound in Great Britain
by Jarrold Printing, Norwich

CONTENTS

INTRODUCTION

Garden plants are continually under attack from all kinds of pests and diseases. Fortunately, a plant's natural defences enable it to withstand most attacks. It is only when the pest or disease threatens the life of the plant, significantly reduces yields from fruit and vegetable crops or spoils your enjoyment of your garden that you need to take action.

The aims of this guide are two-fold. Firstly, it helps you recognise individual symptoms and identify the problem affecting your plants. Brief descriptions of symptoms are highlighted throughout the book and over 240 common problems are illustrated with photographs to make diagnosis easier. Symptoms are listed for each part of each plant. Secondly, the book sets out all the best options for dealing with the cause of each problem, recommending **control** and **prevention** whenever possible.

Control covers anything you can do immediately to remedy the problem, or at least stop it from getting worse. **Prevention** explains how you can take measures to avoid a recurrence of a problem the following year. Wherever possible, several options are given. Often it is not simply a question of organic or chemical approaches. The pragmatic gardener will combine the best of each. In many cases good gardening practice – keeping the plants well fed, watered and pruned, and the garden tidy – will go a long way towards reducing serious pest and disease problems.

Not all problems are caused by pest or disease attacks, and details of those caused by physiological or environmental factors are also included in relevant chapters. In addition there is a short chapter on the problems that affect lawns, and another which will help you identify and deal with troublesome weeds.

PESTICIDES

The use of pesticides is an emotive subject. Whether you use them in your garden or not is a matter of personal choice. This guide will tell you when the application of pesticides is one of the best options and will point you towards the most appropriate product. There are two approaches to using chemicals:
■ To treat them as a last resort (applying only when attacks get out of hand)
■ To use pesticides on a regular basis as part of a preventative programme – worthwhile on soft fruit or roses, for example.

Whichever method you adopt, you will need to concentrate on trying to prevent problems arising in the first place by adopting good garden hygiene, using traps and barriers and planting resistant varieties of plants where appropriate.

GARDEN CHEMICALS GUIDE
On pages 130–136 you will find a guide to all the garden insecticides and fungicides available nationally at the time of going to press. These Tables will guide you to the most appropriate products for dealing with the major pests and diseases in your garden.

However, since labels are updated and changed from time to time and new products are introduced, we intend to update the Garden Chemicals Guide periodically. Details of how you can obtain updates will be published in *Gardening from Which?* In any case, you should always check the label before you buy or use any garden chemical.

The Garden Chemicals Guide also includes information on weedkillers, application equipment and advice on using garden chemicals safely.

COMMON PROBLEMS

Some pests, such as slugs and snails, greenfly and blackfly, and diseases like grey mould and powdery mildew are just as likely to cause problems in the fruit or vegetable patch, ornamental borders or in the greenhouse. This chapter covers in detail these and other pests and diseases that can occur anywhere in the garden.

TOP TEN PESTS AND DISEASES

Listed below are the most common pest and disease problems reported by *Gardening from Which?* readers in regular surveys. Bear in mind that the order is likely to change from year to year.

1. Slugs and/or snails
2. Greenfly
3. Blackfly
4. Blackspot
5. Mildew
6. Whitefly
7. Caterpillars
8. Grey mould
9. Rust diseases
10. There are many candidates for this spot. Depending on what you grow and the season, this could be carrot fly, maggots in fruit, soil grubs or spider mites, for example.

With the exception of blackspot, which attacks only roses, most of these common pests and diseases occur on a whole range of plants. Different species of caterpillar, rust and whitefly attack different types of plant and are covered in the relevant chapters, but the ubiquitous offenders are covered over the next five pages.

NOTIFIABLE PESTS AND DISEASES

Some pests and diseases are considered to be so serious by the Ministry of Agriculture, Fisheries and Food (MAFF), that any occurrence must be reported to them. The list of notifiable pests and diseases changes as new problems are discovered or existing ones get out of hand. For example, fireblight was once a notifiable disease but efforts to contain it have now been abandoned. Most notifiable pests and diseases are rare in the UK, but some commonly occur in Europe: Colorado beetle, for example. You are very unlikely to come across any in your garden, but a few can occur from time to time. If you do find, or suspect, any of the following, contact your nearest MAFF Office or MAFF Harpenden Laboratory, Hatching Green, Harpenden, Herts AL5 2BD, or the Department of Agriculture in Northern Ireland or Scotland: Colorado beetle; plum pox; potato cyst nematode; South American leaf miner; wart disease of potatoes; western flower thrips.

SLUGS AND SNAILS

Common slug

Slug and snail damage to hosta leaves

Garden snails

Nibbled, shredded leaves and trails of slime are the classic signs of slug or snail damage.

Slugs and snails are found in every garden: there could be up to 50 in each square metre of soil. Well-kept gardens provide them with perfect living conditions – water, loose soil and succulent young plants. The warm, moist conditions that are ideal for plant growth are also ideal for slugs and snails. They can consume a large number of seedlings overnight and will have disappeared under stones or into the soil by the time you find the damage.

Apart from the large, surface-feeding garden and field slugs, there are also small, black keeled slugs which feed mainly underground, damaging roots and tubers. Amongst the snails, the garden snail is the most destructive species, but banded snails can also be a nuisance.

Slugs and snails do have natural enemies such as birds, frogs and hedgehogs, but even if you encourage these in your garden, they are unlikely to be effective when conditions for slugs and snails are ideal.

Rather than trying to eradicate slugs and snails from your garden, which is an impossible task, concentrate on protecting your most vulnerable plants: seedlings, young vegetables, emerging herbaceous perennials and strawberries.

CHEMICAL CONTROLS

Chemicals enable you to kill slugs and snails without coming into contact with the pests.

SLUG PELLETS

Most contain metaldelyde, a chemical that breaks down fairly rapidly leaving no soil residue. Methiocarb – the active ingredient in pbi Slug Gard – is more persistent and more toxic to birds and mammals. Blue pellets are less attractive to birds. Apply pellets during mild weather in the spring, before any damage occurs, and again in the autumn, as these are the main periods of slug activity.

Scatter them thinly once a fortnight (as a rough guide, aim for a pellet every 7.5–15cm; 3–6in or so). Be prepared to re-apply them after heavy rain.

LIQUID CONTROLS

Slug killers based on aluminium sulphate can be watered into the soil around vulnerable plants. They are less likely to harm other animals than slug pellets but they can prove expensive.

NON-CHEMICAL CONTROLS

As far as possible remove anything that slugs can shelter under, including unused pots, bricks and rubble, dead leaves and other plant remains.

Dig the soil over to expose the slugs and eggs to birds. Digging in frosty or windy weather is especially effective.

Particularly vulnerable young plants can be very effectively protected with barriers cut from plastic bottles. Cut rings about 10cm (4in) high and push them 2.5cm (1in) into the ground.

SOIL PESTS

Millipede

Chafer grub

Cutworm

Leatherjacket

■ SOIL GRUBS

Several kinds of soil-living grubs can damage garden plants, particularly seedlings and young plants. They are most likely to be a problem in gardens reclaimed from grassland or which have become overgrown.
Chafer grubs These white, C-shaped grubs up to 4cm (1½in) long are the larvae of chafer beetles. They feed mainly on roots, causing plants to wilt and die, and may also damage lawns. Adult beetles nibble leaves.
Cutworms These are plump, pale brown or white caterpillars up to 4cm (1½in) long. They are active during the summer, feeding on the soil surface at night. They often sever young plants and seedlings at soil level.
Leatherjackets These are the larvae of craneflies, up to 4cm (1½in) long. They feed on grass roots and are mainly a problem of lawns (see page 59).
Control If damage is limited search the soil nearby and remove any large grubs or caterpillars found – leave them for the birds to eat.
Prevention Dust vulnerable plants with a soil insecticide (see

right). Winter digging will destroy a proportion of them on borders and the vegetable garden. A few particularly vulnerable plants can be protected with sections cut from plastic drink bottles pushed 2.5–5cm (1–2in) into the soil around them.

■ WOODLICE

Stems and leaves of seedlings and young plants nibbled
Large numbers of woodlice can damage plants raised from seed in the garden or in the greenhouse. However, they usually feed on dead plant material.
Control Dust them in their hiding places with a contact insecticide or scatter pbi Slug Gard pellets thinly around vulnerable plants.
Prevention Keep the garden tidy.

■ MILLIPEDES

Millipedes usually feed on dead plant matter. Occasionally they may also eat the roots of young plants or seedlings, causing them to wilt and die. They have many

legs, are slow-moving and tend to curl up if disturbed.
Control Chemicals are not usually worthwhile. Methiocarb slug pellets (pbi Slug Gard) will kill millipedes.
Prevention Keep garden rubbish and debris to a minimum.

SOIL PESTICIDES

Soil pesticides contain relatively persistent chemicals and they may kill beneficial creatures such as ground beetles, spiders and centipedes. If you use them (see page 132 for those available) always follow the label instructions carefully. Do not use them on vegetables that are nearly ready to be harvested. As there are no organic soil pesticides, gardeners who do not use chemicals should rely on gardening techniques, and natural predators.

BENEFICIAL SOIL CREATURES
Not all the animals you find when digging are harmful. Earthworms break up the soil and incorporate organic matter, and their burrowing helps to improve drainage and aeration. Although their casts can be a nuisance on lawns, worms are worth encouraging because of their beneficial effects.
  Ground beetles and rove beetles, of which their are over 1000 species, are nearly all active predators – of worms, soil grubs, insects and even slugs. Their larvae, too, are useful predators.
  Centipedes, which, unlike millipedes, have only one pair of legs per body segment and move quickly, are also predators.

MAMMALS AND BIRDS

Bird damage to apples

■ MOLES

Moles can deface a lawn with their tunnelling activities and mole hills (see page 59) and can be a nuisance in vegetable plots or bedding displays.

They are very difficult to get rid of. Mole smokes and unpleasant smells like mothballs or creosote-soaked rags may expel them for a while, but they will return. The only long-term solution is to call in a mole catcher to trap or poison them. As mole runs often extend over many gardens you may need to combine forces with neighbours.

■ MICE

Small rodents do most damage in the vegetable garden (see page 91) but may also dig up bulbs (see page 52). Trapping is probably the only long-term solution if damage is severe.

■ RABBITS

Rabbits (and in some areas hares) can damage garden plants, especially vegetables or young shoots. They may also strip bark from young trees in winter.

The only sure way to exclude them from part of the garden is to erect a wire mesh fence 90cm (3ft) above the ground, with 30cm (12in) buried. Half of the buried portion should be bent outwards at right angles to stop rabbits burrowing underneath. Plastic spiral tree guards should protect young trees.

■ DEER

They can damage new growth on garden plants in the spring in some areas. If they are a serious problem consider erecting a wire mesh fence at least 1.8m (6ft) high.

■ BIRDS

Most birds are a welcome sight in the garden but some can be a real nuisance.

Bullfinches damage the buds of gooseberries, currants, fruit trees and ornamental trees and shrubs from November to April. Blackbirds and thrushes may eat or spoil ripening apples and pears, strawberries, raspberries and currants. Tits occasionally damage buds while searching for insects. Starlings will strip cherry trees of fruit. Pigeons and pheasants can strip overwintering brassicas and damage seedling vegetables. Sparrows will tear up brightly coloured flowers and occasionally young vegetables.

The only real answer to bird damage is to erect a physical barrier between them and vulnerable plants.
■ 10cm (4in) mesh plastic netting will keep pigeons off vegetables, 25mm (1in) will exclude most birds from soft fruit too and 19mm (¾in) will exclude all birds including tits.

Stretch the netting tightly and secure the edges firmly. Check netting frequently in case birds or hedgehogs have become entangled.
■ Crop covers (see page 139) laid over vegetables will keep off birds and insect pests.
■ If you use cotton or thread to protect crocuses from sparrows – use brightly coloured thread to avoid entangling birds.
■ Bird scarers may deter birds for short periods, but unless you change them or move them around the birds will quickly become used to them.

FRUIT CAGES

These are large frames covered with netting, big enough to walk inside and fitted with a door. They can be expensive if you buy a kit, less so if you make your own, but are the best way to protect soft fruit.

Netting with 25mm (1in) holes will keep out most birds. Make sure it is kept taut to avoid entangling birds. Mend any small holes immediately.

Secure the bottom of the side nets firmly and surround the base with boards to prevent hedgehogs becoming entangled.

Remove the top net if snow is predicted, to prevent damage.

APHIDS

Rose aphids on rosebud

There are around 550 different species of aphid in Britain. Some, like greenfly on roses or blackfly on cherries and beans, can devastate garden plants. They all breed prodigiously. For the whole of the summer only female aphids occur, giving birth to live young which reach adulthood in a week. A single aphid landing on a plant can produce thousands of offspring in a few weeks.

Some, like the beech aphid, live all their lives on one plant, but most migrate between two types of plant, usually a woody plant through the winter and spring and a herbaceous plant through the summer. For example, the black bean aphid overwinters on *Euonymus* trees; other combinations include peach-potato, willow-carrot and currant-lettuce aphids. Winged aphids are produced at the beginning and end of the summer and migrate between the two host plants. They are poor flyers, but can be carried miles by air currents to rain down on your garden.

Aphids can harm plants in several ways.

Hoverfly larva feeding on aphid

■ They feed by inserting their piercing mouth parts into plants and sucking the sap. Large colonies can greatly reduce a plant's vigour and may affect flowering or yield.
■ They excrete a sweet sticky substance known as 'honeydew'. This often becomes colonised by black sooty mould. When combined with shed aphid skins this can seriously cut down the amount of light reaching the leaf surface.
■ Some aphids spread viruses from plant to plant. It might take just a single aphid to introduce mosaic virus to a courgette plant, with fatal results.
■ Some produce distinct symptoms – causing leaves to curl, blister or turn red, which may reduce vigour and yield.

KILLING APHIDS

Most insecticides claim to kill aphids (see pages 130–133). Contact insecticides, including those derived from plants like derris or pyrethrum, will only kill aphids hit by the spray. Systemic insecticides are absorbed into the plant's sap and kill aphids as they feed, so spraying does not need to be quite so thorough. However, most insecticides will also harm any beneficial insects present, the one exception being ICI Rapid, which will not harm bees, ladybirds or lacewing larvae, though it will kill hoverfly larvae.

It may be necessary to re-apply aphid killers, as a few survivors can rapidly start to recolonise a plant.

NATURAL PREDATORS

Many garden birds, insects and spiders eat aphids, but some insects feed solely on aphids. Ladybirds are the best known, but the larvae of lacewings, hoverflies and some midges are also voracious aphid eaters. Several tiny parasitic wasps also prey on aphids. But even if all these are abundant in your garden, aphids can still get out of control. If you can tolerate some damage, the predators will catch up with them eventually or the aphids will move on to their alternate hosts.

You can attract aphid eaters to your garden – tits will seek out overwintering aphids on roses or fruit trees if offered fat as an inducement. A patch of nettles will support an early colony of aphids and encourage predators to build up. Cut the nettles in late March so the predators spread out into the garden.

You can buy natural predators and parasites to control aphids in the greenhouse. See page 119.

COMMON PLANT DISEASES

Most plant diseases are specific to particular plant families and are dealt with in the relevant sections of this book. A few diseases can affect a whole range of garden plants.

POWDERY MILDEW
White powdery coating on leaves and stems

Apart from specific powdery mildews, such as rose, apple or American gooseberry mildew, all sorts of garden and greenhouse plants can be attacked in some seasons.

Several species of fungi may be responsible but all act in the same way and produce similar symptoms. In severe attacks the leaves may turn yellow and wilt. Powdery mildew is likely to be worst in hot, dry seasons, when plants are crowded or suffering from lack of water. Once established, powdery mildew can be difficult to eradicate.

Control Spray with a systemic fungicide as soon as symptoms are noticed and repeat at 10–14 day intervals according to the instructions.

Prevention If powdery mildews regularly occur, start spraying with a systemic fungicide *before* the disease appears and continue at 10–14 day intervals. Keep plants well watered and thin them to prevent overcrowding.

GREY MOULD
Buds, fruit, leaves or stems covered in grey fluffy mould

The fungus *Botrytis cinerea* can attack almost any garden plant. On woody plants it can cause shoots to die back. It frequently affects ripe fruit and can cause buds and flowers to rot. If affected plants are disturbed, clouds of spores will be released.

Although spores are probably always present in the garden, healthy plants can usually resist grey mould. Weakened plants, for example those suffering from lack of water or plants damaged by frost, pests or other diseases are susceptible. It also attacks dead or dying plants and fallen or over-ripe fruit.

Control Remove badly affected leaves or shoots and spray with a systemic fungicide. In some areas grey mould is becoming resistant to some fungicides. Use fungicides as a last resort and if control is not achieved switch to a different type (see page 86).

Prevention Avoid overcrowded or damp conditions, especially in greenhouses. Spray soft fruit around flowering time (see pages 86–87) and repeat at 10–14 day intervals.

DOWNY MILDEW
Yellow or brown patches on upper surface of leaves, grey or purple mould on undersides
This disease is most serious on vegetables (see pages 94 and 104) but occasionally attacks other plants, especially seedlings. It is likely to be worst in warm, damp weather.

Control Destroy badly affected plants and spray the remainder with pbi Dithane 945.

Prevention None.

LEAF SPOTS
Round or angular brown, black or dark green spots on leaves
Almost all garden plants can be attacked by one or more leaf-spotting fungi. But apart from rose black spot (see page 28) these are rarely serious and do not usually merit fungicidal treatment. In some seasons leaf spots may cause problems on soft fruit or vegetables.

Control Spray with a systemic fungicide.

Prevention This is only really worthwhile on roses. See page 28.

RUSTS
Brown, red or orange powdery spots or streaks on leaves
Different species of rust fungus attack a whole range of garden plants. Leeks and many ornamentals, especially roses, are frequently affected.

Control and prevention See page 106 for leeks, page 23 for ornamentals and page 28 for roses.

CHAPTER TWO

PROBLEM WEEDS

In some gardens weeds can be more of a problem than pests and diseases and are often more difficult to eradicate completely.

Perennial weeds, once established, can keep regrowing from deep roots or rhizomes or from fragments that you miss when weeding.

Annual weeds produce a lot of seed or can flower and seed before you are aware that they are there. Seeds of annual weeds can survive for years in the soil, so that every time the soil is disturbed a fresh crop of seedlings will appear.

among established ornamentals or fruit bushes.

■ Don't put perennial weeds or weeds that have flowered on the compost heap – you'll only help spread them around the garden.

■ Finally, always be on your guard against introducing new weeds with plants from the garden centre. It's a good idea to remove the top 1cm (½in) of soil before planting.

AVOIDING WEED PROBLEMS

■ Prevent weeds seeding, especially annual weeds such as groundsel, shepherd's purse and annual meadow grass, which can produce three generations in a year, by regular hoeing.

■ If the soil already contains a lot of weed seeds then use weed preventers or mulches wherever possible. See page 16.

■ Don't underrate regular hoeing to keep weeds down.

■ Creeping perennials often arrive as wind-borne seeds. Deal with them immediately, before the underground parts creep in

NO DIG BEDS

The solution for a weedy vegetable plot is to leave the soil undisturbed, except for seedbed preparation, so that buried seeds stay buried. Adding layers of organic mulches to flower borders on a regular basis will also prevent weed seeds from germinating, provided the mulch material is itself weed-free.

COMMON WEEDS

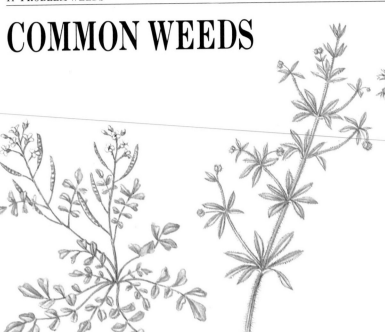

Common chickweed Annual. Height 30cm (12in). A prostrate plant with inconspicuous flowers all year. Can be a persistent problem on vegetable patches. Control by hoeing.

Hairy bittercress Annual. Height up to 20cm (8in). Flowers from April to August. A serious problem in flower beds. Seeds set and are released explosively very soon after flowering. Hoe regularly before it flowers, or hand pull carefully to avoid dispersing the seed.

Cleavers Annual. Inconspicuous flowers from June to August. All parts of the plant, including seed pods, are spiny. Plants grow rapidly, scrambling through garden plants. Trace back to the root and hand pull carefully – if it breaks at the base it will regrow.

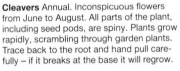

Annual meadow grass Annual. Height up to 30cm (12in). Flowers all year. Control by hoeing or use glyphosate.

Bramble Perennial. Forms spreading thickets. Flowers May to September. Spreads by seed and by arching stems rooting at the tips. Control by digging out roots or cut back and spray new growth with glyphosate or a problem weedkiller.

Broad-leaved willow herb Perennial. Height up to 40cm (16in). Flowers June to August. Spreads by seed. Rosebay willow herb is similar but taller. Control by hoeing before seeds are set.

Creeping buttercup Perennial. Height 15–30cm (6–12in). Flowers May to August. Spreads by surface runners and by seed. Control by hoeing or hand weeding, taking care to trace and remove runners.

Field bindweed Perennial. Height up to 90cm (36in) but may grow prostrate. Flowers (much smaller than hedge bindweed flowers) July to September. Spreads by deep fleshy roots, occasionally by seed. Control both bindweeds by repeated hoeing or spray or paint leaves with glyphosate. May take many years to control.

Hedge bindweed Perennial. Climber with large flowers up to 5cm (2in) across from June. Spreads by shallow creeping roots.

Pink-flowered oxalis Perennial. Height 15–30cm (6–12in). Spreads by seed and by tiny bulbils that develop round the base. Flowers July to September. Difficult to control unless every tiny bulbil is removed. Try glyphosate or Casoron G4 (see page 134).

Field horsetail Perennial. Height 30–60cm (12–24in). A non-flowering plant spread by deep-creeping rhizomes. Often impossible to dig out and may need several weedkiller applications. Casoron G4 may suppress it (see page 134).

Stinging nettle Perennial. Height up to 1.2m (4ft). Spreads by shallow creeping stems and by seed. Flowers May to October. Control by digging out every scrap of stem – tough yellow roots will not regrow – or spray with glyphosate.

Lesser celandine Perennial. Height up to 15cm. Flowers March to May. Spreads by seeds or bulbils which develop round base of plant. Small fragments of tuberous root regrow. Dig out with surrounding soil to remove bulbils or spray with glyphosate.

Ground elder Perennial. Height 40–100cm (16–40in). Spreads by seed and by shallow creeping rhizomes. Flowers May to July. Can be very difficult to control, especially amongst other plants. Use glyphosate or a problem weedkiller (see page 134).

Japanese knot weed Perennial. Height up to 3m (10ft). Flowers from July to October. Forms dense clumps and spreads by tough underground stems. Impossible to dig out. Can be controlled by persistent use of glyphosate.

Couch grass Perennial. Height up to 75cm (30in). Spreads by shallow rhizomes and by seed. Flowers July to September. Dig out rhizomes, taking care to remove every piece (see page 134) or spray with a grass killer, or glyphosate.

CONTROLLING WEEDS

ANNUAL WEEDS

Apart from those illustrated, many other annual weeds can occasionally become a serious nuisance in flower beds and vegetable plots, including dead nettles, fat hen, groundsel, pineapple weed, shepherd's purse and spurges. All can be controlled by hoeing in vegetable plots, flower beds and other areas of bare soil. Among herbaceous perennials and shrubs mulching may be more effective. On large areas a weedkiller like ICI Weedol will be effective against annual weeds. If perennial weeds are present the top growth will be burnt off, but they may regrow from the roots.

HOEING

Hoe regularly to prevent weeds flowering and setting seed. Some annual weeds can seed surprisingly quickly. The most effective time to hoe is early morning on a hot, dry day when the hoed weeds will be quickly dried up. Use a really sharp hoe, keep the blade level with the soil surface to sever weed stems cleanly from their roots and avoid damaging the roots of garden plants.

MULCHES

These are an effective method for preventing annual weeds in certain situations. They can also suppress perennial weeds if left in place long enough.

Old carpets are one of the cheapest and most effective mulches where appearance is not important – on the fruit and vegetable patch, for example. Black plastic is also very cheap and effective, but drainage holes should be made to prevent puddles. It can be covered with bark or gravel where appearance does matter. Some woven plastic mulching materials allow rain to pass through.

In flower beds and borders a 5cm (2in) layer of bark chips looks good and is effective if it is topped up regularly. However, this can work out very expensive. Weeds that do appear are easily pulled out. Gravel or stone chippings are an alternative.

Areas of weed-infested ground can be cleared of most perennial weeds by laying pieces of old carpet on them, but they must be left for at least a year.

PERENNIAL WEEDS

Small numbers of perennial weeds can be dug or pulled out, but they may regrow from fragments of roots or stems left in the ground. Persistent hand weeding or hoeing may eventually eliminate perennial weeds, but weedkillers are worth considering for areas where weeds are more tenacious.

.

◼ PROBLEM WEEDKILLERS

Weeds with underground stems, rhizomes or roots must be treated with a systemic weedkiller. Glyphosate is the most effective and breaks down rapidly in the soil. Although it travels down into the roots, weeds with extensive root systems may need several applications to destroy them. Weeds may not appear to die for a week or two. Take great care when treating weeds among garden plants. Use a watering can with a special spray head or a dribble bar and avoid splashing garden plants. (See page 138 for application equipment.)

Other problem weedkillers contain hormone-type weedkillers (see page 134). These are more suitable for uncultivated areas, such as a neglected garden or for keeping a weed-free strip around a boundary.

.

◼ SPOT WEEDERS

Among garden plants spot weeding may be more practical. Spot weeders are wiped or sprayed on to individual weeds and can be used anywhere in the garden.

.

◼ GRASS WEEDS

Most weedkillers will have no effect on couch and other grasses. Glyphosate will kill all grasses and there are two selective grasskillers (see page 134)

.

◼ PATHS

Use a special path weedkiller which contains a combination of a weedkiller, to kill existing weeds, and a weed preventer, to keep the path weed-free for up to a year. Weeds can be prevented by laying heavy-duty black polythene sheeting before laying slabs or other paving.

CHAPTER THREE

THE ORNAMENTAL GARDEN

Your attitude to pests and diseases on ornamental plants will depend on your style of gardening and on the prominence of the plant under attack. You might tolerate aphids and caterpillars at the back of a border or in a semi-wild area, knowing that they provide food for garden birds and other insects, but find them unacceptable on edging plants. As a rule, treat pesticides as a last resort.

Healthy plants will survive occasional attacks by many pests or diseases. Those that are under stress because they are growing in an unsuitable position or in inhospitable soil, or are suffering from lack of nutrients or water, may be permanently damaged or even killed.

There is little you can do once some of the more serious diseases have taken hold, though if you spot the symptoms early you can often save a tree or shrub by pruning out affected branches.

Digging out and burning diseased plants may sound drastic, but it can prevent the problem spreading to healthy plants.

Preventive use of insecticides is not generally worthwhile in mixed borders and may do more harm than good by killing beneficial creatures. However, a routine fungicide spray programme is advisable to prevent blackspot, mildew and rust on roses. Consider preventive spraying on other plants only if diseases occur regularly.

HOW TO USE THIS CHAPTER
Because some pests and diseases attack a whole range of ornamental plants, we have covered the most widespread problems on pages 20–25. Pests and diseases that attack one specific group of plants are then covered in detail:
Roses: pages 28–29
Rhododendrons and related plants: pages 30–31
Other deciduous trees and shrubs: pages 32–43
Conifers: pages 44–45
Herbaceous plants: pages 46–51
Bulbs: pages 52–53
Bedding plants: page 54

The key to symptoms on pages 18–19 should lead you to the correct page.

There is a checklist for shrubs and trees and their most serious problems on pages 26–27.

KEY TO SYMPTOMS ON ORNAMENTAL GARDEN PLANTS

MAIN SYMPTOMS	DETAILED SYMPTOMS	CAUSE (PAGE NUMBER)
LEAVES		
Leaves holed	ragged holes or stripped to veins	caterpillars (20), Solomon's seal sawfly (46)
	ragged holes, slime trails present	slugs and snails (8)
	irregular holes or notched	leaf weevils (21 and 30)
	semi-circular pieces cut from edges	leaf-cutting bee (33)
	irregular holes in lily leaves	lily beetle (47)
	tattered and distorted	capsids (21)
	leaves peppered with small holes	flea beetle (47)
	yellow spots fall away leaving holes	shothole (32)
Leaves marked	white sinuous lines	leaf miners (22)
	brown or purple blotches	leaf miners (22)
	transparent patches	rose slugworm (29), willow leaf beetle (33)
Leaves spotted	brown, yellow or grey spots	leaf spots (22 and 46)
	dark spots with yellow edges	rose black spot (28)
	brown spots or patches	anthracnose (34)
	black blotches	delphinium black blotch (47)
	olive green or black scabby patches	pyracantha scab (34)
	dark brown powdery spots	rust (23)
	small orange raised spots	rust (23), on rose (28)
	yellow or brown spots or blotches	leaf blight (32)
	off-white raised spots	white rust (23 and 122), dahlia smut (46)
	glistening, raised white spots	white blister (47)
Leaves misshapen	tightly rolled	leaf rolling sawfly (29)
	rolled, webbing present	caterpillars (20)
	narrow, puckered, frilled edges	stem eelworm (25)
	young leaves distorted or puckered	frost (30)
	pale green waxy swellings	azalea gall (31)
	raised or coloured areas	galls (33)
	thickened yellow margins, curled over	bay sucker (33)
	thickened and rolled	violet leaf midge (46)
Leaves small	growth also poor	phosphorus deficiency (40)
	small and sparse	nutrient deficiencies (40, 43)
Leaves flecked	pale green or white	leafhoppers (21 and 30)
	fine yellow or white flecking	spider mites (21), viruses (24 and 46), on bulbs (52)
	flecked yellow	rhododendron lacebug (30)
	flecked silver	privet thrips (34)
Leaves yellowed	yellow between veins	chlorosis (30 and 40), magnesium deficiency (40)
	also small and sparse	phytophthora root rot (39)
Leaves pale	growth poor	nitrogen deficiency (40)
	pale between veins	manganese deficiency (39)
	pale bands or spots	weedkiller damage (43)
	leaves discoloured or pale	waterlogging/compaction (42)
Leaves discoloured	margins and tips brown	potash deficiency (40)
	brown or scorched	frost (42)
	brown and scorched, remain attached	fireblight (32)
	covered in white/grey furry growth	downy mildew (34 and 46)
	covered in white powdery growth	powdery mildew (34 and 46), on roses (28), on rhododendrons (31)
	silvery sheen	silver leaf (32)
	later wilt and die	leaf and bud eelworm (25) wilt (25 and 49), dieback (31)
Insects present	tiny moth-like insects	rhododendron whitefly (30)
	green, black or pink insects	aphids (33 and 46)

MAIN SYMPTOMS	DETAILED SYMPTOMS	CAUSE (PAGE NUMBER)
SHOOTS		
Shoots wilt	tips wilt and die	leopard moth (20)
	plant may also die	wilt (25 and 49)
	die back from tip	dieback (29, 31 and 38)
	tips die back and remain brown	fireblight (32)
	die back to near ground level	clematis wilt (36)
	young shoots wither and wilt	phytophthora root rot (39)
	young shoots wither and wilt, base rots	foot and root rot (49)
Shoots distorted	tightly packed much-branched shoots	witches' broom (36)
Insects present	green, black or pink insects	aphids (28)
STEMS		
Stems damaged	stems stunted and split	stem eelworm (25)
	brown sunken patches	canker (29)
	brown lesions, pale brown or white ooze	fireblight (32)
	flattened areas of bark, oozing gum	bacterial canker (38)
	roughened or raised areas on bark	cankers (38)
	elongated swellings, powdery black spores	smut (46)
Stems distorted	twisted, spiralled and split	splitting (48)
	thickened and twisted	phlox eelworm (48)
	broad and flattened	fasciation (36 and 48)
	hard, rough lumps present	forsythia gall (36)
	hard, knobbly lumps on stems	crown gall (36 and 49)
	masses of small shoots at base of plant	leafy gall (48)
Stems spotted	pink or red spots	coral spot (37)
	small brown scales present	scale insects (37)
Stems holed	small holes in bark	shot-hole borer (37)
Fungal growths	bracket fungi or toadstools present	wood rots (37 and 38)
FLOWERS		
Flowers distorted	petals twisted or puckered	viruses (24)
	flower stems stunted, anthers distorted	anther smut (50)
Flowers damaged	rose flowers fail to open	balling of roses (29)
	tattered holes in petals	earwigs (50)
	young flowers damaged	birds (35)
Flowers discoloured	brown and wither, later mouldy	grey mould (35 and 50)
	brown, fail to open properly	frost (35)
	brown and withered, remain on stems	blossom wilt (35), fireblight (32)
	flecked or streaked	viruses (24)
	flecked silver	thrips (50)
	white or pale brown spots	petal blight (31 and 50)
	petals replaced by green leaves	Michaelmas daisy mite (50)
Flowering poor	buds drop before opening	viruses (50)
	buds fail to open, few or small flowers	dry roots (31)
	buds fail to open, remain hard and brown	bud blast (31)
	buds small and hard, fail to open	various causes (50)
	flowers fail to open or distorted	capsids (50)
	flowers few or short-lived	various causes (35)
	flowering reduced or ceases	dry roots (31)
Insects present	small dark, shiny beetles present	pollen beetles (50)
GENERAL GROWTH		
Whole plant dies	newly planted rose dies	replant disease (29)
	honey coloured toadstools present	honey fungus (39)
	plant wilts during hot weather	clubroot (49), cabbage root fly (49)
	wet brown rot at stem base	sclerotinia (49)
Growth poor	growth poor, plant stunted	impaired root function (49), viruses (24)
	growth poor, plant deteriorates	soil problems (42–43)
	variegated plants revert to green	insufficient light (42)

LEAF PESTS

Brown tail moth caterpillar

■ CATERPILLARS

The caterpillars of many different moths can attack ornamental garden plants. These are the most common.

Angle shades *Buds, leaves and flowers eaten*
Green or brown caterpillars (up to 5cm; 2in long) with distinct V-shaped markings feed mostly at night. Damage occurs from May to October outdoors, but all year in greenhouses.

Brown tail *Plants defoliated and covered in webbing 'tents'*
This pest is most common near the south and east coasts, occasionally further inland. The caterpillars (up to 4cm; 1½in long) can occur in very large numbers and completely defoliate individual trees or shrubs. They overwinter in smaller 'tents' and feed on new growth in spring. Do not touch the caterpillars as they can cause a nettle-like rash.

Buff-tip *Foliage eaten*
Leaves are rapidly stripped in mid-summer, but usually only a few isolated branches are affected. The black and yellow caterpillars (up to 5cm; 2in long) usually feed in groups.

Carnation tortrix *Leaves or leaf margins bound together with silk webbing*
Dark green caterpillars (up to 2cm; ¾in long) attack plants outdoors and in greenhouses (see page 121). Plant growth may be restricted by the webbing.

Hawthorn webber *Leaves eaten; branches covered in silk webbing*
The small (15mm; ⅝in long) red or brown caterpillars are most prevalent in the south of England and attack cotoneasters and hawthorns from March onwards.

Lackey moth *'Tents' of silk webbing spun over woody plants*
Roses, cotoneasters, lilacs and firethorn are commonly attacked between July and September. The grey-blue caterpillars, each up to 5cm (2in) long feed on foliage and twigs within the webbing 'tents'.

Leopard moth *Shoot tips on young trees wilt and may die*
Look for small holes and droppings on branches. The caterpillars tunnel within the shoots.

Goat moth caterpillars cause similar damage to larger branches.

Silver Y *Ragged holes eaten in leaves*
Large quantities of droppings may be seen and extensive defoliation may occur. The green caterpillars, up to 4cm (1½in) long, feed mainly at night. Plants frequently damaged include pelargoniums, *Datura*, chrysanthemums and azaleas. Greenhouse plants may also be attacked.

Small ermine *Foliage eaten and silk webbing produced*
Small (up to 2cm; ¾in long) green-grey caterpillars of several closely related moth species each attack different plants, including cherries, *Euonymus*, hawthorns and willows.

Vapourer *Leaves eaten by brightly coloured caterpillars*
These colourful 2.5cm (1in) long caterpillars attack many types of plant from May to August. Do not touch them – the hairs contain an irritant.

Winter moths *Young leaves and blossoms damaged*
The green or brown looper caterpillars, up to 2.5cm (1in) long, do most damage to deciduous plants in spring when they attack developing buds. See also fruit trees (page 62).

CONTROL

Individual caterpillars can be picked off if infestations are light and are caught early.

Buff tip moth caterpillar

If you prefer not to kill them, leave them for the birds or move them to less noticeable plants.

■ Tortrix caterpillars which are hidden within their webbing can be killed by squashing the affected leaves.

■ Leopard moth caterpillars can be killed by poking a wire down through the holes in the stems or by pruning out severely affected stems.

■ Caterpillars which produce webbing 'tents' can be controlled by cutting out the affected areas or breaking open the 'tent' and spraying.

■ Any contact insecticide can be used to control large infestations of caterpillars.

■ An alternative, biological, control is a spray containing the bacterium *Bacillus thuringiensis*. This kills caterpillars that eat the sprayed leaves, but is harmless to humans and other animals. Caterpillars cannot be prevented from attacking plants.

Lackey moth caterpillar

Small ermine moth caterpillar

Vapourer moth caterpillar

LEAF HOPPERS
Pale green or white flecking on leaves
Adult leaf hoppers, up to 5mm (¼in) long, may be seen feeding on the undersurface of leaves but they jump off when disturbed. White cast skins of the nymphs may be found attached to the leaf. In severe cases the flecks coalesce, giving the leaf a bleached appearance. Many plants can be damaged, including rhododendrons and roses.

Control Spray with a contact or systemic insecticide. Being highly mobile, leaf hoppers quickly reinvade from other areas.
Prevention None.

SPIDER MITES
Very fine yellow or white flecking on leaves
Inspection with a hand lens may reveal the tiny mites on the lower leaf surface.

In severe attacks, silk webbing may be produced. Affected leaves yellow, turning brown as they die, and the whole plant may be killed. This pest can cause considerable damage in warm summers.
Control Remove and burn severely affected plants. Spray with a contact or systemic insecticide as soon as the problem is noticed. See also page 71.
Prevention None.

CAPSIDS
Young leaves tattered and distorted
These sap-sucking pests inject toxins as they feed, killing off tiny areas of tissue and giving the plant a flecked appearance.

These areas tear as the plant grows. The bugs are about 6mm (¼) long and move rapidly when disturbed, so are rarely seen. Plants often attacked include clematis, dahlias, chrysanthemums, fuchsias, hydrangeas and roses. Flowers are also damaged.
Control Spray with a systemic insecticide.
Prevention Control weeds, which may harbour capsids.

LEAF WEEVILS
Leaves holed or notched

Adult weevils are black or brown and up to 1cm (½in) long. They are active from spring to autumn. Although the damage is unsightly, they rarely harm outdoor plants.
Control Collect and destroy the weevils at night. No effective chemical control is available; biological control may become available to gardeners.
Prevention None.

LEAF PESTS AND DISEASES

■ LEAF MINERS

Leaf blemishes can be caused by grubs of flies or moths.

Chrysanthemum leaf miner *Narrow white (and later brown) wiggly lines*
Chrysanthemums, cinerarias and gazanias may be affected. See also page 121.

Holly leaf miner *Pale green or purplish-brown blotches*
The grubs of the fly which form the mines are active in summer. Hollies clipped as hedges may be badly affected.

Laburnum leaf miner *Round brownish blotches*
Laburnum and sometimes *Genista* are attacked from June to September. Moth caterpillars feed within the mines, causing them to enlarge; several mines on a leaf may coalesce.

Lilac leaf miner *Large brown blotches*
Each mine may contain several moth larvae. When they leave, the leaf may become rolled up and bound by silk webbing – the caterpillars continue to feed within this. Lilacs, ash and privet may be attacked in June and again in August and September.

Apple leaf miner *Long, narrow winding white mines (later brown)*
Ornamental *Malus*, *Prunus*, birch and hawthorn may be attacked, mainly in late summer. There may be many mines on each leaf and they may isolate sections of the leaf, causing brown, dead patches to develop.

CONTROL
Not usually necessary. Pick off and burn affected leaves. Burn hedge clippings and fallen leaves at the end of the season. If attacks are severe, spray with a contact insecticide.

PREVENTION
Control weeds, which may harbour the pests.

Leaf miner damage on lilac

Primula leaf spot

■ LEAF SPOTS
Most plants can be damaged by leaf-spotting fungi or, occasionally, bacteria. Although leaf spots are common, they generally do little real damage. Plants which are lacking in vigour are most susceptible. Most leaf spots are worst in damp weather.
These are some of the most common leaf spots on garden plants.

Primula leaf spot *Yellow spots which later turn brown with a yellow halo*
Tiny black fungal fruiting bodies can be seen in the centre of the spot which may be concentrically ringed. Damaged areas may fall away, leaving holes. Several different fungi can cause these symptoms and may attack primroses, polyanthus and auriculas.

Ivy leaf spot *Brown or slate-grey spots*
In severe cases the spots coalesce and the leaf is killed. Tiny black fungal fruiting bodies may be found in the centre of the spot. The spots may be concentrically ringed.

Lavatera leaf spot *Yellowish-brown spots which rapidly enlarge, darken and coalesce* Lavatera and occasionally hollyhocks are affected. Plants may wither and die back as the stems are girdled and the leaves are killed.

Rose blackspot See page 28.

Yucca leaf spot *Slate-grey almost circular, ringed spots* Tiny black fruiting bodies are present in the centre of each spot. Older leaves are generally most severely damaged. Yuccas growing in the open seem to be most at risk.

CONTROL

Control is generally not necessary, except in a few cases when infection is severe. Remove affected leaves as soon as they are noticed. Prune out severely damaged stems if necessary. Spray with a systemic fungicide as soon as the symptoms appear and when new growth is produced.

PREVENTION

Clear up plant debris from affected plants to prevent further spread or overwintering. Improve the growing conditions and general vigour of the plants. Do not use high-nitrogen feeds as these may produce 'soft' foliage that is more susceptible to attack. Feed with sulphate of potash to 'harden up' the foliage. Improve air circulation around plants.

RUSTS

Many plants are affected by rust diseases, most of which are restricted to a few plant species. Rust diseases are encouraged by warm, moist conditions which allow the spores to germinate. These are the most common.

Antirrhinum rust *Dark brown*

Hollyhock rust

Pelargonium rust

spots on the lower leaf surface, yellowish discoloration
Stems may also be attacked. The whole plant may appear twisted and distorted.

Chrysanthemum white rust *Off-white or beige rounded pustules on the lower leaf surface* The leaf may be distorted and puckered. Chrysanthemums growing indoors and outdoors may be attacked. See page 122.

Fuchsia rust *Leaves discoloured, bright orange spots on the lower surface* The same fungal disease can also be found on willowherbs.

Hollyhock rust *Raised, rounded buff, orange or brown spots on the lower leaf surface* Leaves are discoloured and may be distorted. Mallows and lavatera can also be affected.

Hypericum rust *Masses of bright orange spots on the lower leaf surface* The upper surface is flecked

Antirrhinum rust

yellow. Defoliation occurs and dieback may follow if the plant is regularly affected.

Pelargonium rust *Dark brown, powdery spots on the lower leaf surface, often in concentric rings* The upper leaf surface may be blotched yellow. Leaves wither and die and in severe cases the plant may be killed. The disease is most severe on plants grown close together.

CONTROL

Pick off and burn infected leaves and prune out affected stems immediately, where feasible. Dig up and burn severely infected plants. Spray with a systemic fungicide (see page 28) when symptoms are first seen and repeat at 10–14 day intervals.

PREVENTION

■ Improve air circulation by planting wider apart and pruning, where appropriate.

■ Grow resistant varieties of antirrhinums.

■ Avoid high-nitrogen fertilisers.Lush growth is most susceptible.

■ Control weeds, which can harbour rust diseases.

■ Rake up and burn affected leaves in the autumn.

■ Some plants, such as hypericum, can be cut back hard if infection has been severe.

See Tables, pages 130–136 for guide to insecticides and fungicides

VIRUSES

Dahlia mosaic virus

VIRUSES

Leaves or flowers discoloured, flecked, streaked, stunted or distorted

Viruses are extremely common and each virus may attack a number of different garden plants, possibly causing slightly different symptoms in each. Some infected plants do not show characteristic symptoms and so act as a source of infection.

Leaves may turn yellow, often in mosaic patterns, mottling or ring-spots. There may be distinct yellow areas around the veins known as 'vein clearing'. Leaves may be distorted or stunted and are frequently curled, rolled or narrowed.

Flowering may also be reduced. Buds may fail to form or fail to open. Flowers which are produced may be deformed and often have discoloured streaks on the petals – white streaks on the red petals of 'Rembrandt' tulips or cerise streaks on the white petals of *Cyclamen hederifolium* 'Album', for example. This is known as 'flower-breaking'.

Affected plants are often stunted and the general vigour declines. The plant may die off quite rapidly or over a period of a few years. These are the most common virus diseases.

Cucumber mosaic virus (CMV) This is readily transmitted by handling and by aphids. It affects cucurbits and also many herbaceous perennials. Leaves are small, crumpled and flecked with bright yellow areas. Flowers may show breaking symptoms.

Dahlia mosaic virus The visible symptoms are yellow vein banding, together with general distortion and stunting.

Peony ringspot virus This shows as yellow rings or mosaic patterns on the leaves. Infected plants show little loss of vigour.

Arabis mosaic virus This also affects raspberry, strawberry and hosta. It causes yellow mosaic patterns on the leaves.

Narcissus yellow stripe virus Distinct yellow streaks form on the leaves and sometimes the flower stem, too (see page 52).

CONTROL

No chemical controls are available. Infected plants should be destroyed without delay. In some cases symptoms may be very seasonal, being affected by weather conditions or growing conditions, and the plant may not be much affected overall.

Mosaic virus on iris

PREVENTION

■ Some viruses are seed borne. Do not save seed from infected plants.

■ Do not take cuttings from infected plants because virus particles are distributed throughout the plant, not only in the parts showing obvious symptoms. Always obtain healthy plants and, where possible, choose plants that are certified virus-free.

■ Remove and burn affected plants, including weeds, immediately, as they may act as a source of infection.

■ Control aphids and other sap-feeding pests, which spread viruses, by regular spraying as soon as they are noticed and before their numbers start to build up.

■ Some virus diseases are transmitted by soil-inhabiting creatures. Do not plant susceptible plants in the same part of the garden as infected plants.

■ Do not touch healthy looking plants after handling infected ones until you have washed your hands and sterilised pruning tools.

■ Keep weeds under control because many weeds may act as hosts for viruses, but do not show characteristic symptoms themselves.

EELWORMS

Leaf and bud eelworm damage

LEAF AND BUD EELWORM

Leaves discolour, wilt and die
Dark areas may develop between
the leaf veins. The base of the
plant is affected first.

Buds are also attacked and
growth may be stunted. If the
terminal bud is affected, many
lateral shoots are formed.

Stems may be scarred and
any flowers produced may be
deformed. Symptoms are most
obvious in the autumn or in cool,
damp summers.

Chrysanthemums can be
affected as cuttings or established plants. Common weeds
like chickweed and groundsel
can harbour this pest.
Control Destroy affected plants.
Chrysanthemum stools can be
treated by plunging them into
hot water (46°C; 115°F) for 5
minutes and then into cool
water. Repeatedly taking tip
cuttings may eventually produce
clean plants.

Stem eelworm damage

Prevention Always buy plants
from reputable suppliers. Clear
up debris as the eelworms may
persist for a few months in dead
plant material. Keep the garden
weed-free.

HOW TO TELL EELWORM AND VIRUS SYMPTOMS APART

Many virus-infected plants show characteristic yellow flecks, mosaic, stripes or
ring spots. Discoloration is less defined
with eelworm-infested plants.

If eelworm-infested leaves are torn
into small pieces and put in a glass tube
full of water for about 30 minutes, the
pests may be seen at the bottom of the
tube – they are tiny, clear, hair-like
creatures. Without experience, it is
difficult to be sure of your diagnosis.
If in any doubt, consult an expert.

STEM EELWORMS

*Stunted growth, narrow, puck-
ered leaves with a frilled edge;
stems stunted and split*
Bulbous plants can also be
affected.

The symptoms vary with the
species attacked. There are
several distinct races of the eelworm, each of which may attack
a different range of plants. Phlox
eelworm is among the most common (see page 48).
Control Destroy affected plants.
Prevention Buy plants from
reputable sources. Practise good
garden hygiene. Control weeds.

WILTS

FUSARIUM WILTS

*Leaves discoloured and wilted;
stems may wilt too; the plant dies*
A dark discoloration at the base
and a pale pink fungal growth
may be seen. China asters are
particularly susceptible to this
disease. Carnations, pinks and
sweet peas are also affected.
Control and prevention See
'Verticillium wilts'.

VERTICILLIUM WILTS

*Wilting and discoloration of
foliage, followed by dieback*
A wide range of ornamentals can
be affected. A streaked discoloration may be seen just beneath
the surface of stems at the base

of the plant. Weeds harbour the
disease and the fungus can
remain in the soil for several
years.
Control None. Remove and burn

affected plants.
Prevention Obtain plants from
a reputable source. Rotate different types of bedding plants each
year. Control weeds.

A–Z OF SHRUBS AND TREES

GENERA	RESISTS HONEY FUNGUS? [1]	MAIN PEST AND DISEASE PROBLEMS [2]	SOIL TYPE [3]
Abelia	yes	generally trouble-free	neutral–acid
Abies (fir)	yes	adelgids (44)	any
Acer (maples)	no	coral spot (37), honey fungus (39), wilt (25)	neutral
Actinidia (chinese gooseberry)	yes	generally trouble-free	any
Aesculus	–	coral spot (37), phytophthora (39)	any
Amelanchier	–	fireblight (32)	any
Aucuba (spotted laurel)	yes	generally trouble-free	any
Azalea	–	See pages 30–31	acid
Berberis	–	rust (23)	any
Betula (birches)	–	rust (23)	any
Buddleia	–	capsid (21), leaf and bud eelworm (25)	any
Buxus (box)	yes	rust (23)	any
Calluna (heathers)	–	phytophthora (39)	acid
Camellia	–	phytophthora (39), see also page 30–31	neutral–acid
Caryopteris	–	capsid (21)	alkaline–neutral
Catalpa	yes	wilt (25)	neutral–acid
Ceanothus	–	capsid (21)	neutral–acid
Chaenomeles	–	fireblight (32)	neutral–acid
Chamaecyparis	no	honey fungus (44), phytophthora (45)	any
Choisya	yes	generally trouble-free	neutral–acid
Cistus (rock rose)	yes	generally trouble-free	any
Clematis	yes	clematis wilt (36)	any
Cornus (dogwoods)	yes	generally trouble-free	any [4]
Corylus (hazels)	–	generally trouble-free	any
Cotinus (smoke bush)	yes	wilt (25)	any
Cotoneaster	–	fireblight (32)	any
Crataegus (hawthorn)	–	fireblight (32), silver leaf (32)	any
Cupressocyparis leylandii	no	honey fungus (44), canker (44), phytophthora (45)	any
Cupressus	no	honey fungus (44), canker (44)	any
Cytisus (broom)	–	generally trouble-free	neutral–acid
Daphne	–	crown gall (36), leaf spot (22), mosaic virus (24)	any
Deutzia	yes	generally trouble-free	any
Elaeagnus	yes	coral spot (37)	neutral–acid
Erica (heathers)	yes	phytophthora (39)	acid [5]
Escallonia	–	generally trouble-free	neutral–acid
Euonymus	–	generally trouble-free	alkaline–neutral
Fagus (beech)	yes	coral spot (37), phytophthora (39)	any
Fatsia	–	generally trouble-free	any
Forsythia	–	capsids (21), gall (36)	any
Fothergillia	yes	generally trouble-free	neutral–acid
Fraxinus (ash)	yes	generally trouble-free	any
Fuchsia	–	capsids (21), rust (23)	any
Garrya	–	generally trouble-free	any
Gaultheria	yes	generally trouble-free	acid
Genista (broom)	–	leaf miner (22)	neutral–acid
Griselinia	yes	generally trouble-free	neutral–acid
Hamamelis (witch hazel)	no	honey fungus (39)	acid
Hebe	yes	generally trouble-free	any
Hedera (ivies)	yes	leaf spot (22)	any
Hibiscus	–	generally trouble-free	neutral–acid
Hydrangea	no	capsids (21), honey fungus (39), stem eelworm (25)	neutral–acid
Hypericum	yes	rust (23)	any
Ilex (holly)	–	leaf miner (22)	any
Jasminum (Jasmine)	yes	generally trouble-free	any
Juglans (walnut)	–	coral spot (37), honey fungus (39)	any
Juniperus (juniper)	yes	spinning mite (44), webber (45)	any

GENERA	RESISTS HONEY FUNGUS? [1]	MAIN PEST AND DISEASE PROBLEMS [2]	SOIL TYPE [3]
Kerria	yes	generally trouble-free	any
Kolkwitzia	–	generally trouble-free	any
Laburnum	no	leaf miner (22), honey fungus (39), silver leaf (32)	any
Larix (larch)	–	adelgids (44)	any
Laurus (bay)	yes	bay sucker (33), soft scale (37)	any
Lavandula (lavender)	–	leaf and bud eelworm (25)	any
Lavatera (mallow)	yes	rust (23)	any
Leptospermum	yes	generally trouble-free	acid
Ligustrum (privet)	no	honey fungus (39), leaf miner (22), wilt (25), thrips (33)	neutral–acid
Liquidambar	yes	generally trouble-free	any
Lonicera (honeysuckle)	–	aphids (33), powdery mildew (12)	neutral–acid
Magnolia	–	capsid (21), coral spot (37)	neutral–acid
Mahonia	yes	rust (23)	any
Malus (crab apples)	no	fireblight (32), honey fungus (39), silver leaf (32), see also pages 62–68	any
Myrtus	yes	generally trouble-free	any
Olearia (daisy bush)	–	generally trouble-free	neutral–acid
Paeonia	no	leaf and bud eelworm (25), wilt (25), honey fungus (39)	any
Parrotia	yes	generally trouble-free	neutral–acid
Passiflora	yes	mosaic virus (24)	any
Philadelphus (mock orange)	–	aphids (33)	any
Phlomis (Russian sage)	–	generally trouble-free	neutral
Photinia	yes	generally trouble-free	neutral–acid
Picea (spruce)	–	honey fungus (39), pineapple gall (44), spinning mite (44)	any
Pieris	yes	phytophthora (39)	acid
Pinus (pines)	no	honey fungus (44), adelgids (44)	any
Pittosporum	yes	generally trouble-free	neutral
Platanus (plane)	–	anthracnose (34)	neutral–acid
Populus (poplars)	–	bacterial canker (38), leaf beetles (33)	any
Potentilla	–	silver leaf (32)	any
Prunus (flowering cherries, laurel, ornamental almond)	no	bacterial canker (38), blossom wilt (35), honey fungus (39), peach leaf curl (70), phytophthora (39), silver leaf (32)	neutral–acid
Pyracantha (firethorn)	–	fireblight (32), scab (34)	neutral–acid
Pyrus (pears)	–	fireblight (32), see also pages 62–68	any
Quercus (oaks)	yes	generally trouble-free	any
Rhododendron	no	honey fungus (39), see pages 30–31	acid
Rhus	yes	wilt (25)	any
Ribes (flowering currant)	no	coral spot (37), honey fungus (39), silver leaf (32)	any
Robinia	yes	generally trouble-free	any
Rosa (roses)	no	honey fungus (39), silver leaf (32), see also pages 28–29	neutral–acid
Rosmarinus (rosemary)	–	generally trouble-free	neutral–acid
Rubus	no	honey fungus (39)	any
Salix (willows)	–	anthracnose (34), honey fungus (39), leaf beetle (33), silver leaf (32)	any
Santolina (cotton lavender)	yes	generally trouble-free	any
Senecio	–	mildew (12, 34)	any
Skimmia	–	generally trouble-free	acid
Sorbus (mountain ashes)	–	canker (38), fireblight (32)	any
Spiraea	–	rust (23)	neutral–acid
Stranvaesia	–	fireblight (32)	any
Syringa (lilac)	no	blight (32), leaf miner (22), honey fungus (39), phytophthora (39)	neutral–acid
Taxus (yew)	yes	phytophthora (45)	any
Thuja	–	honey fungus (39), spinning mite (44), thuja blight (45)	any
Tilia (limes)	yes	phytphthora (39)	any
Vaccinium	yes	generally trouble-free	acid
Viburnum	–	crown gall (36)	any
Weigela	no	honey fungus (39), powdery mildew (12, 34)	neutral
Wisteria	no	honey fungus (39)	neutral–acid

[1] –=insufficient information   [2] Numbers in brackets refer to the page number of the relevant entry
[3] Acid=pH below 5.5; neutral=below 7.0. Plants indicated may show symptoms of chlorosis (see page 40) at higher pH levels (more alkaline soil)
[4] Some species need an acid soil   [5] Some species will thrive on neutral soils

ROSES

■ APHIDS

Small insects on young shoots and flower buds

The vigour of the plant is reduced by severe attacks and flowers may be spoiled.
Control Spray with a systemic insecticide or ICI Rapid.
Prevention A combined insecticide and fungicide should prevent aphids becoming a problem if it is used regularly.

■ BLACKSPOT

Dark spots with yellow edges on older leaves

Eventually these leaves turn yellow and drop. In severe cases the plant becomes defoliated.

Blackspot is a common fungal disease that overwinters on old leaves, on the stems and in the soil.
Control Remove affected leaves and destroy them. Spray the plants with a systemic fungicide.
Prevention Clear up fallen leaves in autumn and again in spring, before new foliage appears. Apply a mulch around the bushes to prevent the spores in the soil from reaching the plant. Prune and feed annually to encourage strong new growth. Prune out all stems showing blackspot lesions. Spray regularly with a fungicide (see Box right).

■ RUST

Orange spots on the stems and undersides of leaves

The upper surface of the leaf is flecked yellow. Later the spots will turn black. If the rust attack is severe, the leaves become brittle and drop prematurely.
Control Remove any affected stems and spray with a systemic fungicide (see page 134). Repeat at 10–14 day intervals.
Prevention Practise good garden hygiene (see 'Blackspot', left). Spray regularly with a fungicide (see below).

SPRAY PROGRAMME

You can prevent or control the three major rose diseases by following a regular spraying programme through the summer. Choose a fungicide according to the diseases prevalent in your garden (see page 134). Spray at 10–14-day intervals from May or when the leaves start to open until mid-October. Using a combined insecticide and fungicide will also prevent aphids and other pests. However, it is better to control pests only as necessary. Spray the bushes in the evening and don't spray into the flowers as you risk killing bees and other beneficial insects.

Roses may also benefit from spraying with foliar feed to prevent magnesium deficiency and to improve growth and resistance to disease.

■ MILDEW

White powdery deposit on new stems, young leaves and buds

These become stunted and distorted and may even die. The whole appearance of the bush is ruined. This disease is worst in dry periods.
Control Remove the affected shoots and make sure that the bush is kept well watered during dry weather. Spray with a systemic fungicide.
Prevention Spray regularly with a fungicide (see left).

■ DOWNY MILDEW

Leaves are covered with a furry white fungus

The disease is not common but is worse in warm, damp weather or on roses grown under glass.
Control Remove all affected leaves. Spray the plant with pbi Dithane 945. If the attack is very severe, destroy the plant.
Prevention None.

■ LEAF-CUTTING BEE

Semi-circular pieces cut out of leaves

See page 33

RESISTANT VARIETIES

The following show some resistance to blackspot (B), mildew (M) or rust (R). However, they may succumb in some areas or in particularly bad years.

Large-flowered roses
'Alec's Red' B, M, R
'Alexander' B, M, R
'Alpine Sunset' M, R
'Blessings' B, M, R
'Cheshire Life' B, M, R
'Chicago Peace' M, R
'Congratulations' B, M, R
'Freedom' B, M, R
'Grandpa Dickson' B, M, R
'Just Joey' B, M, R
'King's Ransom' B, R
'Peace' B, M, R
'Peaudouce' B, M, R
'Pink Favourite' B, M, R
'Pink Peace' B, R
'Polar Star' B, M
'Red Devil' M
'Remember Me' B, M, R
'Rose Gaujard' B, R

'Royal William' B, M, R
'Silver Jubilee' B, M, R
'Simba' B, M, R
'Sunblest' B, M, R
'Troika' B, M, R

Cluster-flowered or
floribunda roses
'Allgold' B, M, R
'Amber Queen' B, M, R
'Anne Harkness' B, M, R
'Arthur Bell' B, M, R
'Beautiful Britain' B, M, R
'Bright Smile' B, M, R
'Fragrant Delight' B, M, R
'Korresia' B, M, R
'Lover's Meeting' B, M, R
'Matangi' B, M, R
'Mountbatten' B, M, R
'Paul Shiriville' M, R

'Queen Elizabeth' M, R
'Wendy Cussons' B, M, R
'Southampton' B, M, R
'Trumpeter' B, M, R
'Whisky Mac' B, M, R

Climbing roses
'Aloha' B, M, R
'Arthur Bell' B, M, R
'Compassion' B, M, R
'Dublin Bay' B, M, R
'Golden Showers' B, M, R
'Highfield' B, M, R
'Joseph's Coat' B, M, R
'Maigold' B, M, R
'Meg' B, M, R
'New Dawn' B, M, R
'Seagull' B, M, R
'Sympathie' B, M, R
'Wedding Day' B, M, R

■ LEAF ROLLING SAWFLY
Leaves tightly rolled

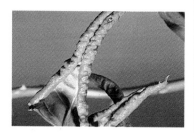

Adult sawflies lay eggs from May to June, causing the leaflets to curl. Rolled leaves usually contain a pale green caterpillar. The leaves may eventually shrivel and die. Roses grown as standards are less prone to attack than those grown as bushes.
Control Spray the bushes with a systemic insecticide during May and June. Pick off and burn affected leaves before mid-July.
Prevention None.

■ ROSE SLUGWORM
Transparent patches on leaves
Pale green slug-like caterpillars up to 15mm (⅝in) long feed on the soft tissue of the leaves. They may appear at any time during the summer. They are sometimes found in large numbers on wild roses.
Control Pick off the slugworms if seen. If necessary treat with a contact insecticide.
Prevention None.

■ DIEBACK
Shoots die back from the tip
Dieback can be caused by a number of factors including frost damage, waterlogging, soil-borne diseases, mildew and blackspot.
Control Cut off affected shoots at a bud at least 5cm (2in) below the area of dieback.

Prevention If dieback is a recurrent problem feed in spring, improve drainage or delay pruning in frost-prone areas.

■ CANKER
Brown sunken patches on stems
Canker usually becomes apparent in spring. It is caused by a fungus that attacks stems which have been weakened by frost or mechanical damage (poor pruning, for example).
Control Prune affected stems at least 5cm (2in) into healthy tissue.
Prevention Do not wound plants; protect from frost.

■ REPLANT DISEASE
Newly planted roses die or do not grow well
If a new rose has been planted on the site of an old rose it may be suffering from replant disease. It is believed to be the result of a build up of nematodes, fungi and other microbial agents in the soil, possibly combined with nutrient depletion.
Control Lift the new rose, shake off soil and replant elsewhere.

Prevention Do not plant a new rose in the same position as an old one unless you change the soil to a depth of about 45cm (18in) over an area of at least 90cm (3ft) diameter.

■ BALLING OF BLOOMS
Buds develop normally but the flowers fail to open

The petals may turn brown. Wet weather usually causes balling, especially on varieties with large, thin-petalled flowers. Balling is worse on roses grown in shady areas. Severe aphid attacks may also cause balling.
Control None.
Prevention Grow rose bushes in a brighter spot. Control aphids.

See Tables, pages 130–136 for guide to insecticides and fungicides

RHODODENDRONS, AZALEAS AND CAMELLIAS

■ RHODODENDRON LEAF HOPPER

Small colourful insects on leaves

Leaf hoppers are about 9mm (⅜in) long with blue-green bodies, red stripes on the wings and yellowish heads. They appear on the foliage from July to October. The yellow nymphs are present from May to August. Both feed on the undersides of the leaves but do little visible damage. However, the adults lay eggs in the flower buds, wounding the bud and allowing the fungus responsible for bud blast disease to enter.
Control and prevention See page 21.

Leaf weevil damage

■ RHODODENDRON WHITEFLY

Tiny white, moth-like insects on undersides of leaves

The adults are under 2mm (less than ⅛in) long and fly up in clouds when the foliage is disturbed during June and July. Immature stages include tiny transparent scales on the undersides of the foliage which may cause yellowing of the leaves in severe cases. They also produce sticky honeydew which encourages the growth of black sooty mould on the leaves.
Control Spray with a systemic insecticide and repeat at three-day intervals until control is achieved.
Prevention None.

■ LEAF WEEVILS

Holes in the leaves and notching around the edges

The lower branches are the most severely affected. The adults do little real harm, but the larvae can cause severe damage to plant roots, especially those growing in containers.
Control and prevention See page 21.

■ RHODODENDRON LACEBUG

Leaves flecked yellow

There may also be brown, sticky patches on the undersurface. Dark brown insects about 4mm (⅛in) long with lace-like patterns on their wings will be present. Rhododendrons grown on shaded sites are less severely damaged than those growing in sunnier positions.

Control Spray the undersides of the leaves with a contact insecticide during early June.
Prevention Grow rhododendrons in a shaded position.

■ CHLOROSIS

Yellowing between veins

Lime-induced chlorosis is common on alkaline soil.
Control and prevention See page 40.

■ FROST DAMAGE

Younger leaves distorted or puckered

Affected leaves may become peculiarly elongated or be distorted, and frequently have a one-sided appearance. There may be a series of tiny holes in them, resembling a pest attack.

Shoots of all ages, but particularly younger ones and those towards the base of the plant, may split. Affected bark may curl away from the split areas. In severe cases this will cause dieback but, in some instances, the splits may heal successfully. Buds may become soft and brown or, if they open, the flowers may be frosted and become discoloured too.
Control Remove badly damaged shoots before they die back.
Prevention Protect the bases of vulnerable plants with sacking during severe weather.

◼ DIEBACK

Leaves discoloured and may fall and stems die from the tip
Frost damage and adverse growing conditions such as drought, extreme malnutrition or waterlogged soil and diseases like honey fungus (see page 39), silver leaf (see page 70) and canker (see page 38) can cause similar symptoms.
Control First establish the cause. Remove affected shoots, pruning back into completely healthy wood. If a fungal disease is responsible take remedial action. Improve drainage on waterlogged soils and feed if necessary.
Prevention Feed and water well to encourage good growth.

•

◼ RHODODENDRON POWDERY MILDEW

Yellow blotches on the upper surface of leaves; off-white or beige felty patches on the lower surface
In severe cases defoliation and dieback may occur.
Control Pick off and burn affected leaves promptly. Spray with a systemic fungicide.
Prevention Water the plant regularly in dry spells.

•

◼ AZALEA GALL

Pale green, waxy swellings on the leaves and occasionally the flowers
Older galls are covered in powdery white fungal spores. These are readily spread by insects and air currents to nearby bushes.
Control Pick off and burn all galls, preferably before they turn white.
Prevention If the disease occurs regularly spray with a copper-based fungicide (Bordeaux Mixture, for example) and remove galls promptly.

Azalea gall

◼ POOR FLOWERING

Flower buds fail to develop, fail to open and/or produce only a few, small flowers
Buds may remain hard and brown on the stem or may be shed. This is usually the result of poor conditions, particularly summer droughts. A shortage of moisture when the buds are being initiated, usually towards the end of the previous summer, even for a couple of days, can greatly reduce flowering.
Control None.
Prevention Water regularly to keep the root area moist, especially during warm weather. Mulch during late winter or early spring with composted bark or garden compost to help retain soil moisture. Do not feed after mid-July.

•

◼ BUD BLAST

Buds fail to open and remain hard and brown
Affected buds are covered with dense blackish bristles and appear silverish.
   This fungal disease is spread by the rhododendron leaf hopper. Affected buds remain on rhododendron bushes for up to two years and flowering may be severely restricted.
Control Remove and burn affected buds, where feasible.
Prevention Control leaf hoppers.

Bud blast

◼ PETAL BLIGHT

White or pale brown spots appear on the flowers which later collapse

This fungal disease affects rhododendrons and azaleas and is worse during humid weather. Within a few days the flowers are spoiled completely. Infected flowers often remain on the stems until the following spring.
Control Remove and burn affected flowers.
Prevention Spray with a systemic fungicide when the buds start to colour up.

See Tables, pages 130–136 for guide to insecticides and fungicides

SHRUBS AND TREES: LEAVES

■ FIREBLIGHT
Dead brown blossom and foliage which remain on the branches

This disease affects some trees and shrubs belonging to the rose family (see Table on pages 26–27). Often certain banches are affected and look as if they have been burnt. Brownish lesions, which exude a pale brown or white bacterial ooze, may be present on the bark of affected stems. The wood beneath the bark around these areas is flecked with a reddish-brown discoloration.

Plants wilt and die back and may be severely damaged or killed in the first year. The bacteria produced in the ooze are spread by rain splash or insects. They enter via the blossom or shoots, then spread down the spurs and into the branches. Fireblight is most troublesome in warm, damp seasons.

Control Removal of the tree or shrub is advisable, but it may be possible to save it if the disease is noticed very early on. Prune out affected stems to a point at least 60cm (2ft) into healthy wood. Dip pruning tools in a household disinfectant after each cut. Burn all prunings to limit spread. See also page 63.

Prevention Check susceptible plants regularly, including hawthorn hedges. Do not grow susceptible plants if the disease is a problem in your area.

■ OTHER LEAF BLIGHTS
Yellow or brown spots or blotches on the leaves

These may coalesce, causing the leaf to die. Several fungi, viruses and bacteria may be involved. The majority cause slight or only cosmetic damage on plants which are in poor condition or are being attacked by a more serious problem. In severe cases or with repeated attacks the tree or shrub may be weakened and dieback may occur.

Control Treatment is rarely necessary. Spray with a copper fungicide if feasible.

Prevention Rake up and burn affected leaves. Feed and mulch to maintain vigour.

•

■ SHOTHOLE (BACTERIAL CANKER)
Yellow spots which later turn brown and fall away

In severe cases the leaves may be riddled with holes, which can give the appearance of pest attack. Young leaves may become yellow as soon as they unfurl, and may wither and die before developing fully. This disease is most serious on flowering cherries and other *Prunus* species, especially laurel. It also causes stem cankers.

Control Prune out affected branches. Spray with a copper fungicide and repeat as necessary. Feed to improve vigour.

Prevention Spray with a copper fungicide three weeks after petal fall and again 14 days later. Remove affected branches promptly.

•

■ SILVER LEAF
Leaves develop a silvery-grey sheen, but do not wither or fall early

The discoloration is often restricted to single branches at

first. It attacks fruit trees (see page 70) and a wide range of other trees and shrubs (see Table on pages 26–27). Some susceptible plants show no foliage symptoms. Similar symptoms can be caused by lack of water and nutrients (see page 70).
Control and prevention See page 70.

GALLS
Raised and discoloured areas

Galls are caused by the plant's reaction to a range of pests, in particular gall-midges, gall-mites and gall-wasps. Galls may be brightly coloured like the long, pointed red nail gall on lime trees or the pin-head red gall on sycamore. Some cause a more subtle colour change like the brown, saucer-shaped spangle gall on oak leaves. The galls are produced by the plant as the result of stimulation by the adult pests when they lay eggs or by the larvae feeding. The larvae then shelter inside the gall. Occasionally gall-mites may cause 'witches' brooms' – see page 36.
Control Difficult and usually unnecessary. Remove affected leaves where possible. Rake up and burn fallen leaves.
Prevention None.

LEAF-CUTTING BEE
Neat, semi-circular pieces cut from the edges of leaves

Many trees and shrubs including roses, lilac, privet and laburnum may be damaged. The bee responsible is solitary. It goes unnoticed until June when the female uses the pieces of leaf to construct thimble-like cells in which eggs are laid. Plants are rarely harmed.
Control and prevention Not usually necessary.

APHIDS
Green, black, pink or brown insects on leaves
Leaves may be distorted or covered in sticky honeydew or black sooty mould and virus symptoms may appear.
Control and prevention See page 11.

BAY SUCKER
Thickened yellow leaf margins which curl over

The thickened areas turn brown and die. Adult bay suckers cause the leaves to curl in late spring and lay eggs in the curled leaf margins. The grey young, which are covered in a fluffy white material, cause more distortion when feeding.
Control Remove affected leaves and stems. Spray with a systemic insecticide in early and late May.
Prevention None.

WILLOW LEAF BEETLE
Leaf surface grazed away
Damaged areas turn brown and dry up. Severe infestations cause extensive defoliation and weaken the tree. Poplars are also attacked. The shiny red, blue or green beetles (up to 6mm; ¼in long) appear during May and June to lay eggs. Larvae feed for about three weeks before pupating in the soil. A second generation of adults causes further damage in late summer.
Control Spray infestations on small trees with a contact insecticide. Feed to compensate for lost vigour.
Prevention None.

SHRUBS AND TREES: LEAVES

PRIVET THRIPS

Extensive silver flecking and pitting on the leaves

In severe cases leaves may appear completely silver and may be smaller than normal. The dark brown adults and yellow larvae (both 2mm; less than ⅛in long) both cause this damage, which is most severe in hot, dry summers.

Control Spray with a contact insecticide as soon as the first symptoms are seen.

Prevention None.

Thrip damage to privet

DOWNY MILDEW

Downy white or greyish fungal growth on the lower leaf surface; yellowish blotches on the leaves

Severely affected leaves soon die off. This disease is rarely very troublesome but is more common in warm, damp seasons. The fungus may produce dormant spores which can overwinter.

Control Pick off and burn affected leaves. Spray with pbi Dithane 945.

Prevention Improve air circulation by pruning and thinning crowded plants.

POWDERY MILDEW

Powdery white fungal growth on the leaf surfaces, yellowish discoloration

Similar symptoms may develop on stems and fruits. Affected leaves may be distorted, wither

and die. In severe cases extensive defoliation occurs.

Control and prevention See page 12.

PYRACANTHA SCAB

Dark olive-green or black scabby patches on the leaves

Similar symptoms also develop on the flower heads and berries. Affected leaves may be slightly puckered and reduced in size and may fall early, gradually weakening the plant. The fungus overwinters in scabby patches on the shoots. Scab is most severe in damp seasons.

Control Prune out and burn scabby shoots and collect up fallen leaves. Spray with a systemic fungicide.

Prevention None.

LOSS OF VARIEGATION

Gradual disappearance of variegated leaves

The resulting foliage may show different shades of green or uniform coloration. A cultivar may 'revert' to its pure green form, particularly if the plant is under some sort of stress. Too much shade is a common cause, particularly with yellow-variegated plants. Drought, waterlogging or

inadequate feeding may also be responsible. The non-variegated foliage is usually more vigorous and quickly becomes dominant.

Control Prune out all stems showing loss of variegation.

Prevention Provide suitable growing conditions.

ANTHRACNOSE

Brown spots or patches on the foliage; cankers on the stems

This is seen mainly on willow and plane trees, especially the golden weeping willow. In severe cases extensive defoliation and even shoot dieback may occur. The leaves often turn yellow and curl before dropping. The fungus responsible overwinters on fallen leaves and stem cankers.

Control Rake up and burn fallen leaves. Where feasible cut out affected stems. No chemical control is available.

Prevention None.

OTHER LEAF PROBLEMS

Discoloured, distorted or dying foliage

A range of problems cause these symptoms, including weedkiller drift, cold winds, frost, bright sunlight, drought or waterlogging. See pages 42–43.

SHRUBS AND TREES: FLOWERS

▇ POOR FLOWERING
No or few flowers produced; flowers small or short-lived
The plant itself may look perfectly normal and be putting on good growth. Flower buds may fail to form or may form but fail to open, often turning brown and remaining on the stem. If the plant is sufficiently mature and established, poor flowering is usually the result of poor growing conditions – dry soil at the stage when flower buds are being initiated is one of the most common causes. This will result in fewer and often smaller buds being formed. An inadequate supply of nutrients, in particular a lack of potash, is also often responsible. Conversely, if excessive quantities of nitrogen are given the plant may produce plenty of lush foliage but few flowers. A plant which is not in an ideal position, perhaps not receiving enough sun, may also produce few flower buds. Incorrect pruning, where the wood on which the flowers are produced is pruned out in error, may also be to blame.
Control None.
Prevention Ensure that the plant is growing in the right conditions and is fed and pruned correctly.

•

▇ GREY MOULD (BOTRYTIS)
Discoloration and withering of the flowers, followed by fuzzy grey fungal growth
Petals may be spotted, usually with white or brown flecks. Whole flower heads may collapse and rot and the grey mould fungus may then spread into adjacent stems, causing dieback. The fuzzy growth bears many fungal spores which are readily spread on air currents and by rain splash. Infection often follows physical damage, from frost or

Grey mould on carnation

hail, for example. The fungus is extremely widespread and often found on plant debris.
Control Prune out badly affected areas. Spray with a systemic fungicide.
Prevention Maintain strict garden hygiene. Prune carefully and avoid unnecessary injury to the plant. Deadhead regularly.

•

▇ FROST DAMAGE
Flowers fail to open fully or are discoloured and soon die off
Injury is most noticeable on camellia (see page 30), magnolia, viburnum and fruit trees (see page 65). Leaves may also be distorted and the bark may split. Affected clematis flowers have a distinct green colour, but later flushes of blooms are normal.
Control None.
Prevention Choose plants which are frost-tolerant and those which are late flowering; avoid planting in frost pockets. Small plants can be protected by wrapping lightly with hessian.

▇ BLOSSOM WILT
Withered brown flowers which remain hanging on the stem
Infection usually occurs within about two weeks of the start of flowering. Ornamental relatives of apples and cherries are the most frequently attacked. Adjacent bunches of leaves wither and die and eventually the whole spur may die back. Tiny beige fungal pustules are produced, which shed spores.
Control Remove infected spurs before the disease spreads. Spray with a systemic fungicide.
Prevention None.

•

▇ OTHER FLOWER PROBLEMS
Birds, particularly bullfinches, may eat or badly damage young flower buds, severely reducing flowering in the spring (see page 10). Virus infection may cause streaking of petals and reduction in flower size and number. This is usually accompanied by other virus symptoms on the leaves (see page 24).

SHRUBS AND TREES: STEMS AND TRUNKS

◼ CLEMATIS WILT

Stems and shoots wilt and die back suddenly

Clematis×jackmanii, other large-flowered types and *C. montana* are most frequently attacked. The youngest parts of the stems are affected first, the petioles discolouring where they join the leaf blade. The stems die off fairly rapidly but the plant is unlikely to be killed completely. Healthy new growth may be produced from below the wilted areas or even from the base. The fungal spores which cause clematis wilt are released from the remains of old stems or from stem lesions and are easily spread, especially by rain splash.

Similar symptoms may be produced by graft failure or unsuitable growing conditions, such as soil compaction, poor drainage, malnutrition or planting too close to a wall. The most common cause of wilting is, however, the fungal disease.

Control Cut back wilted stems completely, to below ground level if necessary. Spray all growth produced later in the season with a systemic fungicide.

Prevention Spray all new growth as it is produced the following spring. Clear up old stems and avoid wounding stems.

◼ FORSYTHIA GALL

Hard, roughened galls on the stems

Large numbers of irregularly shaped galls may appear on one or more stems, particularly those which are upright. The cause of this problem is unknown, but it is not thought to be infectious and is certainly a harmless condition.

Control Prune out affected stems if they are unsightly.

Prevention None.

◼ CROWN GALL

Hard, knobbly galls, often in chains on the stems

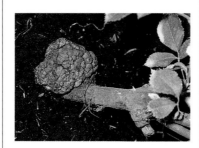

The galls may appear to erupt out from the centre of the stem, causing extensive cracking and splitting. *Daphne*, *Euonymus* and *Viburnum* are often affected. The soil-borne bacteria enter the plant through minute wounds, often being splashed up from the soil.

Control Cut off and burn affected stems before they are invaded by secondary diseases.

Prevention Avoid planting susceptible plants in areas known to harbour the infection.

◼ FASCIATION

Stems and sometimes flower heads are peculiarly broad and flattened

Generally only a few stems are affected on any one plant. A range of trees and shrubs may be affected, but fasciation is very common on *Prunus subhirtella* 'Autumnalis', *Daphne* and forsythia. Leaves and flowers are produced on the shoot but they are often small. The deformity is the result of injury to the growing point; frost damage, insect attack or mechanical injury are probably the main causes.

Control None. Affected stems need only be removed if they are unsightly.

Prevention Avoid injury to plants where possible.

◼ WITCHES' BROOMS

Bunches of short, tightly packed, much-branched shoots in the crown of trees

They gradually enlarge and may completely spoil the appearance of the tree but seem to have little effect on its overall vigour. The foliage is often peculiarly shaped or discoloured. Many trees are affected, particularly ornamental *Prunus*, hornbeam and birch. The cause varies but it is often physical injury or the result of a fungal infection.

Control Prune out brooms if they are unsightly.

Prevention None.

Horse chestnut scale

SCALE INSECTS
Firm, usually brown, scales on stem or bark
The adult scales are sedentary, feeding on the plant's sap and excreting sticky honeydew. Black sooty mould which grows on this can spoil the appearance of the plant. Mobile 'crawlers' hatch from scale insect eggs and move around before developing the scale-like shell. These are some of the most troublesome scales on garden plants.
Soft scale Flat, pale brown, oval scales up to 4mm (⅛in) in length found on stems and leaves of outdoor and greenhouse plants. They produce large amounts of honeydew. Eggs hatch all year.
Brown scale Hemispherical reddish-brown scales up to 6mm (¼in) across on a wide range of woody plants. The eggs hatch from June to August.
Horse chestnut scale A grey-brown, round and fairly flat scale about 4mm (⅛in) across, which sits on a white, waxy egg mass. It is common on maple, magnolia, bay, lime, elm and horse chestnut. Only small quantities of honeydew are produced. The eggs hatch in late June and July.
Mussel scale A dark brown mussel-shaped scale up to about 4mm (⅛in) in length. It is common on hawthorn, cotoneaster, box, *Chaenomeles* and apple trees. The eggs hatch in May and June.
Felted beech scale A small scale up to 1mm (less than ⅛in) in length which is hidden in cracks and crevices in the bark of beech trees. It produces large quantities of white waxy powder which is more clearly visible than the scale itself. It causes little direct damage, but increases the tree's susceptibility to a serious fungus that causes beech bark disease.

Coral spot

Mussel scale

Control Deciduous trees can be treated with a winter wash during December or January (see page 63). Alternatively, spray with a contact insecticide when the eggs are hatching.
Prevention Check new plants to avoid introducing scales.

SHOTHOLE BORER
Small holes in tree bark
The holes are 1–2mm (less than ⅛in) in diameter. Wood dust may be visible at the hole entrance and, with *Prunus* spe-

cies, gum exudes from the hole. The beetles responsible usually attack trees weakened by some other factor, but can attack healthy trees. In extreme cases the tree may die. The adult beetle overwinters and lays its eggs in galleries excavated in the trunk.
Control The pest cannot be reached by insecticides, making control very difficult. Remove badly infested branches.
Prevention None.

CORAL SPOT
Pink or reddish-orange spots on twigs
These spots burst through the bark on dead wood. *Elaeagnus*, flowering currants, maples and magnolia are frequently attacked, but most deciduous trees are susceptible. The disease normally enters through bark wounds or dead wood, but is capable of causing a lot of damage to healthy shoots.
Control Cut out affected areas completely.
Prevention None.

BRACKET FUNGI
Growths on bark
The fruiting bodies of silver leaf (see page 70) appear as brackets or crusty outgrowths with purple undersides. Many other wood-rotting fungi produce fruiting bodies, often in the shape of fungal 'brackets'. Sometimes these are associated with snags or other physical damage. Affected trees sometimes show other signs of deterioration, such as lots of dead branches or a thinning of the crown.
Control Prune out affected areas or remove the whole tree or shrub. For large trees see page 38.
Prevention None.

SHRUBS AND TREES: STEMS AND TRUNKS

■ DIEBACK
Gradual deterioration followed by dying back of stems or branches

Dieback usually starts at the shoot tips and spreads towards the centre of the plant. Often there is no obvious sign of pest or disease damage. A wide range of factors may be responsible, including:
■ Root stress caused by water-logging, drought, soil compaction or poor planting
■ Damage to the roots by soil pests or fungal diseases
■ Physical injury
■ Fungal diseases on the stems themselves, like grey mould, coral spot or silver leaf.
Control Prune out damaged branches. If root damage is suspected prune the top growth to compensate.
Prevention Provide good growing conditions and prevent injury.

■ CANKERS
Roughened or raised, often target-like, concentric rings on bark

The size and appearance of the cankers vary with the host species. Cankers may increase in size until the stem is ringed. In extreme cases the whole stem may die back. Most cankers are caused by fungi and tiny fungal bodies will be seen at certain times of year.
Control Remove affected areas or badly affected branches and use a pruning compound. Spray with a systemic fungicide.
Prevention None.

■ BACTERIAL CANKER
Flattened areas of bark, which may exude amber-coloured gum
The foliage and later the whole stem deteriorates. Buds may fail to develop and leaves may turn yellow and wither. Brown spots and 'shothole' symptoms appear on the leaves. See also page 32.
Control Prune out affected branches. Spray the leaves with a copper-based fungicide at three-week intervals from mid-August (see also page 71).
Prevention None.

ROTS ON LARGE TREES
Brackets or other fungal fruiting bodies on trunks
These may be perennial or short-lived. The bark may be loosened, revealing soft or discoloured wood beneath. Flattened patches of bark may indicate internal decay. Other signs of decay include lots of dead branches, a thinning of the crown, early leaf fall or discoloured leaves.
Control Removing the fungal growths will do no good because the fungus feeds inside the tree. Do not try to remove damaged or rotten wood. Do not drain cavities or treat damaged areas with a fungicide or wound paint. Badly decayed trees could be dangerous. Consult a qualified tree surgeon and leave any remedial work to an expert.
Prevention Avoid unnecessary injury. Any tree surgery work should be carried out by a qualified tree surgeon.

■ IVY AND OTHER CLIMBERS
Climbers wind round or cling on to the bark of trees
Clematis, honeysuckle and ivy may appear to smother young or slow-growing plants or those lacking vigour. They generally do little harm, although the twining stems of honeysuckles can strangle trees and all climbers can hide signs of disease or decay.
Control Prune if necessary. To remove climbers sever the main stem, but do this only when absolutely necessary as they provide important habitats for wildlife.
Prevention None.

■ MISTLETOE
Clumps of fleshy-green leaves growing from trunks
This partially parasitic plant is spread by birds which eat the white sticky fruits. It grows very

SHRUBS AND TREES: ROOTS

slowly on apple, lime, poplar, sycamore and other deciduous trees. It may weaken old trees, but generally does little harm.
Control As it grows so slowly, cutting for decorations should keep it under control.
Prevention None.

HONEY-FUNGUS
Leaves wither and yellow; whole plant deteriorates or dies

This may happen gradually or very suddenly. Trees or shrubs under stress are especially vulnerable; those that are growing well can usually resist it. Prior to death the plant may fail to leaf up normally, producing either very small or sparse foliage. Infected plants may also produce an unusually heavy crop of flowers or fruit or die back branch by branch. Conifers may exude resin from the base of the trunk. Clusters of honey-coloured toadstools appear around the base of the trunk, or occasionally from the main stem or trunk, in September to November, but not necessarily every year. A creamy-white fungal sheet (mycelium) is often visible if the bark is removed near the base of the trunk and on the larger roots. The wood in this area appears rotten and spongy and has a distinct fungal smell. Tough black threads or 'bootlaces' called rhizomorphs can sometimes be found in the soil attached to the plant or under the bark with the mycelium. The disease spreads by means of these rhizomorphs or by root contact, rather than by spores from the toadstools.
Control Armillatox is claimed to control honey fungus. No other chemical controls are available to gardeners. Remove all affected plants with as much root as possible. A complete physical barrier made from thick polythene buried 50cm (20in) deep may prevent spread of the disease.
Prevention remove affected plants quickly before the disease spreads. Remove tree stumps too, as these can harbour the disease.
If honey fungus is present in your garden do not plant susceptible trees or shrubs; choose those that show some resistance (see Table on pages 26–27).

PHYTOPHTHORA ROOT ROT
Leaves small, yellow or sparse, followed by dieback, often up one side of the plant.
The fungus kills the roots, starting with those near to the main stem or trunk and close to the soil surface. Patches of dead bark can be seen at the base of the trunk and the wood beneath may be discoloured. Often a dark, almost black stain can be seen. The affected area may bleed leaving a crusty exudation on the bark. Young trees, both deciduous and evergreen, are frequently attacked, but older trees are sometimes attacked, too. The fungus is carried in soil moisture, so is easily spread. The disease is worst in wet, heavy soils.
Controls None. Remove affected plants and their roots.
Prevention Avoid spreading soil from affected areas around the garden. Improve drainage and do not plant susceptible trees or shrubs (see Table on pages 26–27).

See Tables, pages 130–136 for guide to insecticides and fungicides

SHRUBS AND TREES: NUTRIENT DEFICIENCIES

MAGNESIUM DEFICIENCY
Yellowing between leaf veins
In some cases a brown or pink discoloration may appear. In severe cases the interveinal area turns brown and dies.

Older leaves are affected first because the magnesium in them is moved to the younger, developing leaves.

With conifers the needles turn yellow. The older needles are affected first on *Thuja* and the tips of the younger needles first on some varieties of spruce. If the deficiency persists for several seasons, growth may be reduced.

Magnesium is readily leached from free-draining sandy soils. Excess potash in the soil may make the magnesium unavailable to plants, so trees and shrubs fed with a high-potash fertiliser are particularly susceptible.
Control Where feasible give a foliar spray of Epsom salts. Dilute 225g (8oz) of Epsom salts to 11 litres (2½ gal) of water. Add some detergent or wetting agent to help the solution stick to the leaves. This spray treatment should have a fairly rapid effect in the growing season. During the autumn or winter topdress the soil with 30g of Epsom salts a sq m (1oz a sq yd).
Prevention Feed with a fertiliser containing trace elements. Mulch with organic matter.

NITROGEN DEFICIENCY
Pale leaves and poor growth
Leaves may also be small and in severe cases they may show their autumn colour early. However, this is not a common problem in gardens.
Control Apply a high-nitrogen fertiliser.
Prevention Apply well-composted organic matter and a balanced fertiliser regularly.

PHOSPHORUS DEFICIENCY
Poor growth; small leaves, sometimes discoloured or purple, which may fall early
Needles of conifers may be shorter than normal and appear dull. This is not common in gardens except in upland areas with peaty soils and high rainfall.
Control Apply a phosphate fertiliser, like bonemeal.
Prevention Use a balanced fertiliser regularly.

POTASH DEFICIENCY
Leaf margins and tips brown or scorched
A pinkish coloration may occur on conifers. Affected leaves may also curl at the edges with brown spots on the lower surface. It is often accompanied by poor flowering and fruiting. It is most common on light soils.
Control Apply sulphate of potash or a balanced fertiliser.
Prevention Apply organic matter or a balanced fertiliser regularly, particularly on light soils.

MANGANESE DEFICIENCY
Leaves pale between the veins
In severe cases the whole leaf

may appear chlorotic (see 'Chlorosis'). This deficiency is most common on heavy, wet soils with a pH over 6.5. Young leaves are worst affected.
Control Apply a fertiliser containing trace elements (one based on seaweed, for example), fritted trace elements or a chelated compound.
Prevention None.

CHLOROSIS
Yellowing between the veins and brown spotting, often starting at the edges of young leaves
The symptoms are not easy to distinguish from magnesium deficiency. Acid-loving plants growing on soils with a pH over 6.0 are commonly affected. Other trees and shrubs may be affected on alkaline soil, when the pH is above 7.5. Under these conditions iron and sometimes manganese become 'locked up' in the soil and unavailable to plants. When the soil is very alkaline with a pH over 8.0 and iron alone is locked up, the symptoms are often described as lime-induced. In extreme cases the foliage will appear bleached.
Control Apply chelated iron, which will give short-term improvement. Dig in or mulch with plenty of acidic organic matter, such as pulverised bark, peat or peat substitutes. Check the pH and if it is too high consider moving the plant to a raised bed or a pot containing lime-free or ericaceous compost or soil.
Prevention Never plant acid-loving trees or shrubs or those susceptible to lime-induced chlorosis on alkaline soils. Grow them in raised beds or tubs instead.

Mulch regularly with acidic organic matter and water with rainwater in hard water areas.

Magnesium deficiency on rose

TESTING YOUR SOIL pH

It is essential to know the pH of your soil when starting a new garden. Some plants will not grow well in soil which is alkaline or limy, where the pH is too high (see Table on pages 26–27).

Soil test kits are widely available in garden centres. Testing soil pH is very easy. Take several samples of soil from an area of the garden, about 5cm (2in) below the surface. Mix them together, dry the sample and break up any lumps. Add a small amount to the test tube and add the solution. The colour of the liquid indicates the pH when compared to the colour chart provided.

Kits are also available to test the nutrients in the soil. When these were tested by *Gardening from Which?* they were not as accurate as the pH test kits.

If you move into a new garden consider having a soil analysis carried out by a specialist laboratory.

It is fairly easy to raise the pH, by adding lime, but difficult to lower it.

Potash deficiency on apple

Chlorosis on rhododendron

SHRUBS AND TREES: CAUSES OF POOR GROWTH

Often trees or shrubs appear to be deteriorating or at least not growing as well as you would expect. Pest damage or signs of disease may be apparent but are not necessarily the cause. Plants that are not doing well are susceptible to permanent damage by pests or diseases. The underlying cause of the problem is usually that the plant is in the wrong position or on unsuitable soil or has not been planted correctly.

DRYNESS AT THE ROOTS
Leaves small and discoloured; flowering reduced or ceases
Plants remain small and make little extension growth.

Plants in containers or near to walls are most susceptible. Young or recently planted trees and shrubs are also vulnerable in sunny positions or on free-draining soils.
Prevention Water plants regularly and frequently especially in their first year. Mulch the root feeding area after thoroughly wetting the soil.

Do not plant drought intolerant plants in very dry positions. Plant wall shrubs at least 45cm (18in) away from walls.

WATERLOGGING
Leaves discoloured or chlorotic; growth reduced
Plants grown in containers with inadequate drainage are often affected. A planting hole filled with moisture-retentive material like peat may create a sump, drawing more moisture into the hole. This is most common on heavy soils and when the soil in the bed is not improved as well as the planting hole.
Prevention Improve drainage and soil texture before planting. Consider growing sensitive plants in raised beds.

Frost damage

RAISED SOIL LEVEL
Growth slow; leaves small and discoloured; branches die back
If the soil level is raised around existing plants, the roots can be killed by being deprived of oxygen. The foliage and stems subsequently deteriorate and the bark may also be injured.

FROST
Leaves discoloured; plants stunted; bark and stems cracked
Branches may be cut back by severe frosts, particularly late frosts. Young plants, especially tender species or those growing in exposed spots are particularly vulnerable. Buds and flowers of early varieties of some shrubs can also be damaged (see pages 30 and 35).
Prevention Do not plant tender shrubs in exposed spots or frost pockets. Provide winter protection, for example by wrapping lightly with sacking, until all danger of frost has passed.

COMPACTION
Leaves discoloured or chlorotic; growth reduced
Soil may become compacted if the area is frequently walked on or driven over when it is wet. Heavy vehicles used in construction work may also be a cause.
Prevention Double dig areas that you suspect of compaction thoroughly before planting.

MULCHING TOO NEAR THE BASE
Leaves and stems deteriorate
Close inspection of the stem may reveal deterioration of the bark. The moist environment created by the mulch causes direct damage to the bark and encourages soil-living micro-organisms which may attack the stems. Clear mulches away from plants that have not been seriously damaged. Do not mulch right up to the stem base.

POOR PLANTING
Plants grow normally at first but then start to deteriorate
Bare rooted plants which have suffered root injury or dehydration or which are planted without their roots being well spread out may show these symptoms. Container-grown plants which are pot bound and do not have their roots teased out when planted may produce roots which continue to grow around and around in the shape of the original container. They are then unable to take advantage of nutrients and moisture in the surrounding soil. Lift the shrub, soak the root ball in water and gently tease out the roots. Replant it in a freshly prepared planting hole.
Prevention Prepare a large enough planting hole and spread the roots out well.

INSUFFICIENT LIGHT
Growth poor; unusually coloured or variegated foliage may revert to green
In shade or semi-shade green foliage may predominate. Yellow variegated plants often need full sun. Grey or silver-leaved plants generally do not do well in shade. If possible prune overhanging branches to increase light levels.

REMEDIES FOR POOR GROWTH
In most cases the problem can be prevented, but once symptoms are obvious there is usually little you can do. If the plant is fairly small consider moving it to a new site or, if the soil is wrong, to a raised bed or tub. Improve drainage, break up compacted layers or improve the moisture retentive capacity of the soil when you prepare a new planting hole. The planting hole should be at least 45cm (18in) deep and wider than the plant's rootball. Tease out the roots and spread them out well.

If the plant is too large or too difficult to move, replace it with something more suitable.

Before planting a tree or shrub check that the conditions in your garden are suitable for it.

WEEDKILLER DAMAGE
Pale bands or spots on leaves

These areas later turn brown and wither. The plant should recover and new growth will be normal colour.
Prevention Read the label carefully before using a weed preventer. Choose a cool, still day to spray weedkillers to avoid drift. Take care when treating paths that weedkiller does not run off onto borders.

STARVATION
Leaves small and sparse; growth poor
Plants growing on naturally poor soils or in containers are likely to show this unless they are regularly fed and maintained. In extreme cases dieback may occur. Prune out straggly or dying branches. Apply a foliar feed to provide immediately available nutrients and a slow-release fertiliser or manure, too. See also 'Nutrient deficiencies' on pages 40–41.

TOO MUCH SUN
Young leaves scorched
Golden or yellow-leaved shrubs and maples are particularly vulnerable to sun scorch in spring, especially on dry soils. Keep them well watered.

EXPOSED SITUATIONS
Leaves scorched, especially around the leaf edges and on one side of the plant
The growth may also appear stunted and lop-sided as the plant grows away from the prevailing wind. In extreme cases branches may die back.
Prevention Use wind-breaks to provide shelter for plants growing in exposed positions. Avoid especially susceptible plants such as maples which are easily scorched.

SALT
Leaves small with brown patches of dead tissue; stems die back
Plants growing near roads can be damaged. The salt prevents the normal uptake of moisture and nutrients and may scorch the foliage. Salt-tolerant trees include *Alnus glutinosa*, *Robina pseudoacacia* and, *Salix alba* 'Vitellina.'

CONIFERS

PINEAPPLE GALL

Buds of Norway spruce swell and produce green galls like miniature pineapples

The galls are produced by the feeding of a tiny adelgid (a relative of aphids) and form around the nymph of this pest. Towards the end of summer the gall splits to release the adult, then dries up and turns brown. Infested trees may look unsightly but are not seriously harmed.
Control If necessary, spray with a contact insecticide during February.
Prevention None.

WOOLLY ADELGIDS

Stems and needles covered in white woolly patches

Larch, pine and fir trees are attacked. The insects are covered in waxy white material, so are not visible. Although the plants may look unsightly this pest rarely does any harm, except by excreting sticky honeydew, which in turn encourages black sooty mould.
Control Rarely necessary, but small trees can be sprayed with a contact insecticide during February.
Prevention None.

NEEDLE CASTS

Needles of young trees discolour and fall
Tiny fungal fruiting bodies can be seen on the needles and shoots may die back. The fungi responsible can overwinter on the fallen needles.
Control Spray with a systemic fungicide. Rake up and burn fallen needles.
Prevention None.

CANKER

Patches of needles turn yellow, then brown and die
Cankers that develop on affected branches may exude sticky resin. Tiny black, pin-prick-sized fungal fruiting bodies are formed around the cankers. The cankers may gradually girdle and kill the affected stems. *Cupressus* species and Leyland cypress are frequently attacked. The spores enter the branches through frost cracks, twig crotches and leaf scales, usually during the winter.
Control Remove affected areas by cutting back into healthy wood as soon as the problem is seen.
Prevention None.

COLD WEATHER OR FROST

Foliage bronzed or yellowing, sometimes followed by dieback
Young foliage and young trees are the most likely to be damaged. In extreme cases stems may also be injured or cracked.
Control Where necessary cut out damaged areas.
Prevention Provide young trees with frost protection – by wrapping lightly with sacking, for example.

CONIFER APHIDS

Foliage discoloured or mottled and may drop
Several species of aphid are involved, each attacking specific conifers, including cypress, cedar, spruce and *Thuja*. In severe cases dieback may occur – this can happen very rapidly in hot, dry summers. Damage is most obvious at the base of the tree.
Control Spray with ICI Rapid.
Prevention None.

HONEY FUNGUS

Foliage turns yellow and then brown; tree gradually or suddenly dies
Resin may ooze from the base of the trunk. Honey-coloured toadstools may appear in the autumn. Look for tough, black rhizomorphs (like bootlaces) in the surrounding soil and creamy-white fungal growth under the bark.
Control and prevention The tree will have to be removed. See page 39.

CONIFER SPINNING MITE

Foliage mottled yellow and falls; fine webbing visible
Tiny yellowish-green mites and their red eggs can be seen through a magnifying glass. Hot, dry summers encourage these pests. Dwarf conifers are particularly susceptible, especially spruce, *Thuja* and juniper.
Control Spray with a suitable insecticide as soon as the mites are first seen.
Prevention None.

Effects of phytophthora root death on Leyland cypress

PHYTOPHTHORA
Foliage becomes yellow and sparse and may die back
Areas of the bark at the base of the trunk may deteriorate and a blackish discoloration develops beneath. Young trees and those growing on heavy or water-logged soils are particularly susceptible.
Control No chemical controls are available. Remove and burn affected trees and roots.
Prevention Improve drainage on heavy soils. Leyland cypress and western hemlock are less likely to be affected.

JUNIPER WEBBER
Foliage turns brown in patches and is bound together by silk webbing

Older juniper trees are usually more severely affected. In May small (up to 2cm; ¾in long) brown caterpillars may be found in amongst the webbing and foliage.
Control This is difficult because the webbing is almost impene-trable. Spray, using a hard jet, with a contact insecticide as soon as the caterpillars are seen.
Prevention None.

BRACKET FUNGI
Fungal fruiting bodies, often bracket-shaped, on the trunk
These usually appear near to

ground level, on the ground near to the trunk or on roots. The crown may appear rather thin, branches may die back and growth may be reduced. If the heart wood is rotten, affected trees may be vulnerable to strong winds.
Control Consult a qualified tree surgeon. Removal of the tree is often advisable.
Prevention None.

TRUNK OR STEM SPLITTING
Surface or deep longitudinal cracks or fissures develop
Growth may be stunted but the tree appears healthy. This is particularly common after a dry summer due to inadequate and then fluctuating soil moisture levels. The wounds usually heal over.
Control None.
Prevention Ensure regular and adequate supplies of water. Mulch the root area.

THUJA BLIGHT
Small areas of foliage turn yellow and later brown; small blackish-brown fungal fruiting bodies on the surface of foliage

The lowermost branches are usually worst affected and may die back. *Thuja* grown as hedges seems to be very susceptible.
Control No chemical control is available. Prune out and burn affected areas or in severe cases remove the whole tree.
Prevention Plant Leyland or Lawson's cypress instead.

See Tables, pages 130–136 for guide to insecticides and fungicides

HERBACEOUS PLANTS: LEAVES

NUTRIENT DEFICIENCIES
Leaves discoloured and growth stunted

If feeding is inadequate or if nutrients are made unavailable by poor growing conditions, nutrient deficiencies may occur. Probably the most common is magnesium deficiency, causing a yellow, red or brown discoloration between the veins. It is especially common on free-draining acid soils. The older leaves are affected first. Nitrogen deficiency causes yellowing and often results in the development of small leaves.
Control and prevention See 'Nutrient deficiencies' on pages 40–41.

FUNGAL LEAF SPOTS
Yellow, brown or reddish spots or blotches on leaves, usually with clearly defined margins, sometimes surrounded by a yellow halo
Close examination may reveal concentric rings on the spot and minute fungal bodies in the centre. Leaf spots may coalesce to form large, dead areas and cause considerable damage. They are more troublesome on plants which are not growing strongly.
Control Pick off affected leaves. If necessary, spray with a systemic fungicide.
Prevention None.

DOWNY MILDEW
Yellowish blotches on the upper leaf surface. Greyish or purplish white patches of fluffy fungal growth on the lower surface
Affected leaves may wither and die and damage may be severe if the disease is not checked. It is worse in damp weather.
Control Pick off and burn affected leaves immediately. Spray with pbi Dithane 945.
Prevention Make sure plants are not crowded.

POWDERY MILDEW
Powdery white fungal growth on the upper leaf surface
Leaves may also have yellow patches and may be distorted, particularly if the infection is very heavy or early in the season. Severely affected leaves wither and die. Dry soil conditions encourage this disease.
Control Remove affected leaves. Spray with a systemic fungicide. See page 12.
Prevention Keep plants well watered and mulched. Make sure plants are not crowded.

VIRUSES
Leaves mottled or flecked yellow or with ring-spots
Severely affected plants may be distorted, gradually become less vigorous and eventually die. Some plants may show these symptoms for many years with no apparent effect on their general health. Some viruses affect a very wide range of plants.
Control No chemical control is available. Destroy virus-infected plants.
Prevention Remove infected plants. Control sap-feeding pests, especially aphids. Do not collect seed from plants which may be infected. Wash hands after handling infected plants.

APHIDS
Leaves and growing tips covered in green, black or pink insects
Leaves may be puckered or distorted and, in severe cases, young plants may be stunted or even die. Plants may also be covered in sticky honeydew and black sooty mould. Aphids can transmit viruses. See also page 11.
Control Spray with ICI Rapid or a systemic insecticide.
Prevention None.

VIOLET LEAF MIDGE
Leaves thickened and rolled
Clusters of pale orange or white larvae (about 4mm; ⅛in long) or white cocoons may be found if the leaves are unrolled. In severe cases plants are stunted and flowering is reduced.
Control Pick off and burn affected leaves.
Prevention None.

SOLOMON'S SEAL SAWFLY
Leaves eaten, plants may be stripped bare
Solomon's seal and other polygonatums can be attacked. In July the off-white caterpillars move to the soil where they overwinter. The adults emerge in May the following year and lay rows of eggs in the stem. A purple scar may develop. The plant usually recovers well and produces plenty of foliage the following year.
Control Pick off larvae. Spray with a contact insecticide.
Prevention None.

SMUT
Pale yellow spots on leaves
Dahlias first show symptoms from July. The spots gradually darken and some leaves may be killed. Other smut diseases attack marigolds and anenomes.

Swellings on leaves and stems burst to release masses of black spores.
Control Destroy affected plants.
Prevention None.

•

■ BLACK BLOTCH
Black blotches on the leaves of delphiniums
Severely affected leaves may wither. The spots sometimes spread to the stems and flowers.
Control Remove badly damaged leaves and spray with a copper fungicide.
Prevention Spray shoots with a copper-based fungicide when they emerge above ground.

•

Smut

Lily beetle

■ WHITE BLISTER
Glistening raised white pustules, sometimes in concentric rings
This is common on *Arabis*, honesty and alyssum. See also page 95. Severely affected leaves may be yellowed and badly distorted. The spores are easily spread and this disease is encouraged by humid conditions.
Control Remove and burn affected leaves.
Prevention None.

•

Violet leaf midge damage

■ FLEA BEETLE
Young leaves peppered with 1–2mm (less than ⅛in) holes
The leaves may also appear pitted. The adult beetles, up to 3mm (⅛in) long attack plants during dry spells in March and April. The larvae may attack the roots causing poor growth. Stocks, wallflowers, godetias, alyssum, draba, anemones and vegetable members of the cabbage family are often attacked.
Control Dust young leaves and the soil with derris.
Prevention Encourage strong growth so that plants can grow away well or start them in pots.

■ LILY BEETLE
Irregular holes eaten in leaves and sometimes petals
The larvae start to feed at the tip of the leaf and can cause severe defoliation on lilies. The adult is about 8mm (⅜in) long and bright scarlet with a black head and legs. The larvae are often coated in excreta. The adults overwinter in the soil. This pest is currently confined to Berkshire, Hampshire, Surrey and neighbouring areas.
Control Pick off and destroy the pests. Spray with a contact insecticide at dusk.
Prevention None.

White blister

See Tables, pages 130–136 for guide to insecticides and fungicides

HERBACEOUS PLANTS: STEMS AND ROOTS

Cuckoo spit

stem base and, in severe cases, the wound may allow the entry of fatal diseases. The rest of the plant should remain healthy. This is usually the result of very irregular watering and occurs when a lot of water is supplied after a long, dry period.
Control Cut out affected stems completely.
Prevention Water adequately and regularly. Mulch to maintain soil moisture.

•

PHLOX EELWORM
Thickened, twisted stems which may split; thin distorted leaves

CUCKOO SPIT
Frothy white secretions
Within the froth is the yellowish nymph of a sap-feeding insect called a frog hopper. It is most commonly seen between May and June. Cuckoo spit usually does little harm, but growing tips can be distorted.
Control Pick off the froth.
Prevention None.

•

FASCIATION
Stems broad, flattened and sometimes ribbon-like
The health of the plant is not affected and it should flower normally. The condition is believed to be caused by injury to the growing tips by insects, frost, slugs or even hoeing early in the season. It is frequently seen on delphiniums, primulas, bellis and euphorbias.
Control Not necessary. Cut out affected stems if desired.
Prevention Protect plants from damage.

LEAFY GALL
Masses of small shoots at the base of the plant

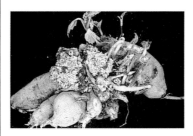

The bacterium responsible enters through wounds and most often attacks chrysanthemum, *Heuchera*, *Pelargonium*, and phlox. The plant may gradually lose vigour.
Control Destroy affected plants.
Prevention Do not grow susceptible plants on that site. Avoid injuring plants.

•

SPLITTING
Stems twist, spiral and split
Splitting is most common at the

The plants are generally stunted and may not flower. Vigour is reduced each year. Phlox, aubrieta, *Gilia*, *Oenothera*, Sweet William, gladiolus and primula may be attacked, together with several common weeds.
Control and prevention See page 24. Propagate plants from root cuttings.

HERBACEOUS PLANTS: CROWNS, ROOTS

■ CROWN GALLS
Rounded but irregularly shaped lumps break through the stem
The galls may measure up to 2cm (¾in) in diameter and frequently appear in chains. Affected stems appear not to suffer, but are vulnerable to secondary infection by more serious diseases. The bacteria responsible may be present in the soil and enter through wounds. Wet soil conditions encourage the disease.
Control Cut out affected stems or remove the whole plant.
Prevention Avoid injuring plants.

■ CROWN ROT OF WATERLILIES
Stems and leaves deteriorate, become slimy and blackened
The microscopic fungi responsible are found in the water.
Control Remove and destroy affected waterlilies.
Prevention None.

■ SLUGS AND SNAILS
Leaves, stems or crowns nibbled
A silvery slime trail confirms the presence of slugs or snails. Young plants or those with basal rosettes of leaves are most vulnerable.
Control and prevention See page 8.

■ CLUBROOT
Plants wilt during hot weather; leaves discoloured
Inspection of the roots reveals swelling and distortion. Impaired root function is responsible for the above ground symptoms, though plants may recover in the evening. Clubroot is most troublesome on heavy, wet, acid soils. Stocks, wallflowers and candytuft are often affected together with vegetables belonging to the cabbage family. The disease is spread on soil, plants, tools and boots, etc.
Control and prevention See page 98.

■ CABBAGE ROOT FLY
Plants wilt, especially during hot, dry weather
This pest attacks wallflowers and vegetables of the cabbage family. Inspection of the base and soil reveals many tiny white maggots which feed on the roots. Young plants may die, but slight attacks may do little harm to vigorous plants.
Control and prevention See page 98.

■ IMPAIRED ROOT FUNCTION
Stunted and poor growth. Stems sometimes crack
Plants wilt in dry, hot weather. This can be caused by a pest or disease problem or where the roots are unable to function normally because of poor soil conditions: compaction, drought or waterlogging. If very pot-bound plants are planted out without first teasing out the roots they may show similar symptoms.
Control Move the plant to a more suitable site. Check the condition of the roots first.
Prevention Choose a suitable site, plant and maintain the plants well.

■ WILT
Leaves and younger stems wilt and may be discoloured
Wilted leaves may remain on the stems. The plant may die off in sections and may take more than one season to do so. Various soil-borne fungi are responsible, each having a restricted range of hosts: for example, asters, chrysanthemums, dahlias, Michaelmas daisies and pinks. The fungi remain in the soil for several years, sometimes in the absence of a host plant.
Control None. Remove and burn affected plants and their roots.
Prevention Do not plant susceptible plants on the site.

■ SCLEROTINIA
Wet-looking brown rot, usually at the stem base
Dahlias, delphiniums, gypsophila, sunflowers and lupins are most often attacked. A white, fluffy fungal growth is often present and large, hard, dark fungal resting bodies are embedded in it. These fall into the soil and overwinter to cause new infections, often via wounded or dying stems, in subsequent years.
Control Dig up and burn affected plants immediately, preferably before the resting bodies are shed.
Prevention Do not grow susceptible plants on the site for at least four years. Keep the area free of weeds, which can harbour the disease.

■ FOOT AND ROOT ROTS
Young stems wither and wilt; the base or crown may be discoloured and later rots
Many roots are lost, while those which remain are blackened. A wide range of herbaceous plants are attacked. Young or poorly growing plants are worst affected and in severe cases may die.
Control Dig up and burn badly affected plants. Slightly affected ones can sometimes be saved by removing the damaged area and replanting the healthy part on a new site.
Prevention None.

HERBACEOUS PLANTS: FLOWERS

ANTHER SMUT
Flower stems stunted and anthers distorted
Carnations grown outside and under glass are affected. The anthers may split open revealing masses of purplish-black fungal spores.
Control Remove and burn affected plants, preferably before the flower buds open.
Prevention Do not take cuttings from affected plants. Do not grow carnations on that site for at least five years.

MICHAELMAS DAISY MITE
Flower petals replaced by rosettes of green leaves
The stems are disfigured by rough, brown scars caused by the mites feeding. The tiny, cream mites live in the leaf sheaths and flower buds. *Aster novi-belgii* types are most severely affected. *Aster amellus* or *A. novae-angliae*, should flower well even when affected.
Control No chemical controls are available. Remove and burn severely infested plants.
Prevention None.

EARWIGS
Tattered holes in the petals
Chrysanthemums, clematis, dahlias, delphiniums, pansies, violas and zinnias are commonly affected. Buds and leaves may also be attacked and, in severe cases, buds may die. Earwigs feed mainly at night. During the day they hide within the flower. Damage occurs from June to September.
Control Trap earwigs in flower pots filled with dry straw placed on top of stakes, or use rolls of corrugated cardboard or hessian. Spray with a contact insecticide.
Prevention Keep the garden tidy to eliminate hiding places.

THRIPS
Petals flecked silver and slightly distorted
The flowers may later turn brown and die off. Leaves and buds are often affected as well. Most of the damage is done during mid-summer. Tiny adults and larvae may be seen. The adults overwinter in plant debris on the soil surface and in the soil.
Control Spray with a systemic insecticide when first seen.
Prevention Water plants regularly.

VIRUSES
Poor flowering, bud drop or flowers with streaks or blotches
Flowers may be distorted. Leaves are often flecked yellow, ring-spotted or streaked.
Control No chemical controls are available. Remove and burn any plants showing symptoms. Do not propagate from them.
Prevention Spray regularly to control aphids and other sap-sucking insects.

PETAL BLIGHT
Small elliptical water-soaked spots on the outer petals
This disease affects anemones, chrysanthemums and other members of the daisy family. The flower head later browns, shrivels and usually becomes covered with grey mould.
Control Remove and burn affected florets or flowers.
Prevention None.

BUD FAILURE
Small hard buds remain on the plants but fail to develop fully and do not open
This is usually the result of unsuitable conditions. Frost, dry soil and malnutrition are often to blame.

Control Remove affected buds and improve conditions.
Prevention Protect susceptible plants from frost. Apply a deep mulch and water well in dry spells. Feed regularly, preferably with a high-potash feed or apply a dressing of sulphate of potash.

POLLEN BEETLES
Flowers infested with small (2mm; $^{1}/_{16}$in), shiny black or green-brown beetles
They appear in spring, but are most troublesome from June onwards. They are more common in areas where oil-seed rape is grown. They are usually harmless and may help to pollinate flowers, but are a nuisance on flowers used for cutting or for showing.
Control Insecticides usually prove ineffective. Shake blooms. Put cut flowers in a dark shed or garage with an open window or door for a few hours. The beetles should fly towards the light.
Prevention None.

GREY MOULD
Brown patches on the petals or buds, later becoming covered in a fuzzy grey fungal growth
Affected flowers soon die off completely and the fungus may spread down the flower stem. Large numbers of spores are produced and are spread by water splash or air currents.
Control Cut out affected flowers and stems.
Prevention Keep the garden free of debris which may harbour the fungus.

CAPSID BUGS
Flowers fail to open or are deformed or ragged
The small bugs inject toxins into the plant as they feed, killing off

tiny areas of tissue. As the petals expand these dead patches tear, leaving holes. Leaves and young shoots may be similarly affected.

Control Pick off badly affected buds or flowers. Spray with a systemic insecticide.

Prevention Keep weeds under control as these may be alternative host plants.

Anther smut

Earwig damage

Petal blight

Pollen beetle

Thrips

See Tables, pages 130–136 for guide to insecticides and fungicides

BULBS

APHIDS
Leaves distorted or discoloured
Leaves, stems and flowers are covered with large clusters of pale green, black or brownish aphids. Apart from causing a general reduction in vigour, aphids spread many virus diseases, so virus symptoms may also occur. See also page 11.
Control Spray with ICI Rapid or a systemic insecticide.
Prevention None.

VIRUSES
Leaves streaked or mottled yellow or brown and may also be stunted and distorted

The buds may fail and any flowers produced may also be discoloured or spotted or show 'breaking' symptoms (see page 24). Some bulbs appear almost unaffected by certain virus infections, but in many instances they gradually deteriorate.

Many viruses are spread by sap-feeding pests, particularly aphids.
Control Remove affected plants promptly to decrease the chance of the disease spreading.
Prevention Spray to control aphids (see left). Plant replacement plants on a fresh site in case soil-inhabiting organisms were carrying the virus.

SLUGS
Ragged holes in the flower stems and young leaves
Silvery slime trails confirm the presence of slugs or snails. Bulbs may also be attacked underground. Much of the damage is done before or as the foliage emerges above ground in spring and early summer.
Control and prevention See page 8.

SQUIRRELS, MICE AND VOLES
Bulbs fail to come up
Excavation reveals that the bulbs have disappeared. Newly planted bulbs are most at risk and are often eaten in the autumn and winter. Gardens in rural locations are usually worst affected.
Control None.
Prevention Firm down soil well after planting. If necessary protect newly planted bulbs with wire netting until the shoots emerge above ground. Plant bulbs for naturalising at twice the normal depth.

GREY MOULD
Flowers discolour and die off, and are covered in a grey, fuzzy fungal growth
The foliage may also be affected. This is a common problem especially in wet seasons. The flower stems of snowdrops may also be

affected and in severe cases, whole clumps can be killed off.
Control and prevention See page 12.

BLINDNESS
Flowering is poor or even non-existent
Buds may be produced but they are dry and empty, although leaves appear healthy. Narcissus are frequently affected, particularly the double or multi-headed varieties. This problem is common the year after a hot, dry summer. One possible cause is that bulbs which have been left to naturalise divide and become overcrowded. Soil-borne pests and disease are sometimes responsible, in which case the whole plant usually dies.
Control Water and feed bulbs through the growing season and flowering should improve after a couple of years. Lift and divide crowded naturalised bulbs.
Prevention Plant bulbs at the correct depth, feed and water them regularly throughout the growing season. Do not cut off the leaves until they start to die back naturally.

BLUE MOULD
Bulbs and corms in store covered in blue-green fungal growth
In extreme cases decay may set in, but often the damage is restricted to sunken patches on the surface scales. Mildly affected bulbs and corms may grow normally when planted.
Control Discard severely affected bulbs and corms.
Prevention Only store bulbs and corms which appear completely sound and healthy. Dip them in a suitable fungicide before storage and keep in cool, dry, well-ventilated conditions.

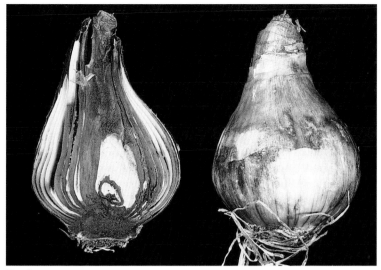

Basal rot

BASAL ROT
Leaves discoloured and growth stunted
The bulb may fail to come up at all. The basal plate and roots of the bulb will be rotted. This disease is worse in dry summers.
Control Dig up and burn affected bulbs. Lift adjacent bulbs in June, before the soil warms up and dip them in a solution of systemic fungicide.
Prevention Always discard any bulbs which do not appear completely healthy. Dip bulbs in fungicide after lifting.

TULIP FIRE
Emerging leaves appear scorched and distorted

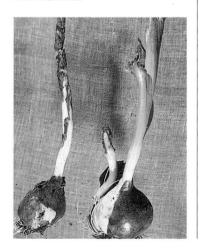

They may be covered in a fuzzy grey fungal growth. Small brown flecks may appear on leaves and petals and flower buds may fail to open.
Hard, black, 1–2mm (1/16in), resting bodies of the fungus, can be found on the bulbs. These fall into the soil and allow the fungus to survive in the absence of bulbs. Fire is common when tulips are grown on the same site several years running.
Control Dig up and destroy affected plants. Spray the leaves with a systemic fungicide to control mild infections.
Prevention Dip bulbs in a systemic fungicide after lifting. Do not grow tulips on the same site for more than two years in succession. If the disease occurs, do not grow tulips on that area for at least four years.

LARGE NARCISSUS BULB FLY
Small, thin, sparse yellowing leaves and no flowers

A cream-coloured maggot kills off the centre of the bulb, which becomes filled with its excreta. Other plants including snowdrop and bluebell may also be attacked.
Control Destroy affected bulbs. Use a soil insecticide.
Prevention Rake up soil around the bulbs when the foliage is deteriorating.

GLADIOLUS THRIPS
Leaves flecked and may wither and die

Small dark insects may be visible. Damage is usually worse in late summer.
Control Spray with a contact insecticide if necessary.
Prevention None.

FUNGAL LEAF SPOTS AND SCORCHES
Leaves covered in brown or yellow patches
Leaves may become stunted or distorted. Several fungi may be involved, each with a fairly restricted host range.
Control Cut off affected leaves and spray the remainder with a suitable fungicide.
Prevention None.

ANNUALS & BIENNIALS

◼ COLD DAMAGE
Leaves discoloured, usually pale yellow. Young leaves and leaf tips silverish
Later the leaves may become distorted. Plants raised under glass before being planted out are particularly susceptible if they have not been adequately hardened off. Foliage may recover and subsequent growth should be unaffected.
Control None.
Prevention Do not plant out too early. Harden off plants before planting out. Provide protection if late frosts are forecast.

Mosaic virus on sweet peas

◼ APHIDS
Leaves distorted and sometimes discoloured particularly at the shoot tips
Flowers may also be affected. Colonies of green, yellow, brown or black aphids will be present. These sap-sucking pests may also spread virus diseases. Their sticky excreta may encourage the growth of black sooty moulds.
Control and prevention See page 11.

◼ PANSY SICKNESS
Leaves wilt and yellow; plant may be loose in the soil
The roots of pansies and violas may be killed by this soil-borne fungus.
Control Remove and destroy affected plants together with their roots and discard their soil.
Prevention Grow susceptible plants on a new site each year. Water seedlings with a copper-based fungicide.

◼ POWDERY MILDEW
Leaves covered in white, powdery fungal growth
Sometimes the stems and flowers are attacked. Affected areas may turn yellow and die. This fungal disease is especially common in hot, dry seasons and may be found on most plants.
Control and prevention See page 12.

◼ DAMPING OFF
Seeds fail to germinate or seedlings collapse and die
This is mainly a problem under glass, but direct-sown annuals can also suffer outside.
Control and prevention See page 122.

◼ SOIL PESTS
Very young seedlings eaten
Woodlice, slugs and millipedes may all be responsible, but slugs cause the most damage.
Control and prevention See pages 8 and 9.

SWEET PEA PROBLEMS

◼ VIRUSES
Plants stunted with discoloured, streaked or mottled leaves
Flowers may fail to develop or are stunted and streaked too. The plants die off early.
Control Remove and burn affected plants immediately.
Prevention Control aphids which can spread viruses.

◼ FLOWER BUD DROP
Buds do not develop fully and are then shed
If plants are otherwise healthy the most likey cause is dry soil.
Control Water well.
Prevention Never allow the soil to dry out. Incorporate plenty of bulky organic matter into the sweet pea trench.

◼ FOOT AND ROOT ROTS
Plants grow well but then collapse. The stem base may appear blackened or shrivelled
Microscopic soil and water-borne fungi attack the roots or stem bases and are most troublesome if sweet peas or peas have been grown on the same site recently.
Control Remove and destroy affected plants.
Prevention Use a fresh site each year. Water seedlings with a copper-based fungicide.

CHAPTER FOUR

THE LAWN

A well-maintained lawn is less likely to suffer from pests, diseases or weeds than grass that is struggling for any reason. However, pests can attack even the best-kept lawn, so it is worth looking out for early symptoms and taking appropriate action. Fortunately, most other lawn problems can be prevented by good maintenance.

Weeds cannot compete with vigorously growing grass. So try to prevent bare patches which may allow weed seeds to gain a foothold.

Moss is more difficult to prevent, especially if the lawn is damp or shaded at any time of the year, but is relatively easy to control.

If you follow the advice on the right you should prevent most lawn problems and gradually improve an existing lawn. If the grass still does not grow well, consider replacing the lawn with ground cover plants or by extending borders. Alternatively, kill the grass and start a new lawn.

AVOIDING LAWN PROBLEMS

■ Mow frequently – once a week on family lawns and twice a week on fine lawns while the grass is actively growing. This encourages dense grass.
■ Set the mower blade as high as possible – 25mm (1in) for family lawns, 13mm (½in) for fine lawns. This should help to prevent weeds and moss.
■ Scarify lightly with a spring-tine rake every month or two to prevent thatch building up and to raise straggling grass stems so they can be cut by the mower.

This does less damage to the lawn than a heavy raking just once a year in autumn. Scarify at right angles to the direction in which you mow.
■ If you mow little and often, leave the clippings on to nourish the lawn.
■ Topdress in early autumn or late spring with a mixture of equal amounts of sharp sand and sieved well-rotted garden compost or soil at a rate of about 1kg a sq m (2lb a sq yd) and brush into the grass.
■ If you neither leave clippings on the lawn nor topdress in early autumn, apply a lawn fertiliser (or 35g a sq m/1oz a sq yd of growmore) in April. If the lawn starts to yellow in summer apply 17g a sq m (½oz a sq yd) of sulphate of ammonia.
■ Try not to walk on the lawn when it is wet, frozen or covered in snow.
■ Aerate or spike the lawn once or twice a year, in late spring and/or early autumn.

LAWN WEEDS

Plantains Perennials forming rosettes of leaves.
Ribwort plantain Common on drier soils.
Hoary plantain Less common, preferring lime-rich soils.
Greater plantain Broader rosettes that spread to form clumps. Common on heavy, compacted soils.

All flower from May to September. All are spread by seeds dispersed by wind or birds. Hand weed or spot treat.

Dandelion Perennial with a deep tap root and a flat rosette of leaves. Flowers from April to June and often again in autumn. Spread by wind-blown seed. Dig out or spot treat rosettes.

Cat's ear Perennial with rosettes similar to dandelion, but prefers drier conditions. Flowers May to September. Spread by wind-blown seed. Dig out or spot treat.

Daisy Perennial, forming dense clumps of small rosettes of leaves. Flowers from January to October. Prefers neutral to alkaline soil. Spread by wind-blown seeds. Hand weed or spot treat.

Yarrow Perennial that spreads rapidly by branched creeping stems that root at the nodes. Common on neutral and fertile soils. Flowers from June to August. Spread by seed, dispersed by wind or birds. Control with a lawn weedkiller.

Mouse-eared chickweed Perennial with long prostrate stems. Common on drier soils. Flowers from April to September. Spread by wind-borne seed. Control with a lawn weedkiller.

LAWN WEEDKILLERS

If the lawn is well fed, use a lawn weedkiller without a fertiliser. Otherwise, it is more convenient to apply a combined weed and feed (see page 137 for Best Buys).

For small or medium-sized lawns, soluble weed and feeds applied using a watering can with a fine rose are easiest, although granules are also a convenient method. For larger lawns it is worth buying or hiring a lawn fertiliser spreader.

Some lawn weeds and feeds also contain a mosskiller. So if moss is also a problem it can be dealt with at the same time. Apply weedkillers on a calm day during April or May when the soil is moist and the grass and weeds are growing vigorously. If it does not rain for 48 hours, water the lawn to prevent scorching. Do not mow the lawn for three days before or after treatment.

If one treatment does not kill all the weeds, repeat it after four to six weeks. Some persistent weeds may require a spot treatment.

Spot treatments Weeds in distinct patches can be treated with a lawn weedkiller without treating the whole lawn. Repeat the treatment after four to six weeks if necessary.

Small patches of weeds or even individual plants can be treated using a lawn spot weeder (see page 137).

HAND WEEDING

On a small lawn or if weeds are few and far between, hand weeding is worthwhile.

Daisy grubbers are special tools designed for levering out rosette weeds like daisies. Dandelions or other tap-rooted weeds such as cat's ear or plantains will regrow from pieces of tap root left in the ground. Remove

Lesser trefoil (*suckling clover*) Annual, producing long creeping stems that cover a large area very quickly, but these trailing stems do not root. Flowers May to September. Spread by seed, which remains dormant for long periods in the soil. Control with a lawn weedkiller, repeating if necessary.

Selfheal Perennial with long creeping stems that root as they go. Common on damp lawns, especially on alkaline soil. Flowers June to September. Spread by seed initially, then by creeping stems. Hand weed or use a lawn weedkiller.

Pearlwort Perennial with creeping stems that root at intervals, producing small cushions of foliage. Superficially, it resembles moss and is often overlooked. Common on close-mown lawns. Flowers (inconspicuously) from May to September. Spread by creeping stems. Use a lawn weedkiller, repeating if necessary.

White clover Perennial with creeping stems that root as they go. Common on poor soil. Flowers from May to October. Spread by seed, which remains dormant for long periods in the soil. Control by spraying, repeating if necessary.

Creeping buttercup Perennial which has strong leafy runners that root as they go. Common on heavy, damp, clay soils. Flowers from May to August. Spread initially by seed, then by runners. Hand weed or use a lawn weedkiller.

Slender speedwell Perennial with long creeping stems that root as they go. Flowers from April to June but spread by fragments of stem which root – it does not produce seed. Use a lawn weedkiller, early in spring and repeat after four to six weeks.

as much of the root as possible with an old knife or a special weeding knife.

GRASS WEEDS

Patches of coarse grass like Yorkshire fog, cocksfoot and creeping soft grass can spoil the appearance of a lawn. Lawn weedkillers will not control them. Repeated cutting of the clump with a knife will weaken it. In severe cases, kill the patch with a total weedkiller, such as Tumbleweed or Greenscape, and reseed. Fine grasses like annual meadow grass cannot compete with well-grown lawn grasses.

Meadow buttercup Perennial. Flowers in June and July. Spread by seed, it does not produce runners.
Bulbous buttercup Perennial. Flowers from March to June. Spread by seed and budding from the main corm. Both are less common than creeping buttercup. Dig out or spot treat.

Field woodrush Perennial often mistaken for grass, but leaves are fringed with white hairs. Common in dry, acid soils. Grass-like flowers in April and May. Spread by seed and short creeping stems. Hand weed or kill the patch with glyphosate and reseed.

LAWN DISEASES

DAMPING OFF
Patches of newly sown grass turn red or yellow and usually die
Established lawns are unlikely to be attacked. The disease is most common in damp, humid and cold conditions.
Control Fungicidal control is difficult.
Prevention Prepare a free-draining seedbed. Rake in a general fertiliser (lack of nutrients also encourages damping off) and sow the seed thinly (no more than 35g a sq m; 1oz a sq yd). Do not try to sow a lawn before April or after mid-September.

RED THREAD
Patches of mottled, light brown grass

Look closely for pink or coral-red needles of fungus. It is most common in summer and autumn on lawns suffering from a lack of nitrogenous fertiliser.
Control Use any of the fungicides recommended for lawns. Apply a lawn fertiliser (but not after mid-September).
Prevention Feed lawns at least once a year in spring.

FUSARIUM PATCH
Small orange or brown spots which enlarge and join up

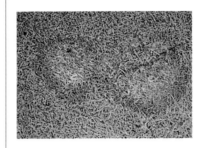

Sometimes pink cotton wool-like fungal growths are visible. This is the most common lawn disease. It often occurs in spring or autumn or any period of damp weather, even under snow (hence its other name, 'snow mould').
Control Use a systemic fungicide during the growing season. Dichlorophen can be used at any time of the year and iron sulphate will control mild attacks, so mosskillers containing either chemical will also control fusarium.
Prevention If possible keep the grass dry, by improving drainage, reducing shade, mowing regularly and removing the clippings. Liming to keep the soil slightly alkaline and using nitrogenous fertiliser sparingly will also help.

FAIRY RINGS
Rings of lush green grass appear and gradually spread outwards
Sometimes rings of stunted grass occur. Small toadstools may also appear, especially in the autumn.
Control No really effective chemicals are available to gardeners. Regular spiking and flushing the area with a dilute solution of washing-up liquid or watering with a strong solution of sulphate of iron (400g in 4.5 litres) may help to discourage the fungus. Physically digging out the affected soil is sometimes suggested, but is impractical.
Prevention None.

TOADSTOOLS
Clumps of toadstools that appear in late summer and autumn are probably living on dead roots under the turf and will do no harm. Brush them off if they are unsightly. Check that they are not honey fungus (see page 39).
Control and prevention Not necessary.

Fairy rings

LAWN PESTS

Effects of dog urine

EARTHWORMS
Wormcasts on the lawn surface
Earthworms can be a nuisance when near the surface in mild, damp spells and especially in the autumn. Wormcasts can serve as seedbeds for weeds. However, worms are generally beneficial, helping to aerate the soil and incorporating and recycling organic matter.
Control Not usually necessary, though Murphy Lawn Pest Killer also kills worms.
Prevention Keep the pH of the lawn low by using acidic fertilisers like sulphate of iron or sulphate of ammonia. Remove fallen leaves in autumn and remove clippings to deprive them of food.

•

MOLES
Soft patches or hollows and occasionally large mounds of loose earth suddenly appear
Moles excavate tunnel systems which often extend over many gardens and adjacent woods and fields. They feed on worms and grubs that fall into the tunnels.
Control Poisons and trapping are the only really effective controls and are best left to experts.
Prevention Discourage soil pests and earthworms to make the lawn less attractive to moles. Mole smokes or other deterrents may scare them off temporarily.

•

LEATHERJACKETS
Irregular yellow patches, especially in dry spells
Leatherjackets (larvae of the cranefly, or daddy-long-legs) are brown legless grubs (5cm; 2in long) which eat grass roots during autumn and late spring, though the effects are not usually seen until the summer. Their presence can be confirmed by digging into affected areas or by watering these areas and laying black polythene overnight. The grubs will move to the surface. The adult craneflies emerge and lay their eggs in late summer. Starlings active on your lawn often indicate the presence of leatherjackets.
Control Dust the lawn with a soil insecticide in October or during mild spells in the spring.
Prevention None.

•

CHAFERS
Irregular yellow patches
Chafers cause similar damage on lawns to leatherjackets. The grubs have legs and usually occur in warmer parts of the country (see page 9).
Control As for leatherjackets.
Prevention None.

•

FEVER FLIES
Irregular yellow patches
The larvae live together in colonies in turf. They generally cause little damage, though the flies can be a nuisance.
Control and prevention Not necessary.

•

ANTS
Small mounds of loose earth
Ants sometimes excavate small mounds when building a nest.
Control Use any antkiller if a problem.
Prevention None.

•

SOLITARY BEES
Small mounds with a hole on top
These are burrows excavated by solitary bees. They look like bumble bees but don't sting. They also pollinate garden flowers.
Control and prevention Not necessary.

OTHER PROBLEMS

DOG URINE
Roughly circular brown patches, surrounded by a ring of lush green grass
If you own a bitch, or one regularly visits your garden, this is the most likely cause. If you catch her in the act flush the area with plenty of water. If the grass has already been killed, rake off dead grass and reseed.

•

GRASS THINNING
If the area is not shaded, suspect poor growing conditions. Give the lawn a thorough spiking to aid drainage and aeration; scarify to remove moss and thatch. Scatter lawn fertiliser and grass seed at 17g a sq m (½oz a sq yd) and brush in. Water during dry spells until the lawn recovers.

•

YELLOWING GRASS
If the cause is not leatherjackets or fusarium patch, suspect lack of nitrogen. Apply a lawn fertiliser in April. A lawn tonic containing iron, or a lawn sand will help to green up the grass. Follow this with sulphate of ammonia (on alkaline or neutral soils) or Nitrochalk (on acid soils). Water in the summer at 17g a sq m (½ oz a sq yd) and water in if dry.

See Tables, pages 130–136 for guide to insecticides and fungicides

MOSS

■ MOSS
Lawn feels spongy underfoot
Footprints may remain in the lawn after you have walked across it. Nearly all lawns can attract moss, but it is most likely on shaded or badly drained lawns or where the grass is growing poorly. It is usually less of a problem in the summer, but in cooler, wetter conditions when the grass is dormant, moss grows rapidly.
Control Use a mosskiller without fertiliser during the spring or autumn or one with a fertiliser in spring. Lawnsand containing iron sulphate is the traditional method of controlling moss. It also feeds the grass. The effect is short-lived, so you will need to apply it every year.

Liquid mosskillers are easier to apply evenly, using a watering can. Some contain iron sulphate, others contain chloroxuron or dichlorophen and although they are claimed to control moss for more than a year, you will probably still need to reapply them annually.
Prevention The long-term answer is to remove the cause of the damp, shady conditions, but this can prove difficult and may be impossible. Poor surface drainage can sometimes be cured by spiking or aerating the lawn at least once a year. This will break up the compacted surface layer to let air into the soil beneath and encourage the grass to grow. You can buy special tools for the job but, for a small lawn, a garden fork is perfectly adequate. Push it into the lawn about 10–15cm (4–6in) deep and wiggle it backwards and forwards. Work across the lawn leaving about 10cm (4in) between each line of holes.

Scarifying the lawn – raking vigorously with a spring-tine rake – will remove dead grass, moss and straggly grass stems and will help to keep the lawn surface dry and aid drainage. If you cannot face the work involved, consider hiring or buying a powered lawn raker.

ALGAE

■ ALGAE
Black or green slimy growths on the soil surface
Several types of algae can invade very wet lawns. The most common is a black featureless slime, another occurs as small green jelly-like spheres. In northern Britain, masses of green frogspawn-like jelly can occur. All indicate poor drainage and are worst after periods of wet weather.
Control Use mosskillers containing dichlorophen or iron sulphate.
Prevention Improve surface drainage by regular spiking and topdress with sharp sand. If this fails install a sub-surface drainage system using land drains or slit trenches.

·

■ LICHENS AND LIVERWORTS
Dark green, brown or grey growths on bare areas
These primitive plants cannot compete with grass but colonise bare patches on improverished, very acid, compacted or badly drained soil.
Control Use mosskillers containing dichlorophen or iron sulphate.
Prevention Good lawn maintenance (see page 55) will encourage vigorous grass growth. If the soil is very acid apply lime until the soil is near neutral.

FRUIT

If your fruit crop does not live up to your expectations, there may not be much you can do in the short term because the damage is often done before the problem becomes apparent. But once you have identified the cause you can take steps to prevent it occurring again.

If you are unlucky enough to encounter one of the really serious diseases, such as honey fungus, fireblight or red core, you have to cut your losses. Remove and destroy the tree or plant (by burning) to prevent the disease spreading and do not replant on the same site. However, most common diseases can be controlled to some extent by good gardening practice or, if necessary, by a preventive spray programme, and you can look forward to healthy crops in subsequent years.

A few pests, such as codling moth and winter moth, can be

prevented using non-chemical methods, but most have to be controlled by other means. Some pests may attack every year without fail, while others come and go for no apparent reason.

Often pests and pest eaters reach a balance, so that damage is limited. If this is the case and the yield from your fruit patch is acceptable, leave well alone. If you do decide to spray, bear in mind that spraying to control one pest may upset this natural balance and lead to other problems in the future.

With larger trees your options are limited because effective

spraying is impractical. But with smaller trees, such as cordons, or soft fruit, you can opt for a preventative spray programme. Timing is important and it is best to start spraying according to the stage of the plant's development rather than the date. The spray programme on pages 86 and 87 should control all major pests and diseases. Adapt the programme to suit the problems that occur regularly in your garden.

USING CHEMICALS ON FRUIT

All insecticides and fungicides sold to gardeners have been approved by the Ministry of Agriculture as safe for use on fruit if used according to the manufacturer's instructions.

Routine spraying with some fungicides year after year can lead to a build up of resistant strains of fungi. If you think that your usual fungicide is losing its effectiveness, switch to another type. It is good practice to change regularly to prevent resistance occurring. Note that benomyl, carbendazin and thiophanate-methyl are all related chemically so little is to be gained by changing from one to the other.

Do not use insecticides on fruit trees or bushes that are in flower. You may kill bees or other pollinating insects. If you have to spray during flowering, do it in the evening and use a non-persistent pesticide such as pyrethrum or derris.

Always read the instructions on the packet carefully and follow the advice given. Pay particular attention to the harvest interval (the time you should allow between spraying and harvesting fruit).

APPLES AND PEARS: LEAVES

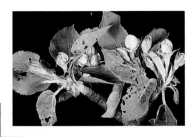

◼ SCAB
Dark green or brown spots

In severe attacks the leaves may fall prematurely. This fungal disease is common and can be serious on some varieties, notably 'Bramley Seedling', 'Cox's Orange Pippin', 'Gala', 'James Grieve' and 'Laxton's Superb'. Branches and twigs may also be affected by scab, producing lesions or swellings which act as a reservoir of fungal spores to reinfect new leaves in the spring. The major source of overwintered spores is fallen leaves. Spread is most rapid during dull, wet weather at blossom time.
Control None. Prune out affected twigs.
Prevention A fungicidal spray programme should prevent scab (see page 86). Clearing away fallen leaves in the autumn will reduce the risk the following year. A few apple varieties show resistance (see Box on page 68).

•

◼ PEAR LEAF BLISTER MITE
Small, pale green or pink blisters on young pear leaves

The blisters darken as the season progresses. Apples are occasionally affected.

These symptoms are caused by mites, invisible to the naked eye, that live inside the leaf blisters. Although leaves can be severely disfigured, the tree is not usually harmed and fruits are unaffected. The mites overwinter under bud scales and invade new leaves in the spring.
Control Light or localised attacks can be controlled by removing affected leaves.
Prevention None.

•

◼ PEAR AND CHERRY SLUGWORM
Dry brown patches on pear leaves
These are caused by slugworms grazing on the upper leaf surface. Leaves become skeletonised.
Control See page 69.
Prevention None.

•

◼ LEAF-EATING CATERPILLARS
Large ragged holes in leaves
The most common caterpillars on apple and pear trees are those of the winter, mottled umber and march moths. All three caterpillars are fairly similar, but the winter moth is green with yellow stripes, the mottled umber moth is dark brown with yellow sides and the march moth is simply green. All move with a looping action and grow up to 3cm (1¼in) long. They attack young leaves early in the spring, often before they have expanded, and may also attack blossom. By the time damage is obvious the caterpillars may have left.

Depending on the species, adult moths emerge in winter or early spring. The females are unusual in having only vestigial wings, so they must climb the trunk to lay eggs near the buds. Caterpillars hatch from March onwards and feed until late May or June. When fully fed they drop to the soil and pupate.
Control Spray with a contact insecticide when caterpillars are seen, but not during flowering.
Prevention Fix grease bands round the trunk about 0.5m (2ft) above the ground to keep females off the tree. Put bands in place in October and check them occasionally to make sure they form a complete barrier.

•

◼ POWDERY MILDEW
Leaves covered in white spores

A common and serious disease of apples, and occasionally pears. The fungus attacks young leaves as the buds open in spring. Whole shoots and flower trusses may also be attacked. Affected shoots wither and drop off and fruits fail to develop. As the summer progresses spores are blown on to other leaves. The fungus overwinters in buds.
Control Removing affected shoots and flower trusses to reduce the primary source of infection may be worthwhile on young trees.
Prevention Remove and destroy any distorted or silvered shoots or buds in winter. A routine spray programme should prevent mildew gaining hold (see page 86). Regular removal of affected shoots or leaves throughout the spring and summer will help.

◼ APHIDS
Colonies of small insects

Several aphid species attack apple and pear leaves in late spring or early summer. The most serious is the rosy apple aphid which can severely reduce the crop by causing the leaves to curl and turn red. Aphids over-winter as eggs in cracks in the bark, hatch during March and move to other host plants in June. See also page 11.
Control Spray with a systemic insecticide as necessary.
Prevention A routine spray programme should be effective (see page 86).

◼ NUTRIENT DEFICIENCIES
Leaves discoloured or generally unhealthy looking
Like all trees, apples and pears can suffer from lack of essential nutrients. See pages 40–41 for symptoms and likely causes.
Control and prevention Regular feeding, mulching with well-rotted organic matter and reducing competition from weeds or other garden plants should prevent nutrient problems. Check occasionally that the pH of the soil is neither too acid nor too alkaline (preferably 6.0–6.5) as this can cause deficiencies.

◼ FIREBLIGHT
Shoot tips wilt and droop; later, the leaves and shoot become dry and brown, as if scorched
This is a serious disease of pears, late flowering apples and related ornamentals (cotoneaster, pyracantha, sorbus, etc.) and also occurs on hawthorns. It is particularly serious on pears. Check that hawthorn hedges are not a source of infection for fruit and ornamental trees. This disease was once notifiable to the Ministry of Agriculture but attempts to confine it have now been abandoned.
During the early stages golden drops of bacterial ooze can be seen on the shoots. The bacterium usually enters through the blossom or sometimes through wounds, rapidly spreading down the shoot to affect the main branch. Infection is most likely in warm, wet periods. Late flowering varieties are particularly vulnerable because flowering occurs under higher temperatures. Cankers develop at the base of affected shoots and act as a reservoir of infection for the next season. You can confirm the presence of fireblight by looking for the characteristic reddish-brown stain under the bark.
See also page 32.
Control If only a few branches show the symptoms cut sections from the affected branches until the reddish-brown stain under the bark disappears and cut off each branch at least 0.6m (2ft) below this point. Be very careful to sterilise all pruning tools after each cut (use a solution of household disinfectant or bleach) to avoid spreading fireblight to healthy stems. If the tree is severely affected the only course of action is to remove the whole tree and burn it.
Prevention None.

REPLANT DISEASE
If a fruit tree is removed and another planted on the same site, the new tree may grow poorly. The cause is thought to be a legacy of bacteria and fungi left by the old tree, which being established could cope with them. A young tree, however vigorous, is less able to fend off attacks by these micro-organisms. The problem affects apples, pears, plums, cherries and raspberries.
Prevention You can reduce the effect by changing a couple of barrow loads of soil from the planting hole with soil from the vegetable plot and by watering well for the first two years after planting. Better still, choose a new site or plant a different type of tree or bush.

WINTER WASHES
At one time, spraying with a tar oil winter wash was part of the standard pest control programme.

Pros A winter wash will kill over-wintering eggs of most aphids, apple suckers and scale insects, and will help to control some caterpillars and woolly aphids. It will also kill moss, algae and lichens.

Cons Winter washes kill the predators that control spider mites and other beneficial insects and spiders.
Even if you succeed in killing overwintering pests you may still have to spray in spring to control blossom weevils, capsids and other pests.

On balance it is probably best to use a modern insecticide during the season if pests are a particular problem (see spray programmes on page 86). Otherwise leave well alone. An occasional winter wash is worthwhile if large numbers of scale insects build up.
If you decide to apply a winter wash, wait until December or January when the trees or bushes are completely dormant. Be careful to avoid drift as winter washes may scorch green leaves nearby. Spray with force to penetrate the bark crevices and do not forget the shoot tips where many pests lurk.
Armillatox, ICI Clean Up, Jeyes Fluid and Murphy Mortegg are all suitable. Follow the instructions.

APPLES AND PEARS: STEMS

■ HONEY FUNGUS

Tree dies suddenly, honey-coloured toadstools present in autumn

If the bark is examined carefully, white growths can be seen underneath it. Occasionally black fungal 'bootlaces' are found in the surrounding soil.

Control and prevention The tree will have to be destroyed. See page 39.

■ WOOLLY APHID

White woolly patches on branches

If examined, small brown aphids will be seen. They secrete a covering of waxy wool as a protection against predators. Colonies develop during spring and early summer and adult aphids overwinter in cracks in the bark. Once established, they will appear year after year but rarely spread far. They cause swellings or galls on the branches which can offer an entry for the fungi which cause dieback and canker. Related plants such as hawthorns and pyracanthas can also be attacked.

Control Spray with a systemic insecticide or brush off obvious colonies with a stiff brush.

Prevention None.

■ SCALE INSECTS

Small brown mussel-shaped scales on stems

These are up to 4mm (⅛in) across and also attack fruits.

Control Only necessary if present in large numbers. See also page 37.

Prevention None.

■ MISTLETOE

Leafy growths on branches, which remain green in winter

Birds spread seeds and deposit them in the crooks of branches,

Woolly aphids on apple tree

usually on old apple trees. These parasitic plants grow very slowly at first and it may be many years before they fruit.

Control and prevention If you do not want it for Christmas, prune out affected branches.

■ APPLE CANKER

Shrunken cankerous patches on shoots and branches

The bark may shrink and crack in rings and shoots may wilt where the canker has girdled them. This can be a very damaging disease of apples and occasionally pears. 'Cox's Orange Pippin', 'Elstar', 'Fiesta', 'Gala' and 'Spartan' are particularly susceptible. The branch may swell around the canker and shoots may die back. Infection occurs through pruning scars, lesions caused by scab on shoots, wounds or leaf scars.

Canker thrives in damp conditions and is often a sign of poor drainage. Look for canker under tree ties or rabbit guards.

Control Remove cankered parts of stems or young shoots as soon as you see them. If a young tree becomes badly infected it is best to replace it. Cut away diseased tissue and affected bark back to sound, green wood. Paint the wound with a wound sealant.

Prevention Improve drainage if possible. Paint pruning cuts with a wound sealant. Spray to control scab (see page 86).

Apple canker

APPLES AND PEARS: BLOSSOM

Apple sucker damage

Frost damage

Blossom weevil damage

BLOSSOM WEEVIL
Some flowers fail to open
Affected buds remain closed and turn brown. Small white grubs or brown weevils up to 4mm (⅛in) may be found inside. The adult weevils overwinter in bark crevices and lay eggs in early spring; the grubs feed on the internal tissue of the developing buds. Adults emerge during early summer and feed on the leaves before hibernating.
Control Not usually necessary.
Prevention If it is an annual problem, spray with a contact insecticide just before the buds open.

APPLE AND PEAR SUCKER
Flowers brown and distorted, buds may fail to open
Similar in appearance to frost damage but for the presence of small insects, which suck the sap from flowers and leaf buds during late spring. Separate species attack apples or pears but the symptoms are similar. Pear suckers can persist throughout the summer, feeding on leaves and, like aphids, producing sticky honeydew. They may transmit virus diseases. Adult suckers are

yellow or pale green, up to 2mm (less than ⅛in) long and superficially resemble aphids. Severe attacks can greatly reduce the amount of blossom and may occasionally reduce yields.
Control None, but pear sucker is often controlled by natural predators through the summer.
Prevention A winter wash (see page 63) will kill overwintering apple sucker eggs. As a last resort, spray with an insecticide containing permethrin in late February or early March.

FROST DAMAGE
Flowers turn brown and wilt
Buds may fail to open, but unlike blossom weevil, frost causes no damage inside the bud. If plenty of blossom is produced this natural thinning may benefit the crop.
Control and prevention None, but do not plant in a frost pocket and choose late-flowering varieties in areas subject to late frosts.

BLOSSOM WILT
Flowers wilt
In severe cases the developing

leaves wilt too and whole shoots may die back.
This disease is worst in warm, wet springs and may not occur every year. Watch out for brown rot on the fruit, caused by the same fungus (see page 68).
Control Remove and destroy all affected shoots.
Prevention Spray with a systemic fungicide when the blossom starts to open and repeat a week later. 'Bramley Seedling' is claimed to be resistant.

BIRD DAMAGE
Buds damaged
The flower buds of pears may be attacked during the winter, whereas apples are attacked in the spring. In severe cases few blossoms will survive. Bullfinches and sparrows are usually responsible. The outer bud scales are discarded in favour of the tender inner tissues.
Control None.
Prevention If bullfinches are common locally, the only solution may be to cover trees with netting, or to enclose small trees or cordons in a fruit cage. Repellent sprays are unlikely to be effective in the long term.

APPLES AND PEARS: FRUIT

Apple sawfly damage

Codling moth caterpillar

Pear midge grubs

▪ APPLE SAWFLY

Fruits misshapen or scarred and may drop prematurely

The sawfly larva first makes a corky, ribbon-like scar, starting at the stalk end of the fruit and then burrows into the flesh. Sometimes the grubs move to fresh fruits, leaving scarred ones. Affected fruitlets often drop in June or July. Cream-coloured grubs (up to 15mm; ⅝in long) may be found inside. The adult sawflies are active in April and May. The grubs pupate in the soil during July.

Control Collect and destroy affected apples.

Prevention Spray with a contact insecticide about a week after three quarters of the petals have fallen.

▪ CODLING MOTH

Apples tunnelled

In some areas of the country a significant proportion of fruit is affected.

Adult codling moths appear in June or July and lay eggs on the young fruitlets. The young caterpillars feed on the flesh of apples or occasionally pears. The grubs depart in late August, leaving the fruits with an exit hole on the outside and messy tunnels inside. You may find grubs of a second generation when you harvest apples. Affected apples ripen early, and can be eaten after the damaged parts are removed. Codling moths pupate and overwinter under loose bark.

Control None.

Prevention A traditional spray programme will prevent attack, but timing is critical to catch the egg-laying females. Corrugated cardboard tied to the trunks in mid-July may trap some pupating caterpillars, which can then be destroyed, but invasion from neighbouring trees will negate this effort.

An alternative is to trap the male moths using a pheromone trap. With fewer males to act as mates many females are unable to lay eggs. Put traps in place in mid-May to protect up to five trees for a season. See page 139 for suppliers.

▪ PEAR MIDGE

Underdeveloped pears drop prematurely

The centre of the fruit is hollowed out and tiny white grubs may be present. Affected fruits initially grow rapidly but then turn black and drop. Mid-season varieties are most at risk. The adult midges, which are small and inconspicuous, lay eggs in flower buds during early spring. The grubs leave the fallen fruits and pupate in the soil.

Control Collect and destroy affected fruits.

Prevention The spray programme on page 87 should control pear midge. Alternatively, spray with a contact insecticide at the 'white bud' stage.

Stony pit virus

■ TORTRIX MOTH
Surface of ripening fruit damaged

This is caused by the feeding of green caterpillars up to 25mm (1in) long. They first feed on leaves and usually attach a leaf to the fruit with silk and feed underneath it. The adult moths are nocturnal and inconspicuous.
Control None.
Prevention A spray programme for codling moth (see page 86) should prevent tortrix too.

■ CAPSID BUGS
Fruits distorted and raised brown patches present
These are caused by the feeding of sap-sucking capsid bugs. The fruit is edible after peeling.
Control None.
Prevention Spray with a contact or systemic insecticide at 'green cluster' and 'petal fall' stages (see pages 86–7).

■ WASPS
Ripe fruits eaten
Sound fruits are not usually attacked but damage, may be enlarged by wasps.
Control Spraying is ineffective.
Prevention If found, the wasps nest can be destroyed. Individual fruits can be protected with bags

made from old nylon tights or muslin. Wasps are effective predators of caterpillars, so try to be tolerant.

•

■ BIRDS
Fruits pecked
Birds may peck at and damage some ripe fruit. Damaged fruits can generally be eaten but should not be stored.
Control and prevention Netting should prevent damage. Stretch it tight to avoid trapping birds, and secure the bottom with pegs. For larger trees, try to protect a few branches.

•

■ FRUIT DROP
Fruitlets drop prematurely; no insect damage is visible
Where too many flowers have been pollinated some natural thinning is necessary to ensure a good crop of ripe fruit. Larger fruitlets dropping, particularly in June, is a normal occurrence for apple trees.
    A cold, wet spring may lead to poor pollination, and tiny fruitlets may be shed in early summer. Late frosts, lack of feeding, crowding or lack of water may be contributory factors and newly planted trees are particularly vulnerable.
Control and prevention None.

•

■ STONY PIT
Pears distorted and pitted; flesh woody and inedible
This is a serious virus disease of older pear trees. It first occurs on one branch, but spreads rapidly and can be spread by insects to affect neighbouring trees.
Control There is no cure, so affected trees should be removed and destroyed.
Prevention Buy certified virus-free trees.

■ BITTER PIT (OF APPLES)
Sunken brown spots on surface, discoloured flesh beneath
If only surface spots occur, the fruit can be eaten after peeling. These spots may also be scattered throughout the flesh, making it bitter and inedible. Apparently sound fruit may develop bitter pit later. This condition is caused by a lack of calcium, or an excess of potash or magnesium, and is usually a result of a period of water shortage. It often affects young, vigorous trees and is common on 'Bramley Seedling', 'Cox's Orange Pippin', 'Crispin', 'Egremont Russett', 'Gala', 'Greensleeves', 'Jonagold', 'Jupiter' and 'Merton Worcester'.
Control None.
Prevention Prune in summer to reduce vigour and improve cropping. Apply lime to acid soils to raise pH to around 6.5. Spray with a solution of calcium nitrate (40g in 4½ litres of water; 1½oz in 1 gal) at least five times between July and September. Water regularly.

See Tables, pages 130–136 for guide to insecticides and fungicides

APPLES AND PEARS: FRUIT

Brown rot

Scab

▇ BROWN ROT
Brown rotten patches
The rot usually starts from a damaged area and spreads rapidly. Concentric circles of grey or white fluffy dots may also be seen. The fruit eventually shrivels and 'mummified' fruit may remain attached to the tree all winter, or may fall.

The same fungus causes blossom wilt (see page 65) and can also attack other related trees (see page 73).

Check fruit in storage for damage or signs of brown rot – the disease spreads by contact between fruit.
Control Remove all affected fruit on the tree and the ground and burn it.
Prevention A spray programme (see page 86) may help to prevent brown rot but good hygiene is equally effective.

▇ SCAB
Brown corky or sooty patches on surface
Both apples and pears are affected. Scab is likely to be worse in mild, damp weather. In severe attacks large areas may be covered and the skin starts to crack as the fruit grows. Scabs may also develop on stored fruit, but the flesh does not usually rot. Affected fruits can be eaten after peeling. Scab also affects leaves (see page 62).
Control None.
Prevention See page 62.

•

▇ RUSSETTING
Skin rough
This is normal on some varieties but may occur on smooth-skinned varieties due to poor growing conditions, frost or cold wind damage to the young fruits. Mildew attacks may also be a cause.
Control None.
Prevention Try to improve growing conditions by mulching and feeding, and spray to control mildew.

•

OTHER PROBLEMS

▇ LOSS OF VIGOUR
Most fruit trees are productive for 10–20 years. After this cropping may start to fall off. On younger trees nutrient deficiencies, waterlogging, shallow soil or lack of pruning may be contributory factors. Viruses may also be to blame.
Control and prevention If good cultivation does not improve vigour, consider planting a new tree on a better site.

▇ POOR CROPPING
Otherwise healthy trees can produce a poor crop for several reasons:
- Winter pruning too drastic
- Bird or pest damage to flower buds (see page 65)
- Poor pollination due to cold weather or lack of pollinating insects at flowering time or the absence of a suitable variety to provide pollen nearby.
Control and prevention Prune lightly in winter or summer prune instead. Use netting to prevent bird damage.

RESISTANT VARIETIES
The following show some resistance to canker (C), mildew (M) or scab (S):

Apples	Pears
'Beauty of Bath' M	'Beurre Hardy' S
'Belle de Boskoop' C,S	'Conference' S
'Charles Ross' S	'Dr Jules Guyot' S
'Discovery' M,S	'Jargonelle' S
'Falstaff' M	
'Fortune' S	
'Greensleeves' M	
'Jester' M	
'Lord Derby' M,S	
'Lord Lambourne' M	
'Red Delicious' M	
'Redsleeves' M,S	
'Sunset' S	
'Winston' S	
'Worcester Pearmain' M	

CHERRIES, PEACHES AND PLUMS: LEAVES

This section also covers almonds and apricots. Ornamental prunus species can be affected by the same problems.

■ PLUM POX

Leaves with pale areas

These symptoms are most noticeable in July. Look also for fruit symptoms (see page 73). Plum pox is caused by a virus that is spread by the leaf-curling aphid.

It is a notifiable disease. If you suspect it, contact your local Ministry of Agriculture office for confirmation and advice.
Control None. Cut down and burn affected trees. Do not forget to inform your local Ministry of Agriculture office.
Prevention None, but buy certified virus-free trees. Control leaf-curling aphids.

■ POWDERY MILDEW

White floury covering on leaves
Powdery mildew is not usually a serious problem on plums, cherries and ornamental species.
Control and prevention See pages 12 and 62.

■ SHOTHOLE

Small holes, often with brown edges

This is the result of dead tissue falling away. Brown spots will also be present. There are two possible causes:
■ Bacterial canker (a potentially fatal disease) – look for wounds (cankers) oozing gum on the stems and for whole branches dying back (see also page 71)
■ a fungal disease – less serious and usually aggravated by poor growing conditions.
Control If bacterial canker, see page 71. If no cankers are visible, feed, water and mulch trees to increase vigour.
Prevention None.

■ PLUM RUST

Orange-yellow dots on leaves
These spots turn dark brown as the season progresses and affected leaves may fall early. This disease is most likely in hot, dry seasons but as it occurs late in the season it is not usually serious. Anemones act as an alternative host for the fungus and it can also overwinter on fallen leaves.

Control None.
Prevention Keep trees well mulched and watered. Rake up and destroy leaves during the autumn.

■ PEAR AND CHERRY SLUGWORM

Surface tissues of cherry leaves damaged

Damaged areas may dry up and turn brown. Small black slug-like caterpillars may be visible throughout the summer.
Control Not usually necessary. Severe attacks can be controlled with a contact insecticide.
Prevention None.

CHERRIES, PEACHES AND PLUMS: LEAVES

◼ PEACH LEAF CURL
Leaves curled and covered in reddish blisters

They may also turn yellow and fall early. The disease, which is spread from leaf to leaf by rain splash, is worse in cold, wet springs.
Control Pick off and destroy affected leaves.
Prevention Spray trees with a copper-based fungicide in late January or early February, before the buds open, and again in the autumn after the leaves have fallen. Cover wall-trained trees with polythene sheeting,

attached to the wall above the tree, from late January to early April to prevent fungal spores being spread by rain.

◼ SILVER LEAF
Leaves become silvered and affected branches die after a year or two
Once the fungus has got into the main trunk, the whole tree may

die. You may also see purple bracket fungi on the affected branches during the autumn. The fungus initially enters through wounds or pruning cuts. It is most common on plums but it can affect other fruit trees.
    If you suspect silver leaf, cut the branch at least 50cm (20in) below the affected leaves. Make repeated cuts towards the branch tip. If you discover a brown stain visible just under the bark, this confirms silver leaf. Sterilise your secateurs (use a solution of household bleach or disinfectant) before further pruning to avoid spreading the fungus.
Control Prune out and destroy affected branches, cut well below the part with obvious symptoms. Sterilise pruning tools between cuts and seal cuts with a wound sealant such as Arbrex.
Prevention Keep pruning to a minimum and confine it to dry spells during or just after flowering, when there are fewer spores in the air. Seal cuts with a wound sealant such as Arbrex. Prevent branches breaking by thinning fruit and supporting heavily laden branches.

◼ FALSE SILVER LEAF
Leaves become silvered
This is a physiological disorder and can easily be distinguished from silver leaf by the absence of staining in the wood and the shoots not dying back. The cause is usually malnutrition and lack of water.
Control None.
Prevention Mulch, feed and water the tree during dry spells.

◼ CHERRY BLACKFLY
Leaves and young shoots covered in black insects

In severe infestations growth may be affected, but the problem does not usually occur every year, so the tree should recover. Ornamental cherries are also vulnerable. Adult aphids feed on the leaves until July, when they migrate to wild flowers, returning in the autumn to lay eggs on the bark.
Control and prevention See page 11, or follow the spray programme on page 87.

CHERRIES, PEACHES AND PLUMS: LEAVES, STEMS

◼ LEAF-CURLING APHID
Leaves stunted and distorted
Apart from causing severe damage and loss of yield, this aphid can also spread plum pox. Overwintered eggs hatch in early spring to infest leaf buds, and later young shoots and leaves. Often by the time the damage is obvious, in May, the aphids have migrated to herbaceous plants such as asters.
Control None once symptoms are obvious.
Prevention Spray with ICI Rapid or a systemic insecticide just before flowering (see also page 87).

◼ MEALY PLUM APHID
Dense colonies of powdery white insects on undersides of leaves
These aphids hatch in April and colonies build up to damaging levels by June. They produce large amounts of sticky honeydew and encourage sooty mould.
Control Spray with ICI Rapid or a systemic insecticide.
Prevention Follow the routine spray programme on page 87.

◼ HONEY FUNGUS
Trees dying, honey-coloured toadstools around base
If examined carefully white growths may be seen under the bark and black 'bootlaces' of fungal tissue in the soil.
Control and prevention The tree will have to be destroyed. See page 39.

◼ SCALE INSECTS
Small, brown mussel-shaped scales on branches
Unless present in very large numbers, these should not cause any real problems.
Control and prevention See page 37.

◼ BACTERIAL CANKER
Cankerous patches on stems oozing gum, branches dying back

Cankers developing from affected buds

This is a serious disease of plums and their relatives, including ornamental prunus species, even if the leaf symptoms do not appear particularly severe. Bacteria released from leaf spots infect the stems, either through leaf scars or wounds. The cankers act as a source of bacteria to reinfect leaves the following year. Leaves on affected branches fail to open or may later wither as the branch dies back. See also 'Shothole', page 69.
Control Prune out and destroy affected branches. Collect up and destroy fallen leaves in the autumn. Spray trees with a copper-based fungicide at petal fall and three times at three-week intervals from mid-August.
Prevention Support heavily laden branches and avoid damaging the trunk.

◼ GUMMING
Gum oozes from the bark
If the tree is otherwise healthy and there are no signs of cankerous areas (see 'Bacterial canker') there is no need to worry. It may be a sign that the tree lacks vigour.
Control None.
Prevention Feed, mulch and water to improve growth.

SPIDER MITES
Leaves speckled yellow, later turning bronze and brittle

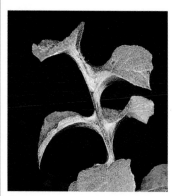

Red spider mite

In severe attacks leaves may fall prematurely. Apple and plum trees and related ornamentals are most often affected. Fruit trees under glass and strawberries may also be attacked by the glasshouse spider mite (see page 118).
If examined with a magnifying glass, minute brown creatures and their cast skins will be seen near the main leaf veins. They are worse in hot, dry summers or if tar oil winter washes are used reguarly. Otherwise they are normally controlled by natural predators.
Severe attacks in June and July will reduce the crop and may also reduce the initiation of fruit buds for the following season.
Mites overwinter as bright red eggs on the bark. Newly hatched mites feed on the young leaves, though an infestation may go unnoticed until late summer.
Control Spray with ICI Sybol or a systemic insecticide and repeat if necessary. Natural predators often control them, but are vulnerable to insecticides containing permethrin.
Prevention Avoid excess nitrogen fertilisers and use winter washes with care (see page 63).

CHERRIES, PEACHES AND PLUMS: FRUIT

◼ PLUM SAWFLY
Fruits tunnelled and fall early
Affected fruits will show holes, covered with messy excreta.

The cream grubs, up to 15mm (⅝in) long, feed on developing fruits all summer and then hibernate in the soil. Adult moths emerge at blossom time. Severe attacks can greatly reduce yields, since each grub attacks several fruits, the damage becoming greater as the grubs grow. The varieties 'Victoria' and 'Czar' are particularly vulnerable.
Control None.
Prevention If it is a regular problem, spray with a contact insecticide 7–10 days after petal fall stage (see page 87). Cultivating the soil around plum trees may expose some cocoons to frost or predators.

◼ FRUIT MOTH
Fruits tunnelled

Damage is similar to that of plum sawfly but occurs later in the season. The grub (up to 15mm; ⅝in long) burrows near to the stone and develops a characteristic reddish colour. Adult moths, which are active from June to August, lay eggs near to developing fruit. The

Plum sawfly

grubs pupate beneath the bark over winter.
Control Destroy affected fruits.
Prevention Spray with a contact insecticide four weeks after petal fall and repeat once or twice at fortnightly intervals if it is a regular problem.

◼ SPLITTING
Fruits or stone inside split
The most likely cause is fluctuating water supply. Other causes might be poor pollination, due to lack of pollinating insects in a cold, wet spring or lack of lime in the soil.

Split fruits are often infected by brown rot or further damaged by wasps.
Control None.
Prevention Keep trees well watered during very dry periods. Hand pollinate in cold, wet springs and lime acid soils in the autumn if necessary.

◼ GUMMING
Droplets of gum at the bottom of the fruit
Sometimes coarse areas, which feel like sawdust, occur in the

flesh. The problem seems to be worse in years with widely fluctuating rainfall.
Control None.
Prevention Try to keep the trees growing steadily by mulching and watering during dry weather.

◼ BIRDS
Ripening fruits pecked
Birds will attack all types of ripe fruit.
Control None.
Prevention If birds are a regular problem, select the branches with the most promising crops and cover them with bird netting before they are fully ripe.

◼ WASPS
Damaged fruits
Wasps are attracted to ripening fruits and cause superficial damage, often enlarging holes made by birds or other pests.
Control If a nearby nest can be located consider destroying it yourself (or hire a professional).
Prevention Small bunches can be protected with bags made of muslin or old nylon tights.

CHERRIES, PEACHES AND PLUMS: FLOWERS, FRUIT

■ BLOSSOM WILT
Flowers wither but do not drop
Sometimes leaves are affected. This disease is worst in a cool, wet spring.
Control None.
Prevention See 'Brown rot' below.

■ BROWN ROT
Fruits turn brown and decay
White fungal bodies in concentric circles are often visible. Infected fruitlets shrivel and dry and remain attached to the tree over winter. Unless removed, they will act as a source of reinfection next season. The fungus usually enters the fruit through wounds caused by pests, but can spread to other fruit by contact (in storage, for example).
Control None.
Prevention Remove and destroy affected fruits to prevent spread. No fungicide treatment is recommended for dealing with brown rot.

■ PLUM POX
Uneven ripening, dark markings on skin
Look for brown areas in the flesh. Fruits may drop prematurely and, when ripe, will taste acid and bitter.
Control See page 69.
Prevention None.

OTHER PROBLEMS

■ FRUIT DROP
If the tree has set more fruit than it can sustain, a proportion may drop, often during June (also called June drop). This is nothing to worry about if there are no signs of pests or disease.
Control and prevention None.

Split fruits and brown rot

■ OVERCROPPING
Where a tree has set too many fruit, it may be worthwhile thinning the fruit yourself.
Control Remove small or misshapen fruits and thin out the most crowded bunches before the 'June drop' (see left). After this, thin remaining fruit to about 8cm (3in) apart. This should give larger, better flavoured fruit, prevent branches breaking and encourage more blossom the next year.
Prevention None.

■ POOR CROPPING
Young trees are often very vigorous and slow to crop. Heavy pruning can make matters worse.
Control and prevention Tie down the strongest growing shoots so that they are near horizontal or loop them back to the main trunk. This should reduce the vigour and encourage fruiting.

Some plums are self fertile, but there may be insufficient pollinating insects in a cold, wet or windy spring. For small trees, use a small paint brush to pollinate individual flowers. Some varieties, gages for example, need a suitable pollinator nearby – 'Victoria' is very good.

RESISTANT VARIETIES
The following show some resistance to bacterial canker (B) or silver leaf (S):

Cherries
'Merchant' B
'Mermat' B
'Merton Glory' B

Plums
'Avalon' B
'Excalibur' B, S

See Tables, pages 130–136 for guide to insecticides and fungicides

CANE FRUIT: LEAVES, STEMS

LEAF AND BUD MITE
Yellow patches on leaves
These are caused by colonies of microscopic mites feeding on the undersides. The symptoms superficially resemble virus diseases, but leaf and bud mites have little adverse effect on the plants. The mites overwinter inside buds.
Control No suitable chemicals are available, but control is rarely necessary.
Prevention None.

APHIDS
Small green or yellow insects on leaves and canes
Several species may attack cane fruits. Apart from distorting leaves and reducing vigour they can also spread viruses (see below).
Control Spray with ICI Rapid or a systemic insecticide before flowering and repeat if necessary after fruiting.
Prevention None.

VIRUS DISEASES
Leaves small and crinkled with pale green or yellow patches
Several viruses, spread by aphids or eelworms can attack all cane fruits. Viruses reduce the vigour of the plants and the consequent fruit yield. Raspberries are particularly prone.

Mycoplasma (micro-organisms that are neither viruses nor bacteria) also attack cane fruit, especially black-berries. These are spread by leaf hoppers (see page 75 for control of this pest) and cause stunting of the plants.
Control None. Remove and destroy affected plants.
Prevention Control aphids (see above). Some raspberry varieties are resistant to aphids (see Box on page 76).

Leaf and bud mite damage on raspberry

Replant new canes which are certified virus-free on a fresh site, well away from existing canes if possible.

NUTRIENT DEFICIENCIES
Yellow or orange patches between the leaf veins
If the soil is naturally alkaline, lime-induced chlorosis could be the cause. In severe cases leaves can appear bleached.

Manganese or magnesium deficiencies could also be to blame. Manganese deficiency shows up as yellowing of the lower leaves.
Control If manganese or magnesium deficiency is suspected, spray with magnesium sulphate (170g in 9 litres; 6oz in 2 gal) or manganese sulphate (30g in 9 litres; 1oz in 2 gal) and repeat a couple of times at 14-day intervals.
Prevention On limy soils, try to reduce alkalinity by adding plenty of organic matter (well-rotted farmyard manure, for example) and using acidic fertil-isers, such as sulphate of ammo-nia. Apply fritted trace elements or chelated iron.

CANE SPOT
Small purplish spots on canes

These appear in May or June on raspberries and hybrid berries. When the spots reach 5mm (¼in) or so they split, giving the canes a rough and cracked appearance. Leaves and flower stalks can also be affected. In severe attacks new shoots may die back. The fungus overwinters on old canes to reinfect new growth the following year.
Control Cut out affected canes.
Prevention Spray fortnightly with a copper or systemic fungi-cide from bud burst until the end of flowering (see page 86).

Spur blight

Cane blight

Cane midge

■ LEAF HOPPERS
Leaves speckled
This is caused by the feeding of these small (up to 5mm; ¼in) jumping insects. They cause little direct damage but can spread mycoplasmas (see 'Viruses', opposite).
Control Spray with a contact insecticide if necessary.
Prevention None.

■ RASPBERRY MOTH
Young shoots wilt and die
If affected shoots are cut open they will be tunnelled and small pink or red caterpillars up to 15mm (⅝in) long will be present.
The young caterpillars also tunnel inside fruits later in the season, but do little damage. They overwinter in the soil, in leaf litter or inside canes. The following spring they invade young shoots and buds. Adults appear from May to June.
Control None.
Prevention Cut out old canes and remove leaves and debris.

■ CROWN GALL
Nobbly growth on canes
This can be introduced on new canes or may be present in the soil. The bacteria enters canes through wounds.
Control Cut out and destroy affected canes.
Prevention Buy certified canes.

■ SPUR BLIGHT
Purplish brown patches around buds on otherwise green canes
The symptoms first appear in August. As the patches enlarge they turn silver and the buds die or produce weak shoots the following season, reducing the yield.
This disease is most common in wet springs, on overcrowded plants or if too much nitrogenous fertiliser has been applied.
Control Cut out affected canes.
Prevention Spray with a systemic fungicide at fortnightly intervals from bud burst until the end of flowering. Do not allow plants to become crowded.

■ CANE BLIGHT
Leaves wilt, lateral shoots are small and withered
Affected canes show dark patches or lesions near to ground level and become brittle. They may snap off during the winter or spring.
The disease enters through wounds caused by low temperatures or through splits in the bark. Often this disease is associated with cane midge attack (see right).
Control Cut out affected canes, below the damaged area.
Prevention A fungicidal programme for other diseases should also prevent cane blight. Control cane midge (see right).

■ CANE MIDGE
Bark of young canes peeling and discoloured
This discoloration often occurs around cracks or splits. If the bark is peeled back small (3mm; ⅛in) pink or red grubs can be seen.
The adult midges lay eggs in cracks in the young canes during April and May. The grubs feed under the bark before pupating in the soil. Two more generations attack canes from July to September. Damaged areas allow fungal diseases to gain entry, producing cankered lesions. Cankered canes are weakened and easily damaged by wind over winter.
Control None.
Prevention Spray canes with a contact insecticide (fenitrothion, for example) during early May when the canes are 45–60cm (18–24in) high and repeat after two weeks. Cultivate soil in winter to expose the cane midge grubs.

■ HONEY FUNGUS
Canes die back; honey-coloured toadstools present
Examine the soil for black 'bootlaces' of fungal tissue and look for white fungal growths under the bark.
Control and prevention The plant will have to be destroyed. See page 39.

CANE FRUIT: BLOSSOM, FRUITS

■ RASPBERRY BEETLE

Fruit damaged by small yellowish-white grubs

Apart from the actual damage, the fruit is unappetising.

Adult beetles emerge from the soil from April to June and lay eggs in the flowers of all cane fruits. The grubs feed on the outside of the fruit, later moving into the plug. They may attack several fruits. When mature and around 8mm (⅜in) long they leave ripe fruits to pupate in the soil. The beetles may damage buds and flowers.

Control Spray with a non-persistent contact insecticide such as derris if the fruits are nearly ripe.

Prevention Spray raspberries with a contact insecticide, such as fenitrothion, when fruits start to turn pink, loganberries at petal fall and blackberries just before the first flowers open. Spray in late evening to safeguard bees.

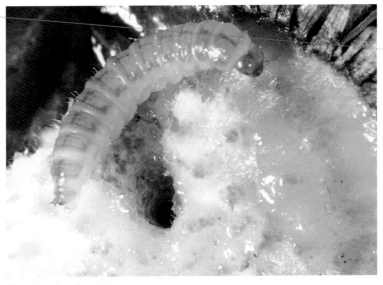

Raspberry beetle grub

■ GREY MOULD

Fruits covered in grey fluffy mould

This disease is usually worse in wet seasons and is common in gardens, affecting many plants (see page 12). It can cause large numbers of fruits to rot.

Control Pick off badly affected fruits to prevent it spreading.

Prevention Thin canes out well. Spray at flowering time with a systemic fungicide and repeat at fortnightly intervals. See spray programme page 86.

OTHER PROBLEMS

■ SMALL FRUIT

The most likely cause, especially for blackberries and autumn-fruiting raspberries, is lack of water in dry summers. But, if the soil conditions are favourable, suspect viruses.

Control None.

Prevention Mulch in spring and water during dry spells.

■ FROST DAMAGE

Flowers die suddenly

Severe late frosts at blossom time can damage flowers and reduce fruit yields.

Control and prevention Little can be done, except ensuring that early varieties are not planted in a frost pocket or growing later varieties.

■ POOR POLLINATION

Fruits deformed

Lack of pollinating insects due to wet, cold or windy weather at flowering time can result in misshapen fruits with flat areas or brown patches.

Control and prevention Nothing can be done. Later varieties should be less prone to the problem.

■ BIRDS

Fruits pecked or missing

Control and prevention If birds are a particular problem, put bird netting in place before the fruit starts to ripen.

RESISTANT VARIETIES

The following varieties show some resistance to large raspberry aphid (A), cane spot (C), mildew (M), spur blight (S) or viruses (V):

Raspberries
'Augusta' A
'Autumn Bliss' A
'Jewel' V
'Joy' A
'Leo' A, C, S
'Malling Admiral' C, S
'Malling Delight' A

Blackberries
'Silvan' C

Hybrid berries
'Jostaberry' M
'Worcesterberry' M

CURRANTS AND GOOSEBERRIES: LEAVES

CURRANT BLISTER APHID
Leaves puckered; bright red or yellow blisters

These symptoms are caused by the feeding of the pale yellow currant blister aphid early in the year. The blisters are red on red and white currants, but may be yellow on black currants. The aphids overwinter on currant bushes, but migrate on to wild flowers from June onwards.
Control Spray plants with ICI Rapid or a systemic insecticide if necessary.
Prevention The spray programme on page 87 will prevent damage by all aphid species.

OTHER APHIDS
Leaves curled or distorted
Look for the presence of small greenish insects on the undersides of leaves and on young shoots. Leaves may also feel sticky, and black sooty mould may be present on them. Several different species of aphids can attack currants and gooseberries, producing similar symptoms. In severe attacks bushes can be stunted and fruiting will be affected.
  Currant-lettuce aphids overwinter on currant bushes, causing some damage before migrating to lettuces in May or June. The other species have weeds as summer hosts.
Control and prevention See 'Currant blister aphid' left.

VIRUS DISEASES
Leaves develop broad yellow bands along veins
This is often accompanied by stunting but fruit yields are not usually affected. The virus is transmitted by aphids.
Control If bushes lose vigour and crop poorly they should be removed. Replace with virus-free stock on a fresh site.
Prevention Control aphids.

SPIDER MITES
Leaves speckled yellow
See page 71.

NUTRIENT DEFICIENCIES
Leaves yellowing or discoloured
If pests are not present, the most likely cause is a nutrient deficiency, waterlogging or poor growing conditions.
  Yellow patches between the veins of older leaves indicate manganese deficiency, while yellow or bleached leaves at the shoot tips are a sign of iron deficiency. Both are often linked with very alkaline soils.
Control and prevention Feed and mulch the bushes with well-rotted organic matter. Use acidic fertilisers (sulphate of ammonia, for example) on alkaline soils. Prune the bushes regularly to maintain the balance between two-year-old fruiting wood and older wood on currants and to keep gooseberry bushes open.

REVERSION
Bushes lose vigour and crop poorly
A general decline in vigour and fruit yield of black currants is often a result of reversion disease. It is thought to be caused by viruses transmitted by big bud mites. Other more specific symptoms can sometimes be discerned. Flower buds may be bright magenta instead of the more usual dull grey. The leaves are narrow with fewer veins than normal – less than five on the main lobe. (The plant on the left shows reversion.)
Control Once bushes have reverted there is nothing you can do except to dig them out and destroy them.
Prevention Plant new bushes on a fresh site away from existing plants.

See Tables, pages 130–136 for guide to insecticides and fungicides

CURRANTS AND GOOSEBERRIES: LEAVES

■ CAPSID BUGS
Young leaves tattered

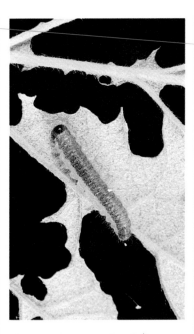

■ LEAF SPOT
Small, dark brown shiny spots

The feeding of sap-sucking capsid bugs in early spring, before the leaves have fully opened, causes holes and tears. The bugs are pale green and up to 5mm (¼in) long. They usually move on to herbaceous plants during the summer months, returning to currant bushes to lay their eggs during the autumn.
Control Spray with a systemic insecticide if necessary.
Prevention The spray programme for aphids will also control capsids (see page 87).

⋅

■ GOOSEBERRY SAWFLY
Gooseberry leaves holed or eaten back to the leaf veins
These and similar species can also damage currant bushes.

The larvae of gooseberry sawflies are extremely voracious feeders and can completely defoliate a bush in a matter of days. Although fruit is not damaged the vigour of the bush can be greatly affected. Eggs are often laid in the centre of bushes, so

the initial stages of an infestation may go unnoticed. The larvae are green with black markings, up to 4cm (1½in) long. Several generations may occur during the summer. They pupate in the soil over winter.
Control Inspect bushes regularly, especially early in the season, and spray with a contact insecticide. Choose a non-persistent chemical such as derris if the fruit is ready to pick.
Prevention None.

⋅

■ MAGPIE MOTH
Leaves eaten
The caterpillars (up to 4cm; 1½in long) are black and white and move with a looping action. They feed on currant and gooseberry bushes in late spring and early summer. The adult moths, which are nocturnal, lay eggs during June or July. The caterpillar overwinters in cracks in the bark.
Control and prevention See 'Gooseberry sawfly', left.

These first appear on currants and gooseberries during May or June and increase in number until the whole leaf is brown. Severe attacks may cause defoliation and a reduction in fruit yield.
Control None. Mulch and feed bushes well the following year to improve vigour.
Prevention The spray programme on page 87 should prevent leaf spot.

⋅

■ SILVER LEAF
Leaves appear silver
Usually the symptoms are confined to one branch which may die back. If cut, affected branches may show a brown staining just under the bark. See also page 70. Bushes may later recover.
Control Branches that have died back should be pruned back to below the area showing browning. All prunings should be destroyed.
Prevention None.

CURRANTS AND GOOSEBERRIES: BUDS, STEMS

BIG BUD MITE
Some buds appear abnormally round and swollen over winter
This problem is specific to black currants where only a proportion of buds are affected, so the contrast between these and normal pointed buds is obvious. The cause is microscopic mites that live inside the buds, causing them to become deformed. Infested buds may not open in the spring. Mites move to new buds or are carried to new plants by insects or air currents. They also spread reversion disease (see page 77).
Control There are no effective chemicals, though there is some evidence that the fungicides benomyl and carbendazim used in a routine spray programme may also control big bud mites.
Prevention Carefully remove and destroy all affected buds during the winter to prevent further spread. Destroy badly affected bushes and plant new stock elsewhere in the garden.

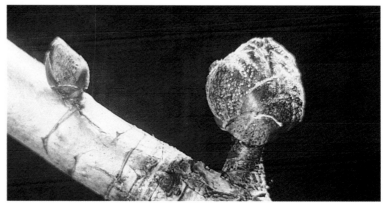
Big bud on black currant

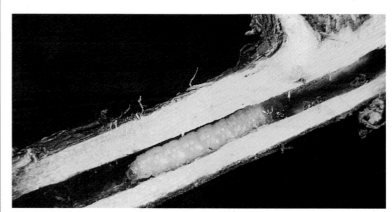
Clearwing moth caterpillar in red currant shoot

BULLFINCHES
Buds eaten or missing
Gooseberries and red currants are most at risk over winter, but other currants can also be damaged in the spring. After severe attacks, fruiting can be significantly reduced.
Control None.
Prevention If bullfinches are common locally, consider protecting bush fruit with fruit cages or bird netting.

CLEARWING MOTH
Young shoots tunnelled
Caterpillars of the clearwing moth burrow into young shoots and tunnel through the core. They generally do little harm but tunnelled shoots may snap. The adult moths are fairly incon-
spicuous and during June lay their eggs on black currant and, occasionally, other bush fruits. The white caterpillars may be found inside affected shoots.
Control If tunnelled shoots are seen when pruning currant bushes, prune out all affected shoots and destroy them along with any overwintering caterpillars.
Prevention None.

CORAL SPOT
Dead twigs covered in small pink spots
Shoots may die back and in severe cases the whole bush may die. The coral spot fungus enters
initially through pruning cuts or wounds and, although it normally attacks only dead wood, it can also attack living wood.
Control and prevention Prune off all affected shoots and dead twigs.

HONEY FUNGUS
Bushes die suddenly
Groups of honey-coloured toadstools may be seen in the autumn. Look also for white fungal growths under the bark and black 'bootlaces' in the surrounding soil.
Control and prevention The plant will have to be destroyed. See page 39.

CURRANTS AND GOOSEBERRIES: FRUIT

■ GOOSEBERRY MILDEW
White powdery coating on shoots, leaves and fruits

This is a common and serious disease of gooseberries, but currants can also be affected. The disease starts as a white powder on young leaves, but as the season progresses the fungus becomes brown and felty. Distortion of young shoots may also occur.

The disease is worse on crowded bushes, or on soft growth caused by excessive application of nitrogen fertiliser. Although fruits are attacked, this superficial mould can be wiped off, so you can still eat them.
Control Spray with a systemic fungicide when first symptoms are seen.
Prevention Prune bushes to keep them uncluttered and open. Cut out and destroy severely affected shoots. Summer pruning also helps to reduce infected shoot tips. Follow the spray programme on page 87.

■ CLUSTER CUP
Fruit leaves and stems covered in red or orange swellings

A disease mainly of gooseberries, prevalent in some areas. Pinhead-sized spots develop in these swellings, from which spores are released. The disease is likely to be worst in a dry spring.

The fungus can also infect sedges, so these are a source of reinfection for gooseberries.
Control Spray bushes a fortnight before flowering with a copper-based fungicide (but not the varieties 'Careless', 'Leveller' and 'Lord Derby').
Prevention None.

■ GREY MOULD
Fruits rotting, covered in grey fluffy growth
In wet summers, serious losses can occur, particularly on currants. The fungus usually enters at flowering time, especially after frost. This fungus can also cause dieback.
Control Remove severely affected fruit trusses.
Prevention The spray programme on page 87 should help to prevent grey mould.

RESISTANT VARIETIES
The following varieties show some resistance to mildew (M) or leaf spot (L):

Black currants
'Ben Lomond' M
'Ben More' M

Gooseberries
'Greenfinch' M, L
'Invicta' M

■ BIRDS
Fruit pecked or missing
Many kinds of bird will take ripe gooseberries and currants if they have the chance.
Control None.
Prevention If birds are a persistent problem consider covering fruiting bushes with bird netting. Alternatively, erect fruit cages as a permanent solution. See also page 10.

OTHER PROBLEMS

■ POOR CROPPING
Possible causes include:
■ Bird or frost damage to the flowers or flower buds (see above)
■ Poor pollination because of cold, wet or windy weather at flowering time
■ Reversion disease (see page 77)
■ Nutrient deficiencies, especially of potash (apply a potash feed in early spring to overcome this problem).

■ SPLITTING
Split fruits are usually a result of irregular water supply.
Control None.
Prevention Mulch bushes in the spring and water regularly in very dry spells.

STRAWBERRIES: LEAVES

STRAWBERRY MITE
Leaves and shoots distorted; plants stunted
Microscopic mites live in the crown and leaf buds, and damage developing leaves. Initially only one or two plants may be affected, but the mites will eventually spread throughout the bed. Eelworms cause similar symptoms (see page 82).
Control Remove and destroy affected plants.
Prevention Buy certified plants and grow on a fresh site.

SPIDER MITE
Leaves speckled, later turning bronze
If the leaf is examined with a magnifying glass tiny brown creatures and fine webbing can be seen, especially on the underside. Damage becomes apparent from June onwards. In severe attacks leaves wither and plants are weakened.
Control Spray the undersides of leaves with ICI Sybol or a systemic insecticide, and repeat twice at weekly intervals.
Prevention None.

APHIDS
Small insects visible on leaves and stalks
Apart from distorting leaves, reducing the vigour of the plants and reducing yields, aphids can spread viruses.
Control Spray with ICI Rapid or a systemic insecticide before flowering.
Prevention Follow the spray programme on page 86.

POWDERY MILDEW
Leaves have purple blotches and curl up
White mould is present on the undersides of the leaves, while stalks, flowers and fruit may also be affected. Mildew is worst in hot summers.
Control Spray with a systemic fungicide. Reduce overwintering spores by removing old leaves after fruiting.
Prevention Follow the spray programme on page 86.

LEAF SPOT
Small purple spots or larger purple- or yellow-bordered brown blotches

Several fungi can attack strawberry leaves. Symptoms are most obvious on older leaves or on starved plants.
Control Remove affected leaves.
Prevention Feed and mulch beds to improve vigour.

LEAF BLOTCH
Brown blotches with purple or yellow borders
This fungal disease is worst in wet seasons and can also affect stalks and fruits.
Control Fungicides are not usually necessary, but you should remove and destroy affected leaves.
Prevention Do not grow strawberries in shaded areas. Remove leaf debris, on which the fungus overwinters, in the autumn.

Leaf blotch

NUTRIENT DEFICIENCY
Yellowing between the veins
This is often a sign of iron deficiency on limy soils.
Control and prevention Check the pH of the soil. If it is very alkaline, add plenty of well-rotted manure or composted bark. Apply chelated (sequestered) iron each year.

LEAF HOPPERS
Small hopping insects
These sap-sucking insects, up to 5mm (¼in) long, cause little direct damage, but they can transmit diseases, such as green petal.
Control Spray with a systemic insecticide if necessary.
Prevention Spray with a systemic insecticide in July and repeat after a fortnight.

TORTRIX MOTH
Leaves eaten and woven together with silk
Green caterpillars (up to 5mm; ¼in) long, of the tortrix moth appear on mature plants in June and July. This is only an occasional problem in strawberry growing areas.
Control Spray with a contact insecticide (such as fenitrothion). Remove webbed leaves.
Prevention None.

See Tables, pages 130–136 for guide to insecticides and fungicides

STRAWBERRIES: LEAVES, CROWNS

■ VIRUS DISEASES
Plants stunted, leaves discoloured or distorted
Several viruses can attack strawberries causing yellow edges, pale spots or crinkling and distortion, and leaves may be smaller than normal. The result is loss of vigour and reduced yield.

Viruses are spread by leaf hoppers, aphids or eelworms. Whole strawberry beds are quickly infected.
Control None. Destroy any affected plants.
Prevention Control aphids. Buy certified stock and plant new strawberry beds on a fresh site.

■ EELWORM
Plants stunted, leaves distorted or crinkled

Leaf symptoms can resemble those caused by strawberry mites or viruses. Other symptoms include soft patches on fruits and thickened leaf stalks. Eelworms are not visible to the naked eye. The whole bed may become infested if affected plants are not removed and destroyed.
Control No suitable chemicals are available. Dig out and destroy affected plants.
Prevention Buy certified stock and replant beds on a fresh site.

SOIL PESTS AND DISEASES

Plants wilt or appear to be suffering from drought
Examine the crowns or roots of affected plants. There are several possible causes.

■ VERTICILLIUM WILT
Outer leaves wilt first
Leaves turn brown and shrivel and plants may die. Outer leaves are affected first; those in the centre will be pale and stunted.

Plants are most likely to be killed in their first year; if they survive this they can fruit in later years, but yields are reduced. This disease is aggravated by compacted soil and is worse if strawberries follow potatoes and under dry conditions. Cut the crowns of affected plants and examine the woody tissue – brownish patches will confirm the disease.
Control Remove and destroy affected plants.
Prevention Some varieties are less susceptible and it might be best to choose these.

■ CROWN ROT
Whole plant wilts and dies
This problem is worst in wet seasons.
Control and prevention See 'Verticillium wilt' above.

■ RED CORE
Roots have red cores
The plants may also be dwarfed and later wilt and die. This is a serious disease of strawberries. If these symptoms are seen in late spring or early summer, dig up an affected plant and cut the roots lengthwise. Healthy roots are white; infected roots have a pinkish or reddish-brown line running down the centre. The disease is more likely on poorly drained soils.
Control Dig up and destroy affected plants.
Prevention Grow resistant varieties. Improve drainage or move to a new site if possible.

■ WINGLESS WEEVILS
Roots nibbled

Adult weevils nibble leaves

Sometimes damage to the roots and crowns is severe before resulting in the plants starting to wilt. Fat white grubs up to 1cm (⅜in) long, the larvae of wingless weevils, are responsible.
Control Dig up affected plants and destroy any grubs found.
Prevention Use a soil insecticide.

■ SWIFT MOTHS AND CHAFERS
Large soil-living caterpillars and grubs eat strawberry roots; plants wilt.
See page 9.

STRAWBERRIES: FLOWERS, FRUIT

■ LACK OF VIGOUR

Strawberries generally crop well for only two to four years, then start to decline. Start a new bed using rooted runners.

Strawberries can suffer from replant disease (see page 63) if new crowns are planted into old strawberry beds.

Control and prevention It is wise to start new beds on a piece of fresh ground after two cropping seasons.

•

■ GREY MOULD

Fruits covered in grey furry growths

One of the most common diseases of strawberries that is particularly damaging during wet summers or where the fruits remain wet for long periods after watering. This is a disease prevalent in most gardens (see also page 12).

Control Remove affected fruits and dead leaves regularly. Spray with a systemic fungicide.

Prevention Water the plants in the morning so that flowers and fruit dry off quickly during the day. Spray with a systemic fungicide when the flowers start to open and repeat at 14-day intervals. Ruffle the foliage with a stick to ensure that the spray penetrates well.

•

■ SEED BEETLE

Fruits nibbled

Shiny black beetles up to 20mm (³⁄₄in) eat the seeds on the outside of strawberries, damaging the flesh. They are active from May onwards, but are rarely seen feeding. They can be found hiding under stones or debris.

Control Spray with a contact insecticide.

Prevention Methiocarb slug pellets (pbi Slug Gard) will also control seed beetles. Scatter them very sparingly and do not use during the fruiting period. Keep strawberry beds free of weeds and debris.

•

■ SLUGS

Fruits tunnelled

Fruits touching the ground are most at risk, and the problem is worst in wet years or on heavy soils. See page 8.

Control Scatter slug pellets sparingly, taking care that they do not touch ripening fruit.

Prevention Put slug pellets underneath a straw mulch.

•

■ BIRDS AND RODENTS

Fruits pecked or missing

Blackbirds, starlings and thrushes can wreak havoc. Squirrels can also be a nuisance.

Control None.

Prevention Stretch 20–25mm (³⁄₄–1in) bird netting over the bed, supported on a cage or wire hoops. Squirrels may gnaw through plastic netting – use wire netting instead.

•

■ GREEN PETAL

Petals greenish, fruits fail to swell

These symptoms are often accompanied by a stunting and distortion of the plants, which may wither and die. The mycoplasma causing the disease is spread by leaf hoppers.

Control None, affected plants die out.

Prevention Control leaf hoppers (see page 81).

•

■ DEFORMED FRUIT

Lack of pollinating insects in cold, wet or windy weather at flowering time can result in unfertilised seeds and uneven swelling of the fruits.

Control and prevention None.

RESISTANT VARIETIES

The following varieties show some resistance to grey mould (G), mildew (M), red core (R) or verticillium wilt (V), but none are totally immune:

'Bogota' R
'Cambridge Favourite' M, V
'Pandora' G, M, V
'Red Gauntlet' G
'Rhapsody' R
'Silver Jubilee' G, M, R
'Tantallon' R
'Totem' R
'Tribute' M, R, V
'Tristar' M, R, V
'Troubadour' R, V

See Tables, pages 130–136 for guide to insecticides and fungicides

GRAPEVINES

■ POWDERY MILDEW
Leaves and shoots covered in white, floury fungus
Powdery mildew is the most serious disease of vines outdoors and under glass. The disease is worst in dry conditions, when plants are crowded or suffering from lack of water. Young fruits may drop, while those nearer maturity will be covered in a white coating and their skins will split or crack.
Control Remove affected leaves and fruits and spray with a systemic fungicide.
Prevention Keep plants well watered and thin out to prevent crowding. Spray with a sulphur-based or systemic fungicide when the first symptoms are seen and thereafter at 10–14 day intervals. This will also prevent grey mould.

■ DOWNY MILDEW
Pale green or yellow spots on top, brownish mould on underside of leaves
This is a less common, but more damaging disease than powdery mildew. It is worst in warm, moist conditions. The leaf spots turn brown and the leaves drop. Affected fruits become shrivelled and leathery.
Control Remove and destroy affected leaves and shoots. Spray with a copper fungicide.
Prevention Spray with pbi Dithane 945 or a copper fungicide every 10–14 days from about three weeks after the buds open in spring. Note that Bordeaux Mixture can check growth for a few days.

■ SPIDER MITE
Leaves speckled and yellowing
If affected plants are examined with a hand lens, tiny creatures and fine webbing will be seen,
especially under the leaves. Spider mites are often a problem under glass, and also outdoors in hot, dry summers.
Control and prevention See page 71, or page 118 for control under glass.

■ SCORCH
Dry brown patches on leaves
This is caused by the effect of strong sunlight on damp leaves under glass. Fruits may also be scorched.
Control and prevention Ventilate greenhouses on sunny days and use a greenhouse shading material.

■ WASPS
Ripe fruits shrivelled
Wasps suck out the contents of ripening fruits.
Control Cover the plant or individual bunches with muslin.
Prevention Search out and destroy nearby wasp nests.

■ SHANKING
Groups of fruits start to shrink
Examine the fruit stalk; if this is shrivelled the most likely cause is lack of water or overcropping.
Control Remove damaged fruits and water regularly.
Prevention Water regularly during dry spells and do not try to get too large a crop.

■ SCALE INSECTS
Round brown scales on stems
These pests suck sap, so large infestations weaken plants and reduce yield. See also page 37.
Control Spray with a contact insecticide during the summer or spray stems with a tar oil winter wash to destroy overwintering scales and eggs (see page 63).
Prevention None.

Shanking

Scale insects

■ MEALY BUGS
Fluffy white patches on young stems
If examined with a hand lens tiny round pinkish-white insects can be seen. They cover themselves with woolly secretions and suck the plants' sap. If large colonies are present the plants may be covered with sticky

excretions that can be colonised by sooty mould.
Control See 'Scale insects' left.
Prevention None.

GREY MOULD
Fruit covered in grey fluffy growth
This disease is usually worst in wet seasons. It gains access through the flowers or through damaged fruit. Once established it can spread rapidly, ruining whole bunches.
Control Remove affected fruits and spray plants with a systemic fungicide.
Prevention Spray with a systemic fungicide when the flowers open and repeat at 10–14 day intervals.

NUTS

HAZELNUT WEEVIL
Small round holes bored in hazelnut shells
This is the exit hole of the adult weevil made in July or August. The grub will have eaten the inside of the nut. The adults are active in June, laying eggs into developing nuts.
Control None.
Prevention If it is a serious problem, spray with a contact insecticide at the end of May. Repeat after two to three weeks.

Shake weevils out of the bush on to a plastic sheet in June.

HAZELNUT MITE
Abnormal swollen buds
The effect is similar to big bud on black currant, but a separate species of mite is involved. The mites feed inside the buds, which may not develop in spring.
Control None.
Prevention Pinch out affected buds and destroy them.

WALNUT LEAF BLOTCH
Yellow or brown patches on leaves
The patches later turn dark brown and the leaves drop. Dark brown blotches may also affect the young nuts.
Control None.
Prevention Rake up and destroy fallen leaves in autumn. Spraying trees with a copper fungicide or pbi Dithane 945 a couple of times in spring may be worthwhile on small trees.

FIGS

SPIDER MITE
Leaves mottled or yellow
If the undersides of leaves are examined, minute creatures and webbing can be seen.
Control and prevention See page 71 or 118.

GREY MOULD
Fruits shrivel or rot
Greyish-white fluffy mould will be present. Infected fruits may drop prematurely. Once established, the disease is spread to other fruits through wounds.
Control Pick off affected fruits; spray with a systemic fungicide.
Prevention Avoid overcrowded or damp conditions.

SCALE INSECTS
Round brown scales on stems
See page 37.

FRUIT DROP
If young fruits fall prematurely, this is usually a result of irregular watering.
Control None.
Prevention Mulch in spring to conserve moisture and water regularly in dry spells, especially plants in pots.

FIG CANKER
Round or oval cankers on branches
Cankers usually occur near the bases of branches or near pruning cuts or wounds. Sometimes branches are killed.
Control Cut out and destroy all affected branches. Paint the cut branches and wounds with a wound paint (Arbrex, for example). Sterilise tools with disinfectant before and after pruning to avoid spreading the disease.
Prevention None.

CORAL SPOT
Pink or orange pinhead-sized spots on shoots
These usually occur on dead or dying shoots.
Control and prevention See page 37 or 79.

FRUIT SPRAYING PROGRAMME

Following the complete programme will work out rather expensive and is not usually worthwhile. Take account of the pests and diseases that are a problem in your area and modify the programme according to your needs.

Time spraying to coincide with the growth stage of the plant, rather than any particular date, because correct timing will vary from year to year and from one region of the country to another.

Large fruit trees are impossible to spray with a conventional garden sprayer, but if the yield is sufficiently heavy, do not worry too much.

Regular spraying may encourage red spider mites to build up to damaging levels by killing their natural enemies. Avoid using permethrin, which kills predators.

STRAWBERRIES

Bud development
(late April) Spray with a systemic insecticide to control aphids.

First open flower
(May) Spray with a systemic fungicide to control grey mould and mildew and repeat at 14-day intervals.

Fruiting (June) Scatter pbi Slug Gard pellets thinly to control slugs and seed beetles, avoiding direct contact with the fruit. Continue fungicide sprays if mildew persists.

After harvest
(August onwards) Continue spraying against mildew and aphids if they persist.

RASPBERRIES

Bud burst (March) When buds are about 1cm (⅜in) long spray with a copper or systemic fungicide to control spur blight and cane spot. Systemic fungicide treatment should be repeated at 14-day intervals. In late April spray with a systemic insecticide to control aphids.

White bud (early–late May) Repeat copper fungicide treatment or continue with systemic fungicide

First open flower (mid-May–early June) Spray with systemic fungicide to control grey mould and repeat twice at 10–14 day intervals.

First pink fruit (June–early July) Spray at dusk (to avoid harming bees) with a contact insecticide to control raspberry beetle and repeat after two weeks. Use derris if fruit is nearly ripe.

APPLES

Bud burst (March–early April) Spray with a systemic fungicide to prevent apple scab and mildew.

Green cluster (early–mid-April) Repeat fungicide spray. Use a systemic insecticide to control aphids and apple sucker. Apply a contact insecticide to control winter moth caterpillars.

Pink bud (late April) Repeat fungicide spray.

Late petal fall (May) Repeat fungicide spray. Spray with systemic insecticide to control aphids, capsid bugs, sawfly larvae or red spider mites.

Developing fruit (mid-June) Repeat fungicide treatment. Spray with a contact insecticide to control codling moth and repeat three weeks later. Spray with systemic insecticide if woolly aphids or red spider mites are present.

Developed fruit (mid-August) Spray with a systemic fungicide to prevent brown rot spoiling stored apples.

PEARS

Bud burst
(late March or
early April) Spray
with pbi Dithane 945
or a systemic
fungicide to
control pear scab.

Green cluster
(early April)
Repeat fungicide
treatment.

White bud (mid-April)
Repeat fungicide
treatment.
Spray with a
systemic
insecticide to
control aphids and
pear sucker, and
a contact
insecticide
to control
caterpillars
and pear
midge.

Late petal fall
(early May) and
Fruitlet stage
(late May) Repeat
the fungicide
treatment.

Developing fruit
(June) Repeat
fungicide sprays
to prevent
scab at
14-day
intervals
until
mid-July.

WEED CONTROL
Keep an area 0.9m (3ft) in diameter
round small trees, 1.2m (5ft) around
larger trees, and 45cm (18in) either side
of soft fruit weed-free by:
■ Applying Casoron G4 to weed-free
ground in February to suppress weeds
for up to a year.
■ Spraying with ICI Weedol, Murphy
Tumbleweed or Monsanto Greenscape,
taking care not to get any on the fruit
foliage.
■ Mulching with a 5–7.5cm (2–3in)
layer of bark chippings or with black
polythene or woven plastic material.
(These also help retain soil moisture).

PLUMS

White bud (early
April) Spray with
a systemic
insecticide to
control aphids
and a contact
insecticide to
control caterpillars.

Cot split (early
May) About eight
days after petal
fall spray with
a contact or
systemic to
control plum sawfly
and aphids.

Developing fruit
(mid-June) If plum
moth is present,
spray with con-
tact insecticide
and repeat three
weeks later. If
mealy aphid is
present spray with a
systemic insecticide.

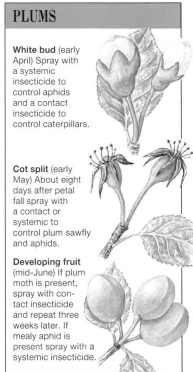

BLACK CURRANTS

Grape stage (March–
April) Spray with a
systemic fungicide to
prevent leaf spot,
grey mould and
mildew.

**First open
flower** (early–
mid-April)
Repeat fungicide
treatment. Benlate
may give some
control of big bud
mite, too.

End of flowering (May)
Repeat fungicide
treatment and
spray with a
systemic insecticide
to control aphids
and capsid bug.

After harvest
(August) Spray
with a systemic
fungicide if mildew
and leaf spot
persist.

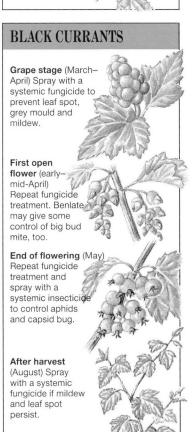

GOOSEBERRIES

First open flower
(April) Spray with
a systemic
fungicide to prevent
leaf spot and
mildew.

End of flowering
(mid-April) Repeat
fungicide treat-
ment. Spray
with a systemic
insecticide to
control aphids
and capsid
bugs.

Developing fruit (May)
Repeat fungicide
treatment. Look
for sawfly cater-
pillars and spray
with a contact
insecticide if
necessary.

After harvest
(August) Spray
with a systemic
fungicide if
mildew and leaf
spot persist.

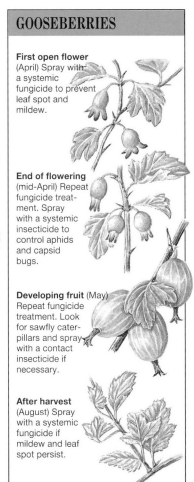

INSECTICIDES AND FUNGICIDES FOR FRUIT
Systemic fungicides ICI Benlate, Boots
Garden Fungicide, pbi Supercarb, May
& Baker Systemic Fungicide, Murphy
Systemic Action Fungicide, ICI
Nimrod-T. In many areas fungi have de-
veloped resistance to the first four,
related fungicides. Switch to Nimrod-T
instead if mildew persists.
Copper fungicides Murphy Traditional
Copper Fungicide, Vitax Bordeaux
Mixture.
Systemic insecticides Boots Greenfly and
Blackfly Killer, pbi Bio Long-Last,
Murphy Systemic Action Insecticide,
Murphy Tumblebug, ICI Rapid (aphids
only).
Contact insecticides pbi Fenitrothion,
ICI Picket, Vitax Py Spray Garden
Insect Killer.

See Tables, pages 130–136 for guide to insecticides and fungicides

PEST AND DISEASE CONTROL CALENDAR

FEBRUARY

■ Apply weed preventer around established soft fruit *before* weeds start to emerge.
■ If peach leaf curl is a regular problem, give a preventive spray of a copper-based fungicide and repeat two weeks later.
■ Use netting to protect buds on fruit trees from birds.

MARCH

■ Begin spraying programme for fruit (see page 86).
■ Put black plastic mulches in place to suppress weeds on the vegetable plot.
■ Sow peas before mid-March to avoid pea moth.
■ In mild, damp spells use slug killers to protect young plants.

APRIL

■ Pinch out the tips of broad bean plants to reduce blackfly damage.
■ Start brassicas in pots if club-root is a problem. Use soil insecticides or cabbage collars to protect plants from cabbage root fly.
■ Use soil insecticides, create a polythene barrier or cover with horticultural fleece or fine netting to protect carrots from carrot fly.
■ Protect young brassicas from flea beetles if necessary.
■ Apply slug pellets or use liquid slug killers as necessary.

MAY

■ Scatter slug pellets around strawberry plants (make sure they do not touch the fruit) and cover beds with bird netting.

■ Watch for the first signs of gooseberry sawfly and mildew and spray if necessary. Hand pick caterpillars.
■ Put pheromone traps for codling moth in place before the end of May.

JUNE

■ Spray potatoes and tomatoes with pbi Dithane 945 or a copper-based fungicide to prevent potato blight, especially in warm, moist periods.
■ Net soft fruit to deter birds.
■ If strawberry beetles are a problem, scatter pbi Slug Gard pellets.
■ Watch for aphids on courgettes and remove plants with virus symptoms.

JULY/AUGUST

Watch for first signs of cabbage caterpillars. Fine netting or horticultural fleece should prevent the butterflies landing to lay eggs.
■ Keep plants well watered in dry spells.
■ Watch for severe attacks of mealy cabbage aphid and spray if necessary.
■ Continue fortnightly sprays to protect potatoes and tomatoes from blight.

SEPTEMBER

■ If canker was a problem on apple trees, spray with a copper-based fungicide before leaf fall and repeat when about half the leaves have fallen.
■ Protect autumn fruiting strawberries from birds and slugs.
■ In mild, damp periods apply slug pellets or other slug killers

to protect overwintering vegetables.
■ Dip apples for storing in ICI Benlate or Murphy Systemic Action Fungicide to prevent brown rot.

OCTOBER

■ Harvest carrots and potatoes early and store, to prevent damage by soil pests.
■ Remove old foliage from strawberry plants after fruiting.
■ Put grease bands in place on fruit trees to prevent winter moths laying eggs.

NOVEMBER

■ Protect overwintered brassicas from pigeons with netting.
■ Replace the top netting on fruit cages with pigeon netting in case of heavy snow.
■ Check stored fruit and vegetables regularly for signs of rotting.
■ Clear up fallen fruit, leaves and other debris around fruit trees and compost them.

DECEMBER/JANUARY

■ Clear out the greenhouse and sterilise the structure, pots and seed trays ready for next year.
■ If required, spray fruit trees with a winter wash to destroy overwintering aphids, scale insects and apple suckers.
■ Prune out weak or diseased branches on fruit trees.
■ Remove abnormally swollen buds from blackcurrant bushes to limit spread of gall mites.
■ Prune gooseberries to keep the bush open and prevent mildew.
■ Cover wall-trained peaches with polythene to prevent peach leaf curl.

VEGETABLES

Nothing spoils the pleasure of growing your own fresh vegetables more than finding maggots in your peas or greenfly in your lettuce.

  Some problems may occur once in a lifetime, while others may return year after year. In most cases, if you identify the problem early enough you can take action to save the crop.

Some common pests and diseases can be controlled easily using pesticides, while others require more drastic action, such as removing and destroying affected plants or even not growing the crop on or near the plot for several years.

  Most soil pests can be prevented by using soil insecticides, and physical barriers will help to prevent adult pests from reaching your vegetable plants to lay their eggs. Some pests can be greatly reduced or prevented altogether by adopting a system of crop rotation (see page 116).

  Some diseases, like parsnip canker, can be prevented by growing vegetable varieties with built-in resistance. Unfortunately, only a few resistant vegetables are available to gardeners, but we have listed these whenever possible. Nearly all physiological problems can be avoided by preparing the soil well, with plenty of organic matter, and by regular feeding and watering. However if all else fails, give up growing vegetables which succumb to a wide range of pests and diseases, and concentrate on those that grow without problems in your garden.

USING CHEMICALS ON VEGETABLES

You may be reluctant to use insecticides and fungicides on edible crops. All garden chemicals have been approved by the Ministry of Agriculture and should be perfectly safe if used according to the manufacturer's instructions. If you are still worried, use pesticides like pyrethrum or derris. These break down very rapidly and are approved by some organic organisations. Never use old chemicals left lying around in the shed as they may not meet modern standards. Always read the label carefully to make sure that the chemical is approved for use on edible crops and follow any advice given about the interval you should leave between application and harvesting.

BEANS AND PEAS: LEAVES

■ BLACKFLY

Leaves and stems covered with small black insects

The commonest pest of broad beans. Blackfly start to congregate on young leaves and especially near the growing tip from May onwards. The leaves may also be sticky and covered with black sooty mould. Blackfly increase rapidly and if they are unchecked the plant will be weakened and distorted and the yield reduced. Newly planted French and runner beans are also attacked from June onwards. Ladybirds and other predators may eventually control blackfly, but usually not before damage has been done. Numbers usually decline from July onwards. Blackfly overwinter on native *Euonymus*.
Control Spray plants with an aphid killer or a systemic insecticide as soon as blackfly appear and repeat as necessary. Use ICI Rapid if ladybird or lacewing larvae are present. Pinch out the growing tips of broad beans once five flower trusses have developed. This removes the most attractive feeding site.
Prevention None.

■ PEA APHID

Large pale green or pink aphids

Pea aphids start to colonise pea plants during May or early June. Large numbers cause damage and need to be controlled.
Control and prevention See 'Blackfly' above and page 11.

■ BEAN MOSAIC VIRUS

Leaves mottled yellow or dark green and crinkled

Plants may also be stunted and pods may be discoloured and distorted. If stems of pea plants are affected whole plants may collapse. The virus is spread by aphids. French and runner beans may be affected.
Control Remove and destroy affected plants.
Prevention Control aphids (see left).

■ PEA AND BEAN WEEVIL

Leaves notched

Adult weevils cut semi-circular notches out of the edges of pea and broad bean leaves. The larvae feed on the roots in late spring. The weevils are grey-brown, 6mm (¼in) long and emerge from the soil in June or July. They feed until the autumn. Damage is rarely severe and strongly growing plants quickly grow out of trouble.
Control Dust affected plants with derris.
Prevention Protect young plants by dusting leaves and surrounding soil with derris.

■ HALO BLIGHT

Small, dry, angular spots surrounded by a yellow halo

This disease, caused by bacteria, affects French and runner beans and is spread by infected seed.
Control None. Remove and destroy plants showing symptoms at the start of the season.
Prevention Do not save seed from affected plants.

■ DOWNY MILDEW

Yellow patches on leaves, lower surfaces covered in mauve or white fungus

A problem on peas in cool, wet seasons. Affected leaves eventually turn brown and die and yield is reduced.
Control Destroy affected plants. Spray others with pbi Dithane 945.
Prevention None.

Blackfly and pea and bean weevil damage

Halo blight

■ POWDERY MILDEW

Leaves covered with white powdery mould

See page 12.

■ CHOCOLATE SPOT

Small red-brown spots on broad bean leaves

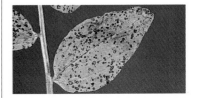

Chocolate-coloured streaks may also appear on stems. Spots or streaks may merge and eventually whole plants may die. Overwintered crops are most vulnerable in a wet spring. Plants that are crowded, or on poor soil are also vulnerable.
Control Destroy badly affected leaves. Spray remaining plants with a systemic fungicide.
Prevention Spring sown crops often escape infection. Ensure soil is fertile and well drained.

BEANS AND PEAS: STEMS AND ROOTS

■ FUSARIUM WILT
Plants wilt starting with the oldest leaves
French and runner beans are affected. When the stem is cut, a brown stain running through the internal tissues confirms the presence of the fusarium fungus.
Control Destroy infected plants as soon as possible.
Prevention Practise crop rotation. Improve soil structure and drainage.

■ FOOT AND ROOT ROT
Leaves turn yellow and die, stems become blackened at soil level and roots rot
Both peas and beans may be attacked by this soil-borne disease. Yield will be affected and plants may be stunted.
Control Destroy affected plants and water remaining plants with a copper fungicide to prevent spread.
Prevention Practise crop rotation. Use a seed dressing when sowing seed.

■ DAMPING OFF
Seedlings fail to appear or collapse at soil level
See page 122.

■ BEAN SEED FLY
Seeds fail to emerge
Soil-living grubs up to 8mm (³⁄₈in) long feed on the seeds and emerging seedlings of peas and beans, especially early in the season and when cold weather slows germination.
Control Soil insecticides applied at sowing time should control them.
Prevention Do not sow too early. Dust seed with a seed dressing containing an insecticide (Murphy Combined Seed Dressing, for example).

Foot and root rot

■ MICE
Seedlings fail to appear
Look for signs of burrowing or seedlings nipped off at soil level. Mice are the most likely culprit and often move systematically along rows.
Control Trapping is effective.
Prevention None, but laying spiky leaves on top of the seed is claimed to act as a deterrent.

ROOT NODULES
Small, round outgrowths on roots
These may be mistaken for a disease but are root nodules produced by a symbiotic bacterium that fixes nitrogen from the air and helps to feed the plant. Nodules are present on peas and broad beans, less commonly on French or runner beans. Leave the roots of peas and beans in the soil to feed next year's crops.

SOIL-BORNE DISEASES
Although peas and dwarf beans are usually rotated around a vegetable plot, it is tempting to leave runner beans in the same place, especially if you have dug a bean trench and erected permanent supports. Crops may grow successfully for many years, but there is always the risk of soil-borne diseases building up. Examples are foot and root rot and fusarium wilt.

SEED-BORNE DISEASES
It is tempting to save seed from peas and beans from year to year. Choose a healthy plant and leave the pods to mature fully and start to dry off. Harvest them and dry the seed indoors before storing.
If you save seed be aware that diseases such as pod spot, anthracnose and halo blight can be carried by seeds. Check saved seed and reject any that is distorted or discoloured. Better still, start with fresh seed each year.

RESISTANT VARIETIES
The following pea varieties have some resistance to downy mildew (D), fusarium wilt (F), mosaic virus (M) or powdery mildew (P):

'Bikini' F	'Titania' F
'Cavalier' F	'Trio' M
'Darfon' D, F	'Tristar' F
'Dark Skinned	'Waverex' F
Perfection' D, F	
'Honeypod' F	
'Hurst	
Greenshaft' D, F	
'Johnsons Freezer' F	
'Markana' D, F	
'Onward' F, M	
'Oregon Sugar Pod' F	
'Sugar Ann' F	
'Sugar Snap' F	

See Tables, pages 130–136 for guide to insecticides and fungicides

PEAS AND BEANS: PODS

▉ PEA MOTH

Grubs eating peas inside pods
Pea moths are active during
May and early June and lay eggs
on pea flower stalks. The grubs
(up to 9mm; ³⁄₈in long) move
inside the developing pods and
feed on one or two developing
peas until August then overwinter in the soil as cocoons.
Control None, but undamaged
peas are still edible.
Prevention Spray with a contact insecticide (at dusk to avoid
harming bees) as they come into
full flower and repeat after 10
days. Crops sown before mid-
March or after mid-May to
flower before early June or after
late July may escape damage.
Winter cultivation will destroy
some caterpillars.

▉ POD SPOT

Brown sunken spots on pea pods
Peas inside may be discoloured.
Leaves and stems may be spotted too. Early crops are most
vulnerable and this disease is
worst in wet seasons.
Control Lift and destroy diseased plants.
Prevention Rotate crops (see
page 116).

▉ PEA THRIPS

Silvery patches on pea pods

Pods may also be distorted and
yield reduced. Silvery patches
may occur on leaves. Attacks are
worse in hot, dry seasons when
the small (2mm; ¹⁄₁₆in) yellow or
black thrips are more numerous.

Pea moth larva

Control Spray with a contact
insecticide.
Prevention Practise crop rotation (see page 116).

▉ MARSH SPOT

Brown cavity inside peas

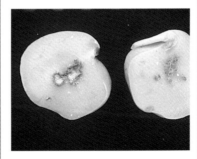

Look also for yellowing of the
leaf veins. The cause is lack of
manganese in the soil. It is most
common on alkaline soils.
Control None.
Prevention Incorporate organic
matter into the soil before sowing. Use a fertiliser containing
trace elements, such as one
based on seaweed, or fritted
trace elements.

▉ ANTHRACNOSE

Brown sunken spots on beans

Brown patches also occur on
leaves and cankers on stems.
Later, the spots may turn pink.
This disease may kill plants and
is worst in cool, wet years, but is
rarely serious.
Control Destroy diseased
plants. Spray remaining plants
with pbi Supercarb.
Prevention Rotate crops (see
page 116). Do not save seed.
Treat seed with a systemic fungicide.

▉ GREY MOULD

*Pods, stems and leaves covered in
grey-brown fluffy mould*
This is worst in wet seasons.
Control and prevention See
page 12.

BEETROOT AND SPINACH

Beetroot and spinach beet (perpetual spinach) are among the most trouble-free vegetables. Spinach is not closely related and is more difficult to grow.

LEAF SPOT
Small spots on leaves

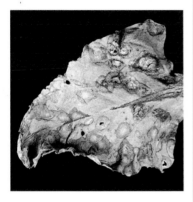

These have a pale brown centre, which may drop out, and a darker border. Weak or crowded plants are more vulnerable, especially in wet weather.
Control Remove and destroy badly affected leaves. Spray with a foliar feed to encourage strong growth.
Prevention Practise crop rotation. Avoid poorly drained soil. Apply a balanced fertiliser or sulphate of potash at around 10g a sq m ($\frac{1}{4}$oz a sq yd) before sowing.

BLIGHT
Yellowing of leaves, starting with the youngest
Leaves may also be rolled or puckered. The cause is cucumber mosaic virus, which is spread by aphids and affects true spinach but not beet.
Control Destroy affected plants.
Prevention Control aphids and weeds, which can also harbour the virus.

LEAF MINER
Brown blisters on leaves

These are caused by groups of small white grubs (up to 10mm; $\frac{3}{8}$in long) feeding inside the leaves. They are active from May to September, but do little harm other than to young plants. The tunnels are yellow-green but later dry up and shrivel. Pupae overwinter in the soil.
Control Pick off badly affected leaves. If damage is severe on young plants, spray with a systemic insecticide.
Prevention Soil cultivation in winter will reduce numbers.

APHIDS
Small insects on leaves
Beet and spinach can be attacked by blackfly or other aphids.
Control and prevention See page 11.

DOWNY MILDEW
Leaves blotched yellow with grey or violet fluffy mould underneath
The disease is worst on crowded plants in damp periods. In poorly drained soils leaves may turn brown and die.
Control Remove badly affected plants and spray remainder with pbi Dithane 945.
Prevention Practise crop rotation, improve drainage and sow thinly.

MANGANESE DEFICIENCY
Yellow blotches between the leaf veins
Mainly a problem on very alkaline soils.
Control Spray with a foliar feed containing trace elements.
Prevention Do not over-lime. If it is a persistent problem rake a fertiliser containing fritted trace elements into the soil before sowing.

VIOLET ROOT ROT
Leaves slightly yellow or stunted
When harvested the roots of beetroot are covered with purple fungal growth.
Control and prevention See page 101.

HEART ROT
Beetroots discoloured inside
Tissues may be black and watery and the rings more pronounced. Rough patches may also appear on the skin and most leaves die. Heart rot is caused by boron deficiency.
Control None.
Prevention If it is a persistent problem apply borax (35g in 10 litres of water to 20 sq m; 1oz in 2 gal of water to 20 sq yd) before sowing.

BOLTING
Plants elongate and produce flowers rather than roots or leaves
See page 105.

SPLITTING
Roots of beetroot split
Caused by heavy rain after a dry spell.
Control None.
Prevention Incorporate plenty of well-rotted organic matter over the years.

See Tables, pages 130–136 for guide to insecticides and fungicides

CABBAGE FAMILY: LEAVES

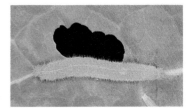

Small white butterfly caterpillar

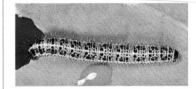

Large white butterfly caterpillar

▇ FLEA BEETLE
Small holes in young leaves

Holes up to 2mm (¹⁄₁₆in) start to appear in April and May when the adult beetles emerge. The beetles are up to 3mm (¹⁄₈in) long, striped yellow and black and leap into the air when disturbed. Strong plants normally grow out of danger, but seedlings and young transplants can be damaged and growth will be checked unless action is taken. The grubs may also nibble roots. Flea beetles hibernate in plant debris, but can fly short distances to attack young plants each spring.
Control Dust leaves and surrounding soil with derris and repeat as necessary until plants are large enough or damage ceases. Some flea beetles can be trapped by passing a piece of card coated in thick grease over the crop – jumping beetles will stick and can then be destroyed.
Prevention Encourage rapid growth of young plants. Clear plant debris away at the end of the season.

▇ MEALY CABBAGE APHID
Waxy grey insects on undersides of leaves and growing tips
Leaves may start to turn yellow. Dense colonies can build up rapidly from a single individual – especially in hot years – and often go unnoticed as they feed on the undersides of leaves. Young plants are very vulnerable and can be permanently stunted. Brussels sprout buttons and the hearts of cabbages can also be ruined. Mealy aphids overwinter as eggs on brassica stems and spread on to new plants from May onwards. Damage occurs from July to September. Mealy aphids also spread viruses.
Control Spray plants, especially underneath leaves and inside hearts, with a systemic insecticide. Protect transplants by dipping the leaves in a solution of aphid killer (wear rubber gloves). Early action is essential as aphids are difficult to control when large colonies have built up.
Prevention Clear away and destroy old brassica stalks. Inspect all young brassica plants regularly for early signs of aphid infestation. Prevention is very difficult if different brassica crops are grown throughout the year or if oilseed rape is grown nearby.

Mealy cabbage aphid

▇ CABBAGE CATERPILLARS
Large ragged holes in leaves
Caterpillars of small and large white butterflies and cabbage moth can be responsible. Diamond back moth caterpillars also occasionally attack cabbages (they eat only the undersides of leaves – the upper skin remains intact). Caterpillars can also get inside cabbage hearts and the heads of calabrese and cauliflowers. Damage is worst in late summer, so seedlings and young plants raised at this time (spring cabbage or sprouting broccoli, for example) are particularly vulnerable.

All cabbage caterpillars have at least two generations a year, so numbers build up through the summer from April until September. Cabbage butterflies overwinter as pupae attached to walls and fences, etc. Cabbage moths pupate in the soil.
Control Inspect plants carefully and pick off any caterpillars or clusters of eggs. Severe infestations can be controlled easily using any contact insecticide. *Bacillus thuringiensis* is a powder containing spores of a bacterium that kills caterpillars only and is applied in the same way as a chemical insecticide.
Prevention Fine-mesh netting or horticultural fleece will stop moths or butterflies reaching the crop to lay eggs and, if the barrier is complete, should prevent all damage.

Ringspot

White blister

Downy mildew

■ CABBAGE WHITEFLY
Small white insects on underside of leaves which fly off when disturbed
Whiteflies and their immobile scale-like larvae suck sap from leaves. Large infestations can weaken plants. They also excrete a sweet sticky honeydew that attracts growths of black sooty mould. Light infestations do no permanent damage on strongly growing plants. Cabbage whitefly are a separate species from glasshouse whitefly and attack only brassicas. They overwinter as adult flies on winter brassicas.
Control Spray with ICI Sybol or any insecticide containing permethrin. The scales are resistant so several applications at weekly intervals will be necessary to destroy adult flies as they hatch.
Prevention None.

•

■ RINGSPOT
Large spots composed of concentric rings on older leaves
The rings, made up of lots of minute black dots are up to 15mm (⅝in) in diameter. This disease is mainly a problem in the South-west and is prevalent in cool, wet years. Affected leaves may turn yellow and die prematurely.

Control None, remove and destroy badly affected leaves.
Prevention Rotate crops.

•

■ WHITE BLISTER
Small shiny white patches on leaves
Also called white rust, it initially causes green blisters, which later form white powdery warts. Heads of cauliflower and broccoli can be distorted and Brussels sprout plants are disfigured, but the disease generally does little harm and yields are unaffected. Overcrowded plants are most vulnerable.
Control Remove and destroy worst affected leaves.
Prevention Practise crop rotation. Thin overcrowded plants.

•

■ DOWNY MILDEW
Leaves yellowing, white fluffy growths on underside
This is often a problem on young plants that are crowded and is worst in cool, wet weather.
Control Remove and destroy severely affected plants, thin out remainder and spray with pbi Dithane 945.
Prevention Sow seeds in fresh soil-less compost, or use a fresh seedbed each year.

■ POWDERY MILDEW
White, powdery mould on leaves
A problem on swedes, sprouts and cabbage.
Control and prevention See page 12.

•

■ SLUGS AND SNAILS
Ragged holes in leaves
Slime trails confirm the presence of slugs or snails. Young plants are most vulnerable, especially in mild, damp weather.
Control and prevention See page 8.

•

■ PIGEONS
Soft parts of leaves between the veins stripped away
Pigeons can attack brassicas throughout the year in some areas and can be a serious problem on overwintered crops.
Control and prevention See page 10.

•

■ CLUBROOT
Leaves discoloured red or purple; plants wilt on hot days
See page 98.

•

■ CABBAGE ROOT FLY
Leaves tinged blue, plants, stunted and wilt in hot weather
See page 98.

CABBAGE FAMILY: PHYSIOLOGICAL PROBLEMS

■ BLOWN SPROUTS
Open leafy sprouts instead of tight buttons.
This problem is caused by unsuitable soil conditions; for example soil that does not contain enough well-rotted organic matter or soil that is too loose. Brussels sprouts, like other larger brassicas, need a firm soil to grow well.
Control Pick off blown sprouts, earth-up stem bases.
Prevention Firm soil before planting and water well in dry spells. F1 hybrid varieties are likely to stand longer before the sprouts 'blow'.

■ WHIPTAIL
Leaves narrow and strap-shaped

Mainly a problem of cauliflowers and broccoli. Young plants become distorted and the growing point fails to develop. It is caused by a deficiency of molybdenum, a trace element present in most garden soils but not available to plants if the soil is too acid.
Control Spray with a foliar feed containing trace elements.
Prevention Check the pH and add lime to acid soils before sowing or planting.

■ SPLIT HEARTS
Hearted cabbages split towards the end of the season
The cause is prolonged drought followed by heavy rain or watering. Heavy frosts can also split overwintered cabbages. Split cabbages can still be eaten immediately, but do not store them.
Control None.
Prevention Plant transplants firmly. Water regularly in dry spells to prevent the soil drying out completely.

■ BOLTING
Loose curds or flowers produced
The edible parts of cauliflower, broccoli and calabrese are immature flower buds. If left too long they will run to flower. A setback or water shortage may cause bolting before good curds or spears are formed.
Control None.
Prevention Incorporate plenty of organic matter. Water regularly in dry periods to prevent the soil drying out completely.

■ BROWN CURDS
Brown patches in cauliflower curds

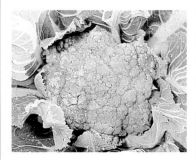

This is caused by a lack of the trace element boron. Young leaves may also be distorted and the heads small. Boron is unavailable to plants if the pH is too high (caused by over-liming).
Control Spray with a foliar feed containing trace elements.
Prevention Incorporate plenty of organic matter into the soil. If it is a recurrent problem apply borax to the seedbed (35g in 10 litres of water to 10sq m; 1oz in 2 gal to 12sq yd). Do not over-lime.

■ BRACTEOLATED CURDS
Leaves growing out of the curds

This condition is caused by fluctuating temperatures when the curds start developing. The curds are still edible.
Control and prevention None.

■ SMALL CAULIFLOWERS
Cauliflowers are difficult to grow well. Disappointingly small curds may be due to several factors, for example trace element deficiencies or early attacks by clubroot or cabbage root fly. The most likely cause is a check to growth early in their lives. The size of the curd depends on the number and size of the leaves produced early in a plant's life. Once it reaches a certain stage of maturity a cold period stimulates it to produce flowers (the curd).
Control None.
Prevention Ensure that seedlings are well supplied with water and nutrients and not overcrowded. Transplant them before they are six weeks old, taking care not to damage the roots. Prepare the soil well with organic matter and fertiliser. Keep the plants well watered during dry spells.

BLINDNESS
Cauliflowers fail to develop curds
Damage to the growing tip by pests or a check to growth are the most likely causes. Lack of nutrients, lack of water or too much water or attacks by clubroot or cabbage root fly could be responsible. It is essential to grow cauliflowers without a check to growth.
Control None.
Prevention See 'Small cauliflowers', opposite.

HEARTLESS CABBAGES
Cabbages fail to develop hearts
The likely cause is loose soil or inadequate humus and the problem is aggravated by drought or lack of nutrients.
Control None.
Prevention Plant firmly into a firm seedbed containing plenty of well-rotted organic matter. Incorporate a balanced fertiliser (growmore, for example). Water regularly during dry periods.

NITROGEN DEFICIENCY
Leaves small, pale and discoloured

Nitrogen deficiency is most common on shallow, sandy or chalky soils which have not been improved with well-rotted organic matter and is exacerbated by long periods of heavy rain leaching out nutrients.

RESISTANT VARIETIES
Brussels sprouts
The following show some resistance to leaf spot (L), powdery mildew (P), ring spot (R) or white blister (W):
'Citadel' L,P
'Cor' L,P,R,W
'Mallard' L,P,R
'Montgomery' P,R,W
'Oliver' P
'Peer Gynt' L,W
'Rampart' L,P,R,W
'Stephen' P
'Troika' L,P,R,W

Cabbages
These summer cabbages show some resistance to powdery mildew:
'Derby Day'
'Stonehead'

Swedes
These show resistance to clubroot:
'Marian' (also powdery mildew)
'Chignetto'

Control Topdress with a nitrogenous fertiliser, such as dried blood or sulphate of ammonia.
Prevention Incorporate plenty of organic matter during winter digging. Add a balanced fertiliser to the seedbed.

MAGNESIUM DEFICIENCY
Yellowing leaves, mainly between veins on older leaves

Control Spray affected plants with a liquid fertiliser containing magnesium.

Prevention Incorporate well-rotted organic matter into the soil. Use a fertiliser containing magnesium (one based on seaweed, for example).

MANGANESE DEFICIENCY
Yellowing leaves
Leaf edges may appear curled and scorched. All leaves are affected.
Control Spray affected plants with a foliar feed containing trace elements.
Prevention Incorporate plenty of well-rotted organic matter.

WEEDKILLER DAMAGE
Rough warty growths on stems

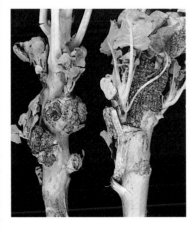

Leaves may be narrow and distorted and plants stunted and unusable. Damage by hormone weedkillers can be due to inadequate rinsing of a sprayer or watering-can that has been used for lawn weedkillers, drifting of spray when treating a lawn or, occasionally, to residues in straw or strawy manure.
Control None.
Prevention Take care to prevent spray drift and rinse equipment thoroughly after applying weedkillers.

CABBAGE FAMILY: ROOT PROBLEMS

■ CLUBROOT
Roots swollen and distorted

The leaves take on yellow, red or purple tinges and plants wilt in hot spells, but may recover when watered. The fibrous roots of swedes and turnips and the main swollen root become galled. Later the galls may decay into a slimy, smelly mass.

Clubroot is caused by a fungus that can remain in the soil for up to 20 years. Once present it is impossible to control. Any movement of soil – on boots, spades, etc. – helps to spread it. It also attacks related ornamental plants and weeds. It is worst on acid or badly drained soils.

Control None. Destroy badly affected plants – never compost them.

Prevention Grow your brassicas from seed, do not buy in plants. Practise crop rotation.

Living with clubroot
■ Lime the brassica plot in autumn to keep the soil between pH 7.0 and 7.5.
■ Improve drainage, by creating raised beds, for example.
■ Dip bare-rooted transplants in a clubroot dip such as May & Baker Liquid Club Root Control.
■ Grow young plants on in large pots (13cm; 5in) containing soil-less compost; when planted out they will have made sufficient root growth to survive attack.
■ Grow spring cabbage and early summer cauliflowers, which do most of their growing before the disease builds up to damaging levels. Grow a resistant variety of swede.
■ Take care not to damage transplants – this will make an entry for the fungus.
■ Alternatively, reserve a special bed for brassicas and keep the pH high.

■ SOIL GRUBS
Young plants nipped off at soil level
Suspect cutworms, swift moths or other soil grubs.
Control and prevention See page 9.

■ CABBAGE ROOT FLY
Leaves bluish and plants wilt in hot weather

Small (up to 6mm; ¼in) white grubs can be seen on the roots. The fine roots are eaten until all that remains is a blackened stump. Young plants can be killed and older plants will have their growth restricted. Cauliflower plants may produce small curds.

Adults, which resemble small houseflies, emerge from pupae in the soil during late April or early May. A second generation occurs in June or July and a third from about mid-August onwards.

Control Little can be done once symptoms are obvious.

Prevention Apply a soil insecticide when sowing and when planting transplants. A second application may be necessary (follow the manufacturer's instructions).

Make collars 15cm (6in) diameter from flexible material like carpet underlay – this will prevent some flies from laying eggs near the plant stem and so reduce damage. Crop covers laid over the top when plants are transplanted should also reduce damage (see page 139).

Above ground symptoms of clubroot

SWEDES AND TURNIPS

GALL WEEVIL

Round swellings on stem base or roots

Superficially, the condition is similar to clubroot, but the swellings are rounded and hollow if cut open. A small white grub may still be inside or there may be a small hole where it has burrowed out. Severe galling can ruin turnips, but established leafy brassicas do not usually suffer. Adult beetles (up to 3mm; ⅛in) lay eggs on young brassicas from March onwards.

Control None. Destroy badly affected plants.

Prevention Remove remains of brassica crops at the end of the season. Thorough soil cultivation will reduce numbers.

Gall weevil damage

SOFT ROT

Slimy rot on crown and inside root

Leaves and the internal tissues of the root rot, though the skin remains intact. The disease is caused by a bacterium that infects leaves which have been damaged by pests or frost and is worst in wet seasons. Stored roots may also develop soft rot.

Control Remove and destroy affected plants.

Prevention Practise crop rotation. Do not apply fresh manure, improve drainage and avoid damaging plants when hoeing around them.

TURNIP MOSAIC VIRUS

Leaves yellow, usually between veins

They may also be distorted or stunted. The virus is transmitted by flea beetles and can affect other brassicas.

Control None, destroy affected plants.

Prevention Control flea beetles (see page 94).

BLACK ROT

Black ring just under the skin

It is evident only when swedes or turnips are cut in half. Leaves of affected plants may be yellow with blackened veins. This is not a common disease.

Control None.

Prevention Practise crop rotation and try to improve drainage.

BROWN HEART

Grey or brown rings running through the interior of swede roots

The roots may also be watery and rough patches may appear on the skin. The cause is lack of boron, so the problem is most likely to occur on light, chalky soils or if excessive lime has been added.

Control None.

Prevention If it is a regular problem apply borax before sowing (30g in 10 litres of water to 10sq m; 1oz in 2 gal to 12sq yd).

RADISHES

FLEA BEETLES

Round holes in young leaves

Provided they have plenty of water radishes grow quickly so are rarely seriously damaged by flea beetle.

Control and prevention See page 94.

CABBAGE ROOT FLY

Radishes tunnelled

Roots may also be eaten, restricting the plant's growth. Attacks are most likely in sowings from May to August in areas where cabbage root fly is a problem.

Control None.

Prevention Do not leave roots in the ground. See opposite.

BOLTING

Flower spikes produced before roots develop

See page 105.

CARROTS AND PARSNIPS

CARROT FLY
*Leaves yellowing or tinged red;
young plants wilt or die*
Symptoms are similar to those of
motley dwarf virus, but can be
distinguished by examining
roots for damage by small (8mm;
⅜in), cream grubs. Seedlings and
young plants are attacked by
carrot fly grubs during June. At
first the side roots are nibbled,
causing discoloured foliage and
wilting or death of some plants.
Later, the grubs begin to tunnel
into the tap roots. A second
generation of flies, which peaks
in the autumn, causes the
characteristic rusty brown tunnels in parsnips. Parsley and
celery are also attacked as well
as related weeds like cow
parsley.
   The adults are small, inconspicuous, shiny black flies with a
12mm (½in) wingspan. The first
generation hatches out in May
and the flies search for carrots or
related plants and lay their eggs
near the stems. A second
generation appears from late
July. Carrot flies pupate in the
soil or in carrot roots that are
missed at harvest.
Control Not usually worthwhile
once damage is obvious.
Cultivate the soil thoroughly
and destroy affected crops.
Prevention is worthwhile if
carrot fly is a regular problem.
There are three main options.
■ Continuous physical barriers
prevent the adult flies, which fly
close to the ground, from reaching the crop. Make barriers to
enclose small patches of carrots
from clear polythene or fine
mesh perforated sheet (such as
Papronet) 75cm (30in) high and
ideally not more than 1.2m (4ft)
across. Alternatively, floating
cloches of horticultural fleece or
very fine mesh netting can be
laid over the crop.
■ Sprinkle soil insecticides into

Carrot fly damage

the seed drill and re-apply after
six weeks or so (follow instructions on the product label) to
give season-long protection.
■ Carrots sown after late May or
dug before early August should
miss the main attacks.

•

APHIDS
Small insects on foliage
Although colonies of small green
willow-carrot aphids are inconspicuous, they spread virus disease (see below).
Control Spray with an aphid
killer (see page 11)
Prevention None.

•

MOTLEY DWARF VIRUS
Foliage distorted and tinged red
The central leaves are mottled
yellow. Plants appear twisted

and roots may be stunted. The
virus is spread by aphids and
also affects parsley.
Control Dig up and destroy
affected plants.
Prevention Watch for aphids
and control them by spraying.

•

LEAF MINER (CELERY FLY)
Pale green blotches on leaves
These areas later become brown
and dry. They are caused by
white grubs up to 8mm (⅜in)
long, tunnelling inside the leaf
tissues. Attacks from April to
June can damage young plants.
A second generation from July
onwards causes superficial damage to established plants.
Control Pick off and destroy
badly affected leaves. Spray with
a systemic insecticide.
Prevention None.

Parsnip canker

Violet root rot

PARSNIP CANKER
Black or orange-brown patches on roots
This disease can be made worse by poor growing conditions, wet seasons or damage by carrot root fly. The cankerous patches usually occur near the crown.
Control None.
Prevention Grown a resistant variety. Practise crop rotation, improve soil drainage and lime to keep the soil near neutral (pH 6.5–7.0).

VIOLET ROOT ROT
Foliage yellow and stunted
Roots are covered by a web of purple fungal growth. An occasional problem on carrots, parsnips and other roots.
Control None. Destroy affected crops.
Prevention Practise crop rotation.

BLACK ROT
Mealy black rotten patches on roots
Symptoms appear on stored carrots but are not obvious when harvested. This disease can also kill seedlings.
Control None.
Prevention Practise crop rotation.

SCLEROTINIA ROT
White fluffy mould on roots
This fungal disease attacks stored roots and, occasionally, growing crops.
Control Destroy any affected plants.
Prevention Store only healthy roots and keep them cool and dry. Check stored roots regularly and destroy any that are diseased.

GREEN TOP
Green tops to roots
Carrot roots exposed to sunlight turn green but, unlike green potatoes, they are safe to eat.
Control None.
Prevention Take care not to expose roots when thinning or harvesting. Earth up if necessary.

SPLIT ROOTS
Roots split lengthways
The cause is often heavy rain or watering after a long, dry spell. The roots are edible, but do not store them.

RESISTANT VARIETIES
Parsnips
'Avonresister', 'Cobham Improved Marrow', 'Gladiator', 'Marrow Improved', 'White Gem' are resistant to canker.
Carrots
No varieties are resistant to carrot root fly, but the following have shown some resistance: 'Nandor', 'Nantucket' and 'Sytan' – they are best used in combination with another control method.

Control None.
Prevention Water as necessary to prevent the soil drying out completely. Improve the soil by adding well-rotted organic matter.

FORKING
Roots forked or otherwise misshapen
This is caused by poor soil. The roots are still edible.
Control None.
Prevention Avoid soil that is very heavy, stony or shallow, or has been freshly manured.

See Tables, pages 130–136 for guide to insecticides and fungicides

CELERY

LEAF MINER
Yellow-brown blotches on leaves
These are caused by grubs of the celery fly tunnelling inside the leaf. They also attack parsnips and parsley (see page 100).
Control See page 100.
Prevention None.

CARROT FLY
Yellowing leaves, stunted plants
Carrot fly grubs tunnel into roots, crown and leaf stalks. Celery planted before mid-June is most vulnerable.
Control and prevention See page 100.

MOSAIC VIRUS
Leaves puckered and veins yellow
Eventually the whole plant may become stunted. Aphids spread the virus.
Control None.
Prevention Spray with ICI Rapid or a systemic insecticide to control aphids.

LEAF SPOT
Small brown spots on leaves

This seed-borne disease is common, but celery seed available to gardeners is normally treated to prevent it.
Control As soon as symptoms are seen, spray with a systemic fungicide.
Prevention None, but buy treated seed.

Leaf miner

BORON DEFICIENCY
Brown horizontal cracks
Growth is also poor and the leaves turn yellow. This is most likely to be a problem on alkaline or very dry soils.
Control Spray with a foliar feed containing trace elements.
Prevention Do not over-lime. Apply borax before planting (30g in 10 litres of water to 10sq m; 1oz in 2 gal to 12sq yd).

SLUGS
Stems and heart nibbled
Small, black keeled slugs are a particular problem. See page 8.

BOLTING
Plants produce flowers
A common problem in dry seasons or on dry soil. Plants that have received a check as seedlings or are too large when planted out may also bolt.
Control None.
Prevention Water celery regularly during dry spells.

HEART ROT
Hearts brown and rotten
The plants may appear normal until harvested. The bacteria causing heart rot enter through wounds made by slugs or other pests or by careless hoeing or earthing up.
Control Destroy affected plants.
Prevention Rotate crops.

SUCCESS WITH CELERY
Celery is a difficult crop to grow well, especially the traditional trench varieties. It also needs a lot of space. Self-blanching types or celeriac are slightly easier.
■ Incorporate plenty of well-rotted organic matter into the soil, by trenching if necessary.
■ Do not plant out until after the last frost; harden off young plants well.
■ Never let celery go short of water – apply at least 10 litres a sq m (2 gal a sq yd) twice a week in dry spells.
■ Feed regularly with a nitrogen fertiliser, such as sulphate of ammonia or Nitrochalk at 35g a sq m (1oz a sq yd) every fortnight.
■ Blanch trench types by earthing up the base.

SCLEROTINIA ROT
White fluffy mould on crown
See also page 101.
Control Destroy affected plants.
Prevention Practise crop rotation.

CRACKING OR SPLITTING
Stalks split lengthways
This is a result of dryness at the roots or an excess of nitrogen fertiliser.
Control None.
Prevention Prepare the soil well, with plenty or organic matter and water regularly in dry spells.

COURGETTES AND MARROWS

Mosaic virus

APHIDS
Small insects on leaves
Several aphid species may attack marrows. Apart from weakening the plants they spread viruses (see below).
Control and prevention See page 11, but note that some insecticides (ICI Rapid and ICI Sybol, for example) can damage marrows.

MOSAIC VIRUSES
Plants stunted, leaves puckered and mottled yellow
Cucumber mosaic virus is the most common disease of marrows. Zucchini yellow mosaic virus produces similar symptoms but the effects are worse. Unless controlled these viruses may spread to the fruits, which will also be distorted and discoloured. Both viruses are spread by aphids.
Control Destroy affected plants as soon as possible. Raise spare plants to compensate for any lost through mosaic virus.
Prevention Control aphids (see left).

SLUGS
Young plants nibbled
Fruits are also vulnerable.
Control Scatter slug pellets when transplanting young plants.
Prevention Surround young plants with 10cm (4in) high sections of plastic bottles. Keep fruits off the soil if possible.

POWDERY MILDEW
Leaves covered in powdery white fungus
See page 12.

GREY MOULD
Leaves, stems and fruits covered in grey-brown velvety fungus
See page 12.

ROOT ROTS
Plants growing poorly, roots blackened and rotting
The whole plant eventually collapses.
Control Destroy affected plants.
Prevention Grow on a fresh site each year.

LETTUCE

Mosaic virus

DOWNY MILDEW
Leaves mottled yellow, white downy mould on undersides

This disease is worst in cool, wet summers and on greenhouse lettuce. It can affect both seedlings and older plants but is worse on older leaves.
Control Remove and destroy affected plants. Spray remainder with pbi Dithane 945.
Prevention Avoid wetting the leaves. Some varieties are resistant (see Box opposite).

•

BIG VEIN
Leaf veins are enlarged and yellow
Affected leaves appear puckered or blistered and plants may not heart up. It is caused by a soil-living fungus.
Control None.
Prevention Rotate crops.

•

MOSAIC VIRUS
Leaves mottled, veins become almost transparent
Affected plants are also stunted. The virus is seed-borne, but aphids can spread it, too.
Control None.
Prevention Control aphids. Some varieties are resistant.

Tipburn

APHIDS
Small green or pink insects on leaves
Also look for black sooty mould, which colonises sticky secretions produced by the aphids. Cast aphid skins may also build up, making crops unappetising. Two main species are involved.
■ Lettuce aphid overwinters on currant and gooseberry bushes and migrates to lettuces in May. Colonies of wingless aphids build up rapidly, sometimes from a single individual, until September when winged forms return to fruit bushes.
■ Peach-potato aphids are pale green, yellow or pink and over-winter on peach trees. Apart from causing damage by feeding they can spread mosaic virus.
Control Spray with an aphid killer (ICI Rapid, for example) as soon as colonies start to appear.
Prevention None.

RINGSPOT
Small brown circular spots with yellow halos on leaves
The centres may later fall out giving a 'shothole' effect. It is most common on winter lettuce or during cold, wet weather.
Control Destroy affected plants.
Prevention Carefully remove all crop remains at the end of the season. Practise crop rotation.

•

TIPBURN
Edges of leaves become watery, turn brown and may rot
These symptoms occur in warm spells and are caused by poor movement of calcium within the plant. The outer leaves are supplied at the expense of the heart leaves.
Control None.
Prevention Water frequently during hot, dry weather. Some varieties have some resistance to tipburn (see Box opposite).

Butt rot

■ BUTT ROT

Plants suddenly wilt

Examine the base, or butt, of the plant. The first sign is a red-brown discoloration inside the stem, where the tissues break down. In severe cases the head may snap off when touched.
Control None.
Prevention Do not over water. Practise crop rotation.

■ GREY MOULD

Leaves and base covered in grey fluffy mould

The stem may also be discoloured red or brown and rotten at soil level causing the plant to wilt suddenly. This disease is worse in cool, wet summers or on greenhouse lettuce.
Control Spray with a systemic fungicide.
Prevention Handle young plants carefully and do not plant them too deeply. Avoid any checks to growth.

■ CUTWORMS

Plants cut at soil level

Severe damage is caused in seed-beds or to young transplants.
Control and Prevention See page 9.

BOLTING

Most garden vegetables are annuals, which naturally flower (run to seed) the year they are sown, or biennials which flower in their second season, often producing bulbs or roots in the first. Where the aim is to produce edible leaves or roots, this can be a problem.

Most vegetables respond to cold and/or lengthening days by switching from vegetative growth to flower initiation.

Leafy crops, like lettuce and cabbages, usually heart up before they start to flower (or bolt), unless they receive an early check to growth; non-hearting 'salad bowl' lettuces stand longer before bolting; newer varieties of Chinese cabbage are less likely to bolt. With spring cabbage, sowing and transplanting at the correct time should prevent bolting. Leaf beet (a biennial) is less likely to bolt than true spinach (an annual).

Root crops like beetroot, radish, leeks and onions are biennials but may bolt if they receive a cold stimulus in the first year, or receive a check to growth. For the earliest sowings use a bolt-resistant beetroot variety (page 93). Carrots and parsnips rarely bolt.

■ SLUGS AND SNAILS

Ragged holes in leaves

Young plants can be destroyed and plants near to harvest can be ruined by slugs or snails.
Control and prevention See page 8.

■ NO HEARTS

Butterhead or crisphead types fail to heart up properly

This is usually caused by poor soil conditions, such as insufficient organic matter or moisture, shade or overcrowding.
Control None.
Prevention Prepare seedbeds with plenty of well-rotted organic matter.

RESISTANT VARIETIES

Lettuce

The following varieties have some resistance to: tipburn (T), some strains of downy mildew (D) or are claimed to be tolerant of mosaic virus (M) or root aphids (A).
'Avondefiance' butterhead A, D
'Dolly' butterhead D, M
'Malika' crisphead M, T
'Musette' butterhead A, D, M
'Sabine' butterhead A, D
'Saladin' crisphead T
'Soraya' butterhead D, M

■ ROOT APHID

Plants wilt in hot weather or suddenly collapse

Examine the roots for tiny aphids covered in white, waxy scales. Their presence may go undetected until a hot, dry spell in July or August. The aphids overwinter on poplar trees, arrive on lettuces in June and July. They are less of a problem in cool, wet summers.
Control Remove affected plants together with their roots and the surrounding soil. Keep remaining plants well watered in dry spells.
Prevention Grow a resistant variety (see Box).

ONIONS AND LEEKS

Leek rust

▪ LEEK RUST

Raised orange spots or streaks on leaves

This is the most important disease of leeks and it can also affect chives. In severe attacks the leaves may turn yellow and die, but usually the blanched stems are still edible.

Control No suitable fungicides are available to gardeners. Remove badly affected plants to limit spread.

Prevention Practise crop rotation. Do not wet leaves when watering. Some leek varieties are more resistant to the disease than others. Destroy affected leaves after harvesting.

▪ LEAF BLOTCH

Oval white or pale brown spots on leaves

The spots darken with age and eventually leaves will die. This disease is worst in wet seasons and most likely in the South-east.

Control Remove and destroy affected plants.

Prevention Rotate crops.

▪ ONION EELWORM

Plants have abnormally swollen base and distorted leaves

Young plants may be killed, older plants produce soft bulbs which may also crack underneath and cannot be stored.

The eelworms feed inside the stems and leaves. They are 1–2mm (less than ¹⁄₁₆in) long but not visible to the naked eye. They move through soil to infest new plants. They also attack carrots, parsnips and beans, although these do not suffer such severe damage. Lettuce and the cabbage family are not affected.

Control No suitable chemicals are available to gardeners.

Prevention Practise crop rotation. Keep weeds under control.

▪ ONION FLY

Plants turn yellow and wilt

Seedlings and young plants may be killed. Older plants will be weakened and the bulbs will be ruined. Onion fly grubs eat the roots and burrow into the developing bulbs.

Adult onion flies look like small houseflies. They first appear in May to lay eggs near onion or leek crops. The cream grubs are up to 8mm (⅜in) long. There may be a second or third generation of flies, but damage is usually worst in June and July. Onion flies overwinter in the soil as pupae.

Control Remove and destroy affected plants.

Prevention Practise crop rotation. Apply a soil insecticide to the seedbed when sowing or planting and reapply later if necessary. Follow the manufacturer's instructions on the product label.

Onion eelworm damage

▪ WHITE ROT

Leaves turn yellow and wilt; fluffy white mould with black pinhead-sized fruiting bodies on base of bulbs

The most serious disease of onions including spring onions and occasionally leeks. Seedlings and young plants may fall over as the bulb rots. The disease spreads rapidly through the crop unless controlled. Spores can remain in the soil for up to 18 years. It is most troublesome in spring and autumn or in cool summers.

Control Lift and destroy affected plants complete with roots.

Prevention Grow onions and leeks from seed on a fresh site. Take great care not to spread infected soil – on your boots, for example – or plant remains.

Onion fly damage

White rot

DOWNY MILDEW
Pale, oval areas on leaves which later turn brown or purple
Affected leaves also die back from the tip. This is mainly a problem on onions and especially when the leaves remain wet for long periods or in cool wet seasons. Bulbs may also be affected, becoming soft and unsuitable for storage.
Control Remove badly affected plants and spray remainder with pbi Dithane 945.
Prevention Practise crop rotation.

ONION THRIPS
White or silvery patches on leaves
These are caused by thrips feeding. Light attacks can be tolerated, but large numbers can build up in hot, dry summers causing leaves to be distorted or even killed. The insects are yellow or black and 2–3mm (⅛in) long. Onion thrips also attack other vegetables including the cabbage family and tomatoes. They overwinter in the soil as adults.
Control Spray severe infestations with a contact insecticide such as one containing malathion.
Prevention None.

BOLTING
A thick flower spike is produced
Onions and leeks do not normally flower (bolt) until their second year, but a check to

growth, such as a cold spell earlier in the year or drought, can trigger off flowering. Cut off the flower stalk and use the bulbs immediately. Do not store them.
Control None.
Prevention Do not let the soil dry out completely. Do not sow or plant too early.

SMUT
Dark streaks on leaves and bulb scales
These streaks remain under the skin at first, but eventually erupt to produce masses of black, powdery spores. Affected leaves are also twisted and distorted and some plants will die. This is a rare but serious disease of onions and to a lesser extent leeks. Spores can remain in the soil for 10 years or more.
Control Destroy affected plants.
Prevention Grow onions and leeks on a fresh site. Practise good hygiene.

NECK ROT
Stored onions start to soften and grey mould develops around the neck
Later, black spore bodies are produced and the bulb starts to rot. This disease does not spread from bulb to bulb but is seed-borne. It is already present on the bulbs when they are harvested, but does not develop for some time in store.
Control Check stored bulbs frequently and remove those affected.
Prevention Do not overfeed onions with nitrogenous fertiliser. Ripen the bulbs off well and store only firm, dry bulbs in a cool, dry, airy place. Dust sets or seeds with Benlate before sowing or planting. Plants grown from seed are less likely to be affected than those grown from sets.

SOFT ROT
Stored onions become soft and start to smell
This disease is caused by a bacterium. Other storage diseases are caused by fungi and stored bulbs may be infected by several different rotting organisms.
Prevention Well-grown, ripe, dry, undamaged bulbs should store until the spring in a cool, dry, well-ventilated place. Tie them in strings or store them on wire netting to allow adequate ventilation.

BULLNECK
Neck of bulb abnormally thick
This is usually caused by too much nitrogen fertiliser in the soil, fresh manure or a very wet summer. The onions can be eaten, but do not store them.
Control None.
Prevention Feed with a liquid fertiliser containing more potash than nitrogen.

SADDLEBACK
Bulb splits underneath
The bulb is found to be cracked when harvested or sometimes it splits into two separate bulbs. Fungi may enter and cause rotting. The most likely cause is heavy rain following a long period of drought and the condition is common with onions grown from sets. Affected bulbs can be eaten but are not suitable for storing.
Control None.
Prevention Water in very dry spells to prevent the soil completely drying out. Lift mature bulbs to sever the roots before drying them off for storing.

POTATOES: LEAVES

BLIGHT
Small dark spots or blotches on leaves

In damp weather these are surrounded by fluffy white growths, especially on the undersides of the leaves. Spots enlarge and spread, and in severe cases all of the foliage may rot and collapse. The disease spreads rapidly to neighbouring plants and also to tomato plants. The first symptoms sometimes appear in May but do not become severe until later in the summer.

Potato tubers are also affected. Grey or brown patches on the surface spread inwards to produce reddish-brown patches in the flesh. Badly affected tubers may remain dry and mummified in store or may be attacked by secondary rots. The disease can survive on tubers left in the ground to infect next year's crop.
Control Remove all, even the smallest, tubers and destroy the stems and leaves.

Prevention Grow resistant varieties. Spray plants with pbi Dithane 945 or a copper fungicide at fortnightly intervals from early July onwards, especially in wet years. Bury tubers deeply and earth up to prevent infection from the foliage.

APHIDS
Small insects on leaves
Two species commonly attack potatoes: the peach-potato aphid (yellow, green or pink) and the larger, more active potato aphid (green or pink). Both can weaken plants by feeding but, more importantly, can spread viruses. They are more numerous in hot, dry summers.
Control Watch for early signs of colonies building up and spray with an aphid killer such as ICI Rapid.
Prevention None.

MOSAIC AND OTHER VIRUSES
Leaves mottled or crinkled; plants stunted
Several different viruses can attack potatoes, some of which are spread by aphids. Potato virus Y is the most serious. In severe cases leaves can shrivel and drop and the yield of tubers is much reduced. Tubers are not usually affected.
Control None. Remove and destroy affected plants.
Prevention Use certified seed (see page 112) and control aphids. A few varieties show resistance to some but not all of the common viruses.

LEAF ROLL VIRUS
Leaves roll up and turn brittle
Lower leaves are usually affected first, gradually becoming dry and turning brown at the edges. This is a common disease,

Leaf roll virus

See page 139 for suppliers of non-chemical pest controls

transmitted by aphids, that can
reduce yields, although the tubers are unaffected.
Control None.
Prevention Use certified seed
(see page 112); control aphids.

•

■ CAPSID BUGS
Small ragged holes in leaves
These are caused by the feeding
of capsid bugs early in the season. The bugs are small (up to
6mm; ¼in), active sap-sucking
insects. In severe attacks the
leaves may be tattered and distorted. Yield is rarely affected.
Control Spray severe attacks
with a contact or systemic insecticide.
Prevention None.

•

■ COLORADO BEETLE
*Leaves eaten, conspicuous yellow
and black beetles present*

The red and black larvae also
feed voraciously and plants can
be rapidly defoliated. Both beetles and larvae are about 10mm
(⅜in) long.
This pest is common in
Europe and it is occasionally
found in Britain, usually
imported with plant material. It
has yet to establish itself here.

Blackleg

Control Phone your nearest
Ministry of Agriculture office or
send specimens in a well-packed
tin to MAFF Harpenden Laboratory, Hatching Green, Harpenden, Hertfordshire AL5 2BD,
and leave them to deal with the
pest.

•

■ BLACKLEG
*Leaves roll and wilt, stem black-
ens*
Usually the upper leaves are
affected first. These eventually
turn yellow and wilt. The base of
the stem will be blackened and
rotten. This bacterial disease
usually occurs early in the season, especially if the weather is
dry. The plant may die before
any tubers are formed. If tubers
have formed they may be infected. Do not store tubers from
infected plants. This disease
cannot survive in the soil and it
cannot spread to healthy plants.
Control Dig up and destroy
affected plants.
Prevention Buy certified seed
potatoes (see page 116). Do not
save tubers.

■ FROST DAMAGE
*Yellow torn leaves or blackened
shoots*
Mild frosts can damage leaves,
especially young shoots, causing
a temporary setback, but severe
late frosts can kill off all above
ground shoots. Plants will
eventually recover, but the yield
of early potatoes will be delayed
and reduced.
Control None.
Prevention Earth up potatoes
regularly and if frosts are predicted cover plants with newspaper, straw or sacking.

•

■ MAGNESIUM DEFICIENCY
Leaves yellowing between veins
The leaves later become brown
and dry and the plants are
stunted. Magnesium is likely to
be deficient only on light, acid,
sandy soils.
Control Water with a solution
of magnesium sulphate (Epsom
salts) or apply a foliar feed containing magnesium.
Prevention Prepare the soil
well with plenty of well-rotted
organic matter.

POTATOES: ROOTS AND TUBERS

▮ POTATO CYST EELWORM
Plants weak and stunted, lower leaves wither and die
The upper leaves appear pale and may wilt on warm days. Eventually the whole plant dies and tubers do not swell. If the roots are examined pinhead-sized golden or reddish-brown swellings will be present on the roots. These are eelworm cysts and usually develop in July and August. The cysts can remain in the soil for up to eight years even if potatoes are not grown. Tomato plants and 'volunteer' potatoes growing from tubers missed at harvest also harbour this pest.
Control None. Lift and destroy affected plants, with as many roots as possible and even the tiniest tubers. Do not grow potatoes or tomatoes on infested land for at least eight years.
Prevention Crop rotation is essential to prevent eelworm numbers building up in the soil. Early varieties often escape damage. Some resistant varieties are available (see page 112).

Potato cyst eelworm damage

▮ WIREWORMS
Small round holes on surface; interiors riddled with narrow tunnels

Wireworms are the larvae of click beetles, 25mm (1in) long and golden brown. They are most numerous in wet seasons and are a particular problem on gardens and vegetable patches newly reclaimed from grassland. Numbers will be reduced by three or four years of cultivation.
Control None.
Prevention Lift main crop potatoes as early as possible. Rake soil insecticide into the soil before planting.

▮ KEELED SLUGS
Large holes on surface, interiors riddled with large irregular cavities
Small, black keeled slugs are mainly responsible, especially during wet seasons and on heavy soil. Damage is not usually apparent until tubers are lifted. Holed tubers are edible, once affected parts are cut out, but do not attempt to store them.
Control None.
Prevention 'Pentland Dell' is less susceptible to slug attack. Scatter slug pellets when earthing up the rows or, if the weather is wet, water with a liquid slug killer based on aluminium sulphate. Lift main crops as soon as you can to minimise damage.

▮ OTHER SOIL PESTS
Millipedes, cutworms, leatherjackets and chafer grubs can occasionally be a serious problem, especially in wet seasons. They nibble potato tubers or enlarge holes made by slugs or wireworms. They are most likely to be a problem in new or weedy gardens.

▮ COMMON SCAB
Raised corky scabs

They may occur as single scabs or in severe cases may merge to cover the whole tuber. This disease is common on light, free-draining soils and in dry years. It is encouraged by alkaline conditions.

The tubers are edible after peeling. The disease does not spread in store, but severely affected tubers should be used first.
Control None.
Prevention Incorporate plenty of well-rotted organic matter into light or chalky soil and water well in dry spells. Use a less susceptible variety (see page 112). Do not lime soil before growing potatoes. Use acidic fertilisers like sulphate of ammonia on chalky soils.

· · ·

WART DISEASE
Rough warty growths on surface

Wart disease is very serious and is notifiable. You must inform the Ministry of Agriculture if it occurs. Certified seed potatoes are guaranteed free of this disease. Legislation prevents non-immune varieties being grown on infected land.
Control None.
Prevention Buy certified seed.

· · ·

SPLITTING
Tubers split or cracked
Large, deep cracks make peeling difficult and increase waste. The cause is heavy watering or prolonged rain following a long, hot, dry period. Use cracked tubers immediately as they may rot if stored.
Control None.
Prevention Keep plants well watered in very dry spells.

Powdery scab

POWDERY SCAB
Circular scabs with raised edges which release brown, powdery spores
In severe cases tubers may become deformed and cankerous. Small nodules may also occur on the roots.
This disease is not common but may occur in heavy soils, especially in cool, damp weather. Spores can remain in the soil for up to 10 years.
Control Destroy diseased tubers and haulms and do not grow potatoes on that part of the garden for at least three years.
Prevention Practise crop rotation and try to improve drainage.

· · ·

HOLLOW HEART
Brown cavities inside tubers

Tubers appear normal until cut open. Large tubers are most

likely to be affected. This condition is caused by heavy rain following a long drought.
Control None.
Prevention Keep plants well watered during very dry periods.

· · ·

SPRAING
Semi-circular reddish-brown marks in the flesh

The tubers appear normal until cut open. Spraing is caused by a virus spread by a soil-living nematode. It is most common in light, sandy soils.
Control None.
Prevention Practise crop rotation; control weeds; do not save tubers from affected plants.

· · ·

GANGRENE
Dark irregular depressions on the surface of tubers
This gradually spreads through the tubers causing them to shrink and decay. They may also be hollow and rotten inside. There is usually a clear demarcation between diseased and healthy tissue. The fungus is common in most soils and enters damaged tubers. The disease may not appear on stored tubers until December or January and is encouraged by cold.
Control None.
Prevention Try to avoid damaging tubers when lifting. Store only sound tubers.

POTATOES: ROOTS AND TUBERS

▓ DRY ROT
Tubers shrivel and white, pink or blue-green mould appears
Eventually the tubers collapse and become unusable. The disease is worst in warm, damp conditions and can affect seed potatoes. The fungi that cause dry rot are present in the soil and can enter the tubers before harvest, through eyes or wounds. Rotting may not become obvious for some months in store.
Control None.
Prevention When you buy seed potatoes, take them out of the bag and spread out on trays in a cool, dry, airy place to sprout.

•

▓ INTERNAL RUST SPOT
Brown flecks or spots in flesh

The exact cause is unknown, but it may be due to poor growing conditions.
Control None.
Prevention Incorporate plenty of organic matter and water regularly in dry summers.

•

▓ OTHER ROTS
Tubers soft and discoloured
Various fungi and bacteria can cause stored tubers to rot. Sometimes the flesh is discoloured and it may also smell.
Control None.
Prevention Store only sound tubers. Inspect stored tubers from time to time and destroy any that are rotting.

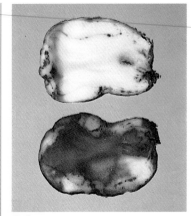

Soft rot

BUYING SEED POTATOES
All sorts of diseases can be introduced on potato tubers, so resist the temptation to save tubers from year to year or accept tubers from other gardeners. It is also risky to plant potatoes sold for eating. Seed potatoes may be a lot more expensive, but if they are 'classified' (certified) they will have been grown on land free of wart disease and in parts of the country where viruses are not present. Bags or tubers sold loose in garden centres must be labelled by law with the variety, the growers identification number and the class and the size range of the tubers. Class 'AA' or 'Basic seed' is the best quality, 'certified' or class 'CC' is perfectly acceptable. Although crops grown from classified seed may contract viruses the effects will not be as severe as when already infected tubers are planted.

RESISTANT VARIETIES
Varieties differ in their susceptibility to pests and disease.
The Table gives ratings for widely available varieties [1]

	blight (leaves)	blight (tubers)	blackleg	common scab	powdery scab	mosaic virus	spraing
First early							
'Arran Pilot'	●●	●	–	●●●	–	●●	●●●
'Dunluce'	●	●	–	●●	●●●	●●●	●●
'Foremost'	●●	●●	–	●●●	–	●●	–
'Home Guard'	●●	●	●●	●●●	●●●●	●●	●●●●
'Maris Bard'	●●	●●	●●	●●●	●	●●●●	●
'Pentland Javelin' [2]	●●	●●	●●●	●●●●	–	●●●●	●
'Sharpes Express'	●●	●	–	–	–	●●	–
'Ulster Chieftain'	●●	●●	–	●●●	–	●●●	●●●●
Second early							
'Estima'	●●●	●●●	●	●●●	●●	●	●●
'Maris Peer'	●●●	●●●	●●●	●●●	●●●	●●	●●
'Red Craigs Royal'	●●●	●●●	●●	●●	●●●●	●●	●●
'Wilja'	●●	●●●	●●●	●●●●	●●	●	●●●
Main crop							
'Cara' [2]	●●●	●●●●	●●●	●●●	●●	●●●●	●●●
'Desirée'	●●	●●●	●●	●●	●●●	●●●●	●●●
'King Edward'	●●	●	●●	●●●●	●●●	●	●●●
'Kerrs Pink'	●●●	●●	–	●●	–	●●	●●●
'Majestic'	●●	●●●	–	●●	●●	●●●	●●●
'Maris Piper' [2]	●●●	●●	●●●	●	●●	●●	●●●
'Pentland Crown'	●●	●●	●●●	●●●●	●	●●●●	●●
'Pentland Dell' [3]	●●●	●●●	●●	●●	●●	●●	●
'Pentland Squire'	●●●	●●●	●●●	●●●	●●	●●	●●
'Romano'	●●●	●●●	●●●	●●●	●●	●●●●	●●●●

Key:
●–●●●● very susceptible – very tolerant, – no information
[1] based on information from National Institute of Agricultural Botany
[2] resistant to cyst nematode   [3] less susceptible to slugs than most varieties

OUTDOOR TOMATOES

■ BLIGHT
Brown patches on leaves
These patches spread and eventually kill the leaves. Blackened patches may also occur on the stems. Green fruit may be spotted; ripe fruit rots and develops fluffy grey mould.

Blight is also a serious problem of potatoes (see page 108) and is worst in damp weather. It can survive from year to year on infected potato tubers.
Control Destroy affected plants.
Prevention Spray with pbi Dithane 945 or a copper-based fungicide every two weeks from early July.

■ WEEDKILLER DAMAGE
Leaves narrow and twisted
Leaves produced later in the season will be perfectly normal, but some fruit may be misshapen. The cause is a hormone-type weedkiller, to which tomatoes are particularly sensitive. This may be from traces of lawn weedkiller in a watering can, drifting from a lawn or residues in straw or strawy manure.
Control None.
Prevention Take great care when applying lawn weedkillers, rinse out sprayers or watering cans thoroughly and compost straw or manure before using it.

Weedkiller damage

■ LEAF ROLL
Young leaves roll up
This is caused by cold nights following hot days. It is nothing to worry about. Even though affected leaves will remain rolled, growth and the fruit will be unaffected.
Control and prevention Not necessary.

■ VIRUSES
Leaves mottled, distorted or stunted
Several viruses attack tomato plants. Some are spread by aphids. The symptoms can be confused with leaf roll or with hormone weedkiller damage.
Control Destroy affected plants.
Prevention Watch for aphids and spray with an aphid killer as often as necessary.

■ MAGNESIUM DEFICIENCY
Older leaves turn yellow between the veins
This occurs naturally on some acid or sandy soils, but can be aggravated by high-potash fertilisers.
Control Water with a solution of magnesium sulphate (Epsom salts), and repeat as necessary or switch to a liquid feed that contains magnesium.
Prevention Incorporate plenty of well-rotted organic matter into the soil before planting.

> **OTHER TOMATO PROBLEMS**
> Many other pests, diseases or physiological problems can occasionally affect outdoor tomatoes. These are covered in detail under 'Greenhouse tomatoes' on pages 124–128.

OUTDOOR CUCUMBERS

■ BITTER FRUITS
Fruits have a bitter taste
The usual cause is either a problem in the soil, such as too much nitrogen, waterlogging or drying out, or a check to growth.
Control None.
Prevention Grow cucumbers on well-prepared soil with good drainage and water regularly during dry spells.

■ MOSAIC VIRUS
Leaves are mottled and puckered
Fruits may also be discoloured or distorted. The virus is spread by aphids. See also page 103.
Control None.
Prevention Control aphids (see page 11).

> **OTHER CUCUMBER PROBLEMS**
> See 'Greenhouse cucumbers' on page 123.

OTHER VEGETABLES: ASPARAGUS

ASPARAGUS BEETLE
Foliage covered with small yellow and black insects
The adult beetles are quite striking and up to 6mm (¼in) long. They first appear on plants in May and successive generations develop until September. The buff-coloured larvae also eat leaves. If left uncontrolled, they can completely defoliate plants, weakening the crowns and reducing future crops. The beetles overwinter as pupae in the soil. The adults can fly.
Control Apply a contact insecticide and repeat if necessary.
Prevention Clear plant debris at the end of the season.

VIOLET ROOT ROT
Leaves turn yellow and wilt
The roots and crowns will be covered with purple fungal growths. This disease will spread rapidly through asparagus beds.
It can also attack carrots, parsnips and beetroots and will remain in the soil.
Control Dig out and destroy affected plants. In severe cases abandon the bed and start a new bed on a fresh piece of land with new crowns.
Prevention None.

FROST DAMAGE
Spears blackened and twisted
This is caused by sudden sharp frosts in late spring. Subsequent spears will be unaffected.
Control None.
Prevention If late frosts are predicted, cover asparagus beds with straw or sacking.

Asparagus beetle and larva (left)

POOR CROP
Spears spindly and sparse
The usual cause is cutting spears over too long a period or too soon after planting, so that insufficient foliage is produced to build up the crowns.
Control None.
Prevention Do not cut spears in the first two years after planting. In the third year cut until late May. Only in subsequent years continue cutting until late June. Keep asparagus beds well supplied with well-rotted manure and fertiliser. After 10 years or so start again on a new site with fresh plants.

ARTICHOKES

GLOBE ARTICHOKE

PETAL BLIGHT
Pale brown spots on petals
Eventually the whole head may turn brown and rot. This is not a common problem but is worse in wet seasons. It can also affect dahlias and chrysanthemums.
Control Remove and destroy affected heads. Spray remaining plants with pbi Dithane 945.
Prevention None.

ROOT APHID
Light coloured insects present on roots
Severely affected plants may wilt or growth may be checked.
Control No suitable chemicals are available.
Prevention None.

Root aphid

JERUSALEM ARTICHOKE

SLUGS
Tubers nibbled or tunnelled
Small, black keeled slugs are the usual cause.
Control and prevention See page 8.

SCLEROTINIA ROT
Stem bases covered in white, fluffy mould
Tubers may also rot. The fungus can remain for many years in the soil.
Control Dig up and destroy affected plants.
Prevention Replant sound tubers on a fresh site.

HONEY FUNGUS
Crowns rot and die
Look for white streaks in the tissue of dead plants and orange toadstools. This disease usually affects trees and shrubs, but can occasionally attack perennial vegetables if present in the garden.
Control and prevention The plant will have to be destroyed. See also page 39.

SWEET CORN

◼ FRIT FLY
Young plants twisted and ragged
Frit fly larvae burrow into young plants, occasionally killing them. Side shoots are produced but any cobs are late and undersized. Plants with more than five leaves are unlikely to be damaged. Adult flies appear in May and any damage occurs during June and July. A second generation attacks other cereals.
Control None.
Prevention Plants raised in pots or sown after late May are less vulnerable.

◼ SMUT
Large, green or white swellings
These can appear on cobs, male flowers or stems and the plants may be distorted. If left these swellings will eventually burst

Smut

revealing masses of black spores. This disease is usually a problem only in hot, dry years.
Control Remove and destroy affected parts, before spores are released.
Prevention Destroy the remainder of the crop at the end of the season. Grow sweet corn on a new site next year.

RHUBARB

◼ LEAF SPOT
Brown spots on leaves
The centres may fall out leaving holes. This disease is rarely serious, but may indicate that the plant is not growing well.
Control Remove badly affected leaves. Apply a liquid fertiliser.
Prevention Feed and mulch annually with well-rotted manure.

◼ CROWN ROT
Clumps deteriorate until only a few poor shoots remain
The crown is hollow and rotten; the main buds rot and fail to produce shoots. The disease is usually worse in poorly drained or waterlogged soils.
Control None. Replant using fresh material on a new site.
Prevention None.

HERBS

◼ MINT RUST
Small orange spots on leaves and stems

This is a serious problem that is difficult to control. It affects all types of mint and related plants like marjoram, and will rapidly infect the whole bed.
Control Remove and destroy affected roots. If it is well established, cut all top growth to the ground and burn it. Spray the soil with Murphy Tumblelite. A more drastic alternative is to cover the bed with dry straw at the end of the season and set light to it, or to use a flame gun.
Prevention Start a new bed, using fresh plants or a heat-treated piece of rhizome from the old bed. Immerse it in a pan of water (heated to 41–46°C; 105–115°F) for ten minutes, then cool in cold water and replant.

PARSLEY

◼ LEAF MINER
White blisters or wiggly lines in leaves
These are caused by grubs of the celery fly burrowing inside the leaves.
Control and prevention See page 100.

◼ LEAF SPOT
Small brown spots on leaves
Parsley leaf spot is very similar to celery leaf spot.
Control Destroy affected leaves.
Prevention Practise crop rotation.

◼ CARROT FLY
Leaves tinged red; young plants wilt and die
The grubs feed on parsley roots.
Control and prevention See page 100.

◼ MOTLEY DWARF VIRUS
Plants stunted; leaves tinged red
This virus disease is spread by aphids.
Control None.
Prevention Control aphids (see page 11).

CROP ROTATION

The main method of controlling soil pests and diseases in a vegetable garden is to rotate groups of vegetables on a three or four-year plan. A four-year rotation is worthwhile on large plots or where lots of potatoes are grown.

There are two major advantages.

■ Soil pests and particularly diseases are prevented from building up to damaging levels. If a disease does occur, moving the crop to a new site can usually prevent a recurrence.

■ Related crops often have similar soil requirements – for example brassicas all benefit from an alkaline soil.

THREE YEAR ROTATION			
	Year 1	Year 2	Year 3
Plot A	brassicas	potatoes/roots	peas/onions
Plot B	peas/onions	brassicas	potatoes/roots
Plot C	potatoes/roots	peas/onions	brassicas

FOUR YEAR ROTATION				
	Year 1	Year 2	Year 3	Year 4
Plot A	potatoes	peas	brassicas	onions/roots
Plot B	peas	brassicas	onions/roots	potatoes
Plot C	brassicas	onions/roots	potatoes	peas
Plot D	onions/roots	potatoes	peas	brassicas

■ THE BRASSICA FAMILY
Includes broccoli, Brussels sprouts, cabbage, calabrese, cauliflower, Chinese cabbage, kale, kohl rabi, swede, turnip, radish, mustard and rape (both used as green manure), and many leafy oriental vegetables.
Rotation will help to control ring spot, white blister, downy mildew (to some extent), soft rot and black rot of swedes and turnip and will prevent clubroot building up to damaging levels.
Soil requirements Brassicas benefit from a fertile soil, so they should follow legumes in a rotation. Mulch with organic matter, such as garden compost if any can be spared. They also need an alkaline soil, so check pH and apply lime if necessary in the autumn, or early spring on light soils. Brassicas also benefit from generous fertiliser applications.

■ THE PEA FAMILY
Includes peas, mange-tout, French beans, broad beans, runner beans and green manures such as agricultural lupins, field beans, tares and vetches.

Rotation can help to prevent diseases like anthracnose, fusarium wilt, pod rot, foot and root rot and to some extent downy mildew and pea thrips.
Soil requirements Plenty of organic matter, but little fertiliser (none in the case of peas). Roots of the pea family 'fix' nitrogen which will benefit next year's crops. Cut plants at soil level after harvest so the roots remain to rot down.

■ THE ONION FAMILY
Includes onions (also spring and Welsh onions), chives, garlic, leeks, shallots.
Rotation will help to control leaf blotch, smut, white rot, stem and bulb eelworm and downy mildew and leek rust to some extent.
Soil requirements Members of the onion family benefit from heavy applications of organic matter. Work fertiliser into the soil before planting or sowing.

■ THE POTATO FAMILY
Includes potatoes and tomatoes (sweet peppers, chillies and aubergines are also related but are not usually grown outside).
Rotation will help to control potato cyst eelworm, potato blight (which can be spread from tubers left in the ground to regrow) and powdery scab.
Soil requirements Members of the potato family need plenty of fertiliser, but no lime. They will benefit from organic matter. Earthing up potatoes ensures the soil is well cultivated for the crops that follow.

■ ROOT CROPS
Include carrot, parsley, parsnip, salsify, scorzonera (and can also include beetroot and spinach for convenience).
Rotation will help to prevent violet root rot, parsnip canker and black rot.
Soil requirements Do not apply fresh manure as this can cause forked roots. They need moderate amounts of fertiliser.

■ OTHER VEGETABLES
These are not related to any of the main families. In theory they can be put on any spare ground within any rotation group. But in practice they can suffer from soil pests and diseases and should be included in a rotation scheme, or at least grown on a different site each year.
Beetroots are often grouped with the other roots for convenience. They need plenty of fertiliser but not organic matter.
Celery, celeriac need a rich, water-retentive soil, so are best grown on a well-manured area. For convenience they may be grown with peas, beans or marrows.
Lettuces benefit from organic matter, and nitrogenous fertiliser. They're useful as a catch crop on any spare land, but can be grown with brassicas for convenience.
Marrows and courgettes can be grown on any spare well-manured land.
Spinach, leaf beet have similar requirements to beetroot.
Sweet corn is generally trouble-free and not fussy about organic matter.

CHAPTER SEVEN

THE GREENHOUSE

The enclosed environment of a greenhouse provides near ideal conditions for growing a wide range of plants. It also offers the perfect breeding ground for many pests and diseases, some of which would not survive outdoors. But you can turn this to your advantage, because the greenhouse environment also presents opportunities for control methods which cannot be applied outdoors.

BIOLOGICAL CONTROL

Biological control involves introducing beneficial insects, that may not survive outdoors, to eat or parasitise certain common pests. This can be an extremely effective alternative to using chemical sprays.

SMOKE CONES

If a pest or disease, such as grey mould, gets out of control, fumigation with a smoke cone is one way you can overcome the prob-lem. Follow the instructions carefully and ensure it is the right size for your greenhouse.

Pros:
- No special equipment is needed
- The whole greenhouse is treated effortlessly
- Doesn't increase humidity
- Penetrates every part of the greenhouse.

Cons:
- The greenhouse must be fairly airtight
- You cannot enter the green-house for several hours
- Pesticides are distributed in-discriminately

A WINTER CLEAN UP

The greenhouse should be thoroughly cleaned each winter to minimise the risk of pests and diseases gaining a foothold in the first place, and to make sure existing problems do not survive to cause trouble the following year.

Remove all plants. Wash the glass with a soft brush and household deter-gent. Remove algae, dirt and debris from between glass panes and from crevices in the frame. Use a stiff brush or wire wool if necessary. Scrub any brickwork or paving. Spray glass, frame and benches with a greenhouse disin-fectant, such as Armillatox, ICI Clean Up, Murphy Mortegg or Jeyes Fluid, and leave to dry. Check plants for signs of pests and diseases and deal with any problems before returning the plants to the greenhouse.

Put old compost from tomatoes, cucumbers, etc., to use elsewhere in the garden.

Clean and sterilise pots, trays and propagators before storing for the winter.

See Tables, pages 130–136 for guide to insecticides and fungicides

GENERAL GREENHOUSE PESTS

◼ APHIDS

Leaves and shoots covered in small insects

Aphids can survive all year on greenhouse plants, but are most likely to be a summer problem.
Control See page 11. Note that melons and cucumbers can be damaged by ICI Rapid. Biological control is worthwhile (see opposite).
Prevention None.

◼ SOOTY MOULD

Leaves covered with powdery black mould

This mould lives on the sugary secretions produced by aphids, whitefly and other sap-sucking insects rather than on the leaves themselves. Severe attacks can reduce the plant's ability to photosynthesise.
Control On large, tough leaves sooty mould can be wiped off. Spraying with soapy water may also help.
Prevention Control pests.

◼ SPIDER MITES

Leaves speckled yellow, later turning bronze

Examine growing tips and undersides of leaves frequently with a hand lens. Fine webbing and tiny, pale, greenish-brown slow-moving creatures may be visible. By the time the webbing becomes noticeable to the naked eye or the leaves begin to dry up and fall, it may be too late to control the pest.

Plants attacked by spider mites include aubergines, cucumbers, melons, begonias, impatiens, fuchsias, pelargoniums and primulas.

Spider mites live only a few weeks, but breed very fast under warm (over 25°C; 77°F) and dry conditions. They overwinter in cracks and crevices in the greenhouse.
Control Remove badly affected leaves. Spray with ICI Sybol (not melons or cucumbers) or a systemic insecticide.

Try biological control (see opposite).
Prevention Regular daily misting, or maintaining a moist atmosphere will slow the population growth, but will not control existing infestations. Disinfecting the greenhouse at the end of the season should reduce the number of overwintering mites.

◼ WHITEFLIES

Undersides of leaves covered in white insects

Whitefly scales (white) and scales parasitised by Encarsia *(black)*

The first signs of an infestation are often clouds of whiteflies in the brightest part of the greenhouse. They do little direct damage, but severe infestations can cover plants with sticky honeydew and attract sooty mould (see left).

There is also a 'crawler stage' that hatches from the egg and moves around before settling as a flattened transparent scale. These cause damage by sucking the plant's sap. Finally, the scale turns into a pupa, which is very difficult to kill and often accounts for infestations reappearing after control measures have been applied.
Control Try the following:
◼ Yellow sticky traps, positioned just above the tops of plants, will trap large numbers of flies.
◼ Use a small car vacuum cleaner to suck them off the leaves twice a week.
◼ Use biological control (see opposite).
◼ Spray every three days with a contact insecticide.
Prevention None.

See page 139 for suppliers of non-chemical pest controls

BIOLOGICAL CONTROL

This technique is widely used in commercial greenhouses. On a small scale it is fairly expensive, but worth considering as an alternative to insecticides. The control agents usually die off over winter or when they run out of prey, so you need to release them each year.

KEYS TO SUCCESS

■ Keep a look out for the first sign of the pest
■ Obtain biological control as soon as the pest appears
■ Release the control agent uniformly over the whole infested area
■ Accept some pest damage
■ Be patient
■ Do not spray with an insecticide other than those recommended (see right).

SPIDER MITE CONTROL
Phytoseiulus persimilis is a fast-moving, orange, pear-shaped mite, slightly larger than its prey. It eats about 30 spider mite eggs or five adults a day. *Phytoseiulus* is normally supplied on bean leaves with a few spider mites as food. Cut the leaves if necessary and place one piece on each infested plant. Distribute *Phytoseiulus* evenly as it spreads very slowly. Leave the pieces of leaf on the plants for at least a week to allow any eggs to hatch. Within a week you should see orange *Phytoseiulus* wherever spider mites are found. If not, move leaves with *Phytoseiulus* around the greenhouse. After two or three weeks new growth should be clean, and within two to six weeks of release the spider mites should have disappeared – depending on temperature (22°C; 71°F is ideal). *Phytoseiulus* should

survive for up to three weeks to deal with fresh outbreaks. A minimum temperature of 13°C (55°F) should ensure control all season.

•

WHITEFLY CONTROL
Encarsia formosa is a parasitic black and yellow wasp smaller than a whitefly. Females lay eggs inside up to 50 whitefly scales and the young parasite feeds on the larva within the scale. After about nine days the scale turns black, and after a further 11 days the adult parasite emerges through a hole in the upper surface and flies to find fresh scales. The parasite develops slowly: its life cycle takes about three weeks at 25°C (75°F) and up to ten weeks at 15°C (60°F). *Encarsia* may be supplied as black parasitised whitefly scales on leaves. Hang the leaf pieces half-way up the infested plants, out of direct sunlight and leave them for about three weeks. Black scales should start to appear on the undersides of leaves in two to five weeks, depending on the temperature. For best results, the greenhouse should be above 21°C (70°F) on most days.

•

MEALY BUG CONTROL
Cryptolaemus is a black and orange predatory ladybird. Its larva looks like its mealy bug prey but is twice as large. An adult consumes about three mealy bugs a day and a larva about nine. Release at least one on each plant as they search only a small area. Keep the doors and vents of your greenhouse closed until *Cryptolaemus* is established to prevent the adults flying off. If possible maintain a temperature of 20–26°C (68–80°F) and high humidity.

APHID CONTROL
Two controls are available. *Aphidoletes* is a tiny midge whose orange grubs are voracious aphid eaters. They are supplied as grubs on moist tissue paper. Shake them gently on to leaves near aphid colonies. Midges will start to appear within two weeks and more grubs will follow soon after.

Aphidius is a tiny parastic wasp that lays its eggs into aphids. Parasitised aphids have a bloated appearance and remain stationary.

Both these controls can live outside the greenhouse and will leave once the supply of aphids runs out. A minimum temperature of 18°C (65°F) should suit them. They may overwinter on pot plants and reappear the following year.

'Mummified' aphids parasitised by the wasp Aphidius

GENERAL GREENHOUSE PESTS

VINE WEEVIL
White grubs in compost, roots nibbled

Often these go unnoticed until plants are repotted. The grubs are up to 8mm (⅜in) long and feed on roots and tubers before emerging as adult weevils in the autumn. These feed on leaves.

This pest is unusual in that males are very rare. Female weevils reproduce parthenogenetically, so a single weevil crawling into the greenhouse (they cannot fly) can start an infestation. They are often introduced with new plants.
Control No suitable chemicals are available. Remove and destroy any grubs when repotting. Biological controls should become available.
Prevention Incorporating gamma-HCH dust into potting compost should prevent this pest. A band of non-drying glue around pots may deter egg-laying weevils (see page 139).

WOODLICE
Leaves nibbled
You may find large colonies of woodlice in damp corners or under pots or debris. They do not usually damage plants, but may occasionally nibble lower leaves or small seedlings.
Control Pbi Slug Gard pellets will also control woodlice. Dust large concentrations with gamma-HCH or derris.
Prevention None.

FUNGUS FLIES (SCIARIDS)
Small black flies in compost
These are a nuisance but do little real damage. They are attracted by organic matter, so they are most common in peat-based composts. The tiny larvae feed mainly on fungi, but may also attack fine root hairs.
Control Yellow sticky traps (see page 139) will dispose of some. Chemical control is not necessary.
Prevention None.

THRIPS
Leaves flecked or distorted
Flowers may also be affected. Long, thin yellow or brown 'thunder flies' up to 3mm (⅛in) long, are present and especially prevalent during warm spells.
Control Spray with a contact insecticide if necessary.
Prevention Regular watering and adequate shading will minimise the risk of attacks.

WESTERN FLOWER THRIPS
Chrysanthemum flowers stunted and papery

They can attack other greenhouse plants, and outdoor plants in warm summers. They also transmit a virus.
Control Spray with a contact insecticide, such as malathion.
Prevention None.

SPRINGTAILS
Tiny jumping insects in compost
These tiny (1–5mm; less than ⅛in) primitive insects do no harm to healthy plants, but feed on fungi or dead organic matter.
Control Not necessary, but if they are a nuisance spray the compost with malathion.
Prevention Repot plants regularly. Springtails are discouraged by dry conditions.

MEALY BUGS
White, fluffy patches on stems or leaves

Small hairy insects up to 7mm (¼in) long can be seen inside this covering of waxy fibres. Cacti and succulents are most vulnerable. They can weaken plants if large numbers are present and spoil the appearance by secreting honeydew and wax.
Control Remove badly affected parts. Spray with a systemic insecticide. If several plants are affected consider biological control (see page 119).
Prevention None.

SCALE INSECTS
Leaves or stems covered in round, brown, raised spots
These are immobile sap-feeding insects which can weaken plants. They can be prised off like limpets.
Control Wipe off with a cloth moistened with soft soap.
Prevention None.

LEAF PESTS

Leaf miner damage on chrysanthemum leaf

◼ CATERPILLARS

Leaves tattered or holed
If the slime trails of slugs are absent, suspect caterpillars. The commonest on greenhouse plants is the caterpillar of the carnation tortrix moth.

Yellow or green caterpillars up to 20mm (¾in) long feed on leaves, buds and shoot tips of carnations and other ornamentals. They spin leaves together with silk and feed inside, which makes them difficult to spot in the early stages.
Control Pick off individual caterpillars or webbed leaves and destroy them or place them outside where they will do less harm. Control severe infestations with a contact insecticide.
Prevention None.

◼ EARWIGS

Puncture marks in leaves and flowers
Earwigs can be a nuisance in hot, dry summers. They feed at night.
Control Dust hiding places with a contact insecticide. Trap them under sacking or in flower pots stuffed with straw and then destroy them.
Prevention None.

◼ CHRYSANTHEMUM EELWORM

Brown patches on leaves
As these patches grow and join the whole leaf withers and dies. Eelworms are microscopic worms that feed and multiply inside the leaves. Many different plants can be infested.
Control No suitable chemicals are available. Dormant shoots can be heat treated to kill any eelworms present. After washing plunge them into water at 46°C (115°F) for 5 minutes then into cool water.
Prevention None.

◼ LEAF HOPPERS

Leaves mottled or spotted white
In severe attacks leaves may appear almost white. Look for pale yellow adults, 7mm (¼in) long, and their cast skins on the undersides of leaves.
Control Remove badly affected leaves. Spray with a contact insecticide. In severe cases fumigate the greenhouse with a smoke cone (see page 117).
Prevention None.

◼ SLUGS AND SNAILS

Ragged holes in leaves; slime trails present
Because slugs and snails feed at night, search for them in a damp corner or under a pot.
Control If you cannot locate the individuals responsible or if damage is severe, scatter slug pellets thinly around vulnerable plants.
Prevention Keep the greenhouse tidy to eliminate hiding places.

◼ LEAF MINERS

White wiggly lines on leaves
The chrysanthemum leaf miner attacks chrysanthemums and related plants. The tiny grubs live inside the leaves eating the green tissue and leaving only the upper and lower skins. In severe cases the leaf may lose most of its colour. The adults are small, black flies.

Two American leaf miners are pests in mainland Europe, and are currently notifiable in the UK. This means you must inform your local Ministry of Agriculture office immediately if you spot them. The symptoms are very similar to chrysanthemum leaf miner and they are most likely to be found on imported greenhouse plants.
Control Remove badly affected leaves, or locate the grub and squash it in the leaf. Alternatively, spray with ICI Sybol as soon as symptoms are seen and repeat if necessary.
Prevention None.

◼ FROG HOPPERS ('CUCKOO SPIT')

Frothy patches on stems
Each patch is occupied by a small, pale hopping insect. They do no real harm.
Control and prevention Not necessary.

See Tables, pages 130–136 for guide to insecticides and fungicides

GREENHOUSE DISEASES

White rust

GENERAL DISEASES

■ DAMPING OFF
Seedlings or young plants collapse at soil level, often in distinct patches

This is a common and serious problem with seed-raised plants. Whole seed trays can be devastated rapidly. A white mould may appear on the compost surface. Affected seedlings are thin at the base and the roots may have rotted away. It is difficult to control once established.
Control Water affected seedlings with Murphy Traditional Copper Fungicide or pbi Cheshunt Compound as soon as symptoms are seen.
Prevention Try the following:
■ Keep the greenhouse, trays, pots, etc., clean
■ Use fresh compost
■ Use tap water, not rain water, and avoid overwatering
■ Water from below
■ Sow thinly
■ Water with one of the copper fungicides mentioned above when you prick out seedlings.

■ POWDERY MILDEW
Leaves covered in dusty white mould
Powdery mildew can attack many greenhouse plants, but begonias, chrysanthemums, cinerarias, cucumbers, melons and vines are particularly susceptible. The disease is worst in hot, dry conditions or when plants are crowded or suffering from drought.
Control Remove badly affected leaves. Spray with a systemic fungicide and repeat at 10–14 day intervals.
Prevention Ventilate the greenhouse well in hot weather. Keep plants well watered but avoid wetting the leaves. Give plants plenty of space to maintain good air circulation.

■ DOWNY MILDEW
Leaves with yellow-brown blotches and downy tufts below
It also causes angular yellow patches that turn dry and brown, with greyish down on the undersides of leaves. This disease thrives in warm, damp conditions. Lettuces, cinerarias and seedlings of brassicas, wallflowers and stocks are most likely to be attacked. Downy mildew can also occur on cucumber leaves, which show the characteristic angular yellow patches.
Control Remove badly affected leaves. Spray with pbi Dithane 945. No chemical controls are available for cucumber downy mildew, although it is no longer a notifiable disease.
Prevention Ventilate the greenhouse to prevent it becoming too humid.

GREENHOUSE ORNAMENTALS

■ RUST
Dark brown or orange spots on leaves and stems
Rust diseases can attack many different greenhouse plants including carnations, chrysanthemums, fuchsias and pelargoniums.
Control and prevention See page 23.

■ WHITE RUST
Yellow spots on undersides of leaves
This is a rare but serious disease of chrysanthemums, usually introduced with bought plants raised from cuttings.
Control It is no longer a notifiable disease. Try a fungicide recommended for rust.
Prevention None.

■ BLACKLEG
Base of stems become soft, black and rotten; plants die
This is a common problem on pelargoniums raised from cuttings and occasionally affects plants raised from seed.
Control None.
Prevention Destroy affected plants. Keep greenhouse clean and use sterile potting compost. Ventilate the greenhouse well.

OTHER PROBLEMS

OEDEMA
Pale pimples on undersides of leaves
These pimples may eventually burst, becoming brown and warty. Stems are also affected. Ivy-leaved pelargoniums, camellias, begonias, and tomatoes are all susceptible. The cause is overwatering or excessive humidity.
Control None.
Prevention Water sparingly and ventilate the greenhouse.

SUN SCALD
Brown or scorched areas on leaves
Strong sunlight can scorch sensitive plants.
Control and prevention Ventilate or shade the greenhouse in hot spells. Do not wet the leaves when watering around midday.

CUCUMBERS AND MELONS

LEAVES

ANTHRACNOSE
Pale green sunken spots
The spots grow and turn brown and in severe attacks the whole leaf may wither. This disease is worst in humid conditions.
Control Spray weekly with a sulphur-based fungicide as soon as symptoms are seen.
Prevention Ventilate the greenhouse well. Clean and sterilise the greenhouse thoroughly at the end of the season (see page 117).

•

CUCUMBER MOSAIC VIRUS
Leaves puckered and mottled

This disease also frequently affects courgettes and marrows outdoors (see page 108).
Control Destroy affected plants.
Prevention Spray to control aphids (see page 11).

•

WILT
Lower leaves turn yellow, later turning brown and wilting
This gradually spreads to higher leaves. If the stems are cut, brown streaks can be seen inside them. This soil-borne disease is most likely to occur in cold, damp weather.
Control Keep the greenhouse warm and do not overwater the plants.
Prevention Do not grow cucumbers in the same border year after year. If there is no alternative, grow them in pots of fresh garden soil or compost, or in growing bags.

FRUIT

GUMMOSIS
Fruits covered in small grey oozing spots

This fungal disease is most likely to occur in cool, wet conditions.
Control Destroy affected fruits.
Prevention Raise the greenhouse temperature and improve ventilation.

•

WITHERING
Young fruits wither and die
There are several possible causes including low temperatures, overwatering, poor growth or general lack of vigour. Plants should recover to produce sound fruits later in the season.
Control Remove all fruits and spray with a foliar feed to increase vigour.
Prevention Water plants regularly but do not overwater early in the season.

ANTHRACNOSE
Pale sunken green spots near flower end of fruit
These areas later turn yellow and the fruit dies.
Control and prevention See 'Leaves' left.

•

BITTER FRUITS
Cucumber fruits taste bitter
Pollination by insects of older varieties, like 'Telegraph', can result in bitter and misshapen fruits. Irregular watering or excessive use of nitrogen fertiliser can also cause this.
Control None.
Prevention Remove male flowers or grow a modern all-female F1 hybrid. Promote even growth by watering and feeding regularly.

STEMS AND ROOTS

FOOT AND ROOT ROT
Stems rot at soil level and the whole plant collapses
Several common soil-borne fungal diseases can destroy the root system causing the plant to wilt. This is mainly a problem if cucumbers are grown repeatedly in the same greenhouse border.
Control None.
Prevention See 'Wilt'.

•

STEM ROT
Stems covered in white fluffy growth near soil level
Eventually black spots will appear amongst the fungus and these 'resting spores' can remain in the soil to reinfect future cucumber plants.
Control Remove and destroy plants before the spores are released.
Prevention See 'Wilt'.

TOMATOES, PEPPERS, AUBERGINES: LEAVES

◼ POTATO BLIGHT
Brown areas on the edges of leaves
These patches spread and the affected leaves die. Stems may also have blackened areas. Potato blight is caused by a fungus which thrives in warm, wet conditions.
Control If the disease takes hold there is no treatment.
Prevention Spray with Dithane 945 or a copper-based fungicide when the plants have been stopped. Repeat every two weeks. Spray any potatoes growing nearby (see page 108).

◼ LEAF ROLL
Leaves roll up and remain rolled for the whole season
Leaf roll is caused by large fluctuations between day and night temperatures. It is not a disease; it is an indication that the plant is growing well, and is no cause for concern.
Control and prevention Not necessary.

◼ LEAF MOULD
Lower leaves have purplish-brown mould patches on undersides and yellow patches on upper surfaces

The fungus is encouraged by humid, warm conditions.
Control Spray with a systemic fungicide when the problem appears and repeat at 10–14-day intervals.
Prevention Keep the greenhouse well ventilated and water plants early in the day. If leaf mould is a persistent problem, grow a resistant variety (see page 128).

◼ VIRUSES
Leaves mottled or curled, foliage thick and distorted or stems have dark vertical streaks
These are all symptoms of viral infection. The growth of the plant may be stunted and the fruit mottled.
Control None. Remove and destroy affected plants. Feed any remaining healthy ones with a tomato fertiliser.
Prevention Some viruses are spread by aphids, so spray regularly to control them (see page 11). Always wash your hands after handling infected plants as viruses can easily be spread to healthy plants. Grow resistant varieties if the problem is persistent (see page 128).

◼ MAGNESIUM DEFICIENCY
Leaves develop irregular yellow or brown patches between the veins
Growth is also poor. Magnesium deficiency is serious and quite common; it is made worse by normal feeding – especially with high-potash tomato fertiliser.
Control As soon as a yellowing appears, spray the leaves with magnesium sulphate (Epsom salts). Use 230g (8oz) dissolved in 11 litres (2½ gall) of water, add a wetting agent such as soft soap.
Prevention Use a tomato feed containing magnesium.

Tomato mosaic virus

Magnesium deficiency

◼ WEEDKILLER DAMAGE
Stems and leaf stalks are twisted and leaves are fern-like
Weedkiller drift is the most likely cause. It will also cause hollow, seedless fruit.
Control None.
Prevention Use weedkillers on still days and close the greenhouse while you are using them.

ROOTS AND STEMS

FOOT AND ROOT ROT
Plants wilt but do not recover

The stem may appear brown at soil level and the roots rot. This is a common problem of seedlings or young plants but may also affect older plants. Several common soil-borne fungi are responsible, but the disease occurs only when plants are damaged while being transplanted, or when the roots are weakened by waterlogged or cold soil.

Control Slightly affected plants can sometimes be saved by watering with pbi Cheshunt Compound. Mulch around the stem to encourage new root growth and spray with a foliar feed.

Prevention See 'Avoiding soil problems' Box.

VERTICILLIUM WILT
Plants wilt but may recover overnight, lower leaves turn yellow
If the stem is cut, brown streaks will be seen inside. A soil-borne fungal disease is responsible.

Control No effective treatment. Sometimes new root growth can be encouraged by mulching around the stem with fresh compost. Drench the soil with a spray-strength solution of a systemic fungicide. Keep the greenhouse temperature at 25°C (75°F) for two weeks.

Prevention See 'Avoiding soil problems' Box.

STEM ROT
Plants wilt; brown sunken cankers on stem at soil level
The roots are not rotten, but this disease is caused by a soil-borne fungus.

Control destroy badly affected plants and spray others with a systemic fungicide.

Prevention See 'Avoiding soil problems' Box.

EELWORMS
Plants wilt; minute growths on roots
Tiny, round yellow, white or brown cysts of the cyst eelworm or large brown swellings caused by root knot eelworms will be present on the roots.

Control No suitable chemicals are available to gardeners. Destroy affected plants.

Prevention Do not grow tomatoes in the same greenhouse border for more than two consecutive years.

You can buy seed of root knot-resistant strains. The young plants are grafted to the variety you want to grow, so it can grow in infested soil.

GREY MOULD
Grey-brown mould on stems above soil level
Grey mould can affect all parts of the plant.

Control and prevention See page 12.

CROWN GALL
Large irregular swellings on stems
These galls are caused by a bacterium. Although they look unsightly they do little harm to the plant.

Control None and rarely necessary.

Prevention None.

Verticillium wilt

ROOTS ON STEMS
Growths appear on the stems
This is nothing to worry about. Tomatoes root very readily all along their stems.

Control and prevention Not necessary.

AVOIDING SOIL PROBLEMS
If tomatoes or related plants are grown repeatedly in the same greenhouse border soil, pests and diseases can build up and are then difficult to eradicate, except by replacing the border soil.

Even if you cannot rotate these crops around different parts of the greenhouse, you may have no problems for years.

Where problems do arise or you want to avoid them:
- Use growing bags, which should be free of disease
- Grow in large pots containing fresh garden soil or multipurpose compost, or a mixture of the two
- Use ring culture – plants are grown in bottomless pots sitting on a bed of gravel, which is kept moist.

The first two methods will require more frequent feeding and watering than when plants are grown in the border soil.

Always clear away all plant debris at the end of the season and sterilise the greenhouse structure, staging and equipment (see page 117).

TOMATOES, PEPPERS, AUBERGINES: FRUIT

■ TOMATO MOTH
Fruits eaten

Large green or brown tomato moth caterpillars up to 4cm (1½in) long may be responsible, but they are not common. They also eat leaves.

Other pests may be the cause, notably slugs and snails – look for the characteristic slime trails. Woodlice may be found on fruits that have split or been damaged but do not usually damage sound fruit.
Control Remove caterpillars and eggs. Chemical control is unnecessary.
Prevention None.

•

■ POTATO BLIGHT
Tough, dry rot on surface

Sometimes fruits may appear healthy but rot within a couple of days of picking.

Dark spots can occur on green fruit and the leaves are also affected (see page 124).
Control None. Remove and destroy affected fruits.
Prevention See page 108.

•

■ BRONZING
Bronze patches on green fruits

The bronzing may be masked when the fruit ripens but brown corky patches will be present in the flesh. These symptoms are caused by tobacco mosaic virus which also affects potatoes and some bedding plants like petunias. It is spread by infected seed or by physical contact, not by aphids. Leaves will also be affected, and may be mottled, undersized or distorted.
Control None. Destroy badly affected plants.
Prevention Clean and sterilise the greenhouse thoroughly. Some resistant varieties are available. Wash your hands after handling affected plants.

•

■ GHOST SPOTTING
Light coloured rings on surface
These symptoms occur where the grey mould fungus has landed,

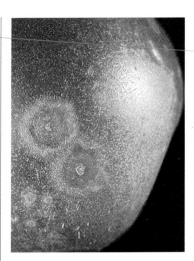

but has failed to cause any significant rotting. The marks remain as the fruit matures, but it is perfectly edible.
Control None necessary.
Prevention Try to prevent grey mould (see page 12).

•

■ BUCKEYE ROT
Brown concentric rings on the skin

Sun scald

This is caused by a soil-borne disease and usually affects the lower trusses, splashed with soil by careless watering. It also occurs on outdoor tomatoes, where heavy rain is responsible for spreading the fungus spores.
Control Remove and destroy affected fruits.
Prevention Try not to splash soil on to fruits when watering.

UNEVEN RIPENING
Ripening fruits blotchy, with hard yellow unripe patches

The most likely cause is lack of potash and the problem is frequently associated with dry soil or compost or a diseased root system. Excessive heat may also be responsible.
Control None.
Prevention Feed regularly with a high-potash tomato feed. Water regularly and frequently in hot weather.

SUN SCALD
Pale brown circular patches
These patches occur on the side facing the glass and result from exposure to very strong sunlight.
Control None.
Prevention Ventilate the greenhouse well in hot weather. Apply a greenhouse shading material to the glass.

FLOWER DROP
Flowers drop without producing fruits
Often the flowers start to open, but are not pollinated. The cause is dry air and lack of moisture at the roots. The flower usually breaks off at the 'knuckle'.
Control None.
Prevention Water regularly and frequently during hot periods, especially if plants are in pots or growing bags. Keep the humidity high by damping down the paths or mist the plants in early morning, but avoid wetting the flowers.
    Tapping the plants daily may aid pollination.

SMALL FRUITS
Flowers do not fall but fruits fail to develop
Often the fruitlets grow no bigger than a match head. The causes are poor pollination and dry air.
Control None.
Prevention See 'Flower drop' above.

SPLITTING
Ripe or nearly ripe fruit splits

PREVENTING FRUIT PROBLEMS
Many common fruit problems can be prevented easily. Plants in growing bags or pots have a limited reservoir of water. They need watering every day early in the season, but two or three times a day during late summer. As a rough guide reckon on 1.1 litres (2 pints) per plant per day from June to August.
    Prevent wide temperature fluctuations by ensuring there is adequate ventilation. Ideally the area of the roof vents should be about a sixth of the floor area. Fit automatic vent openers.
    Maintain a reasonable humidity in the greenhouse by damping down the path or misting plants lightly each morning.
    Shade the south-facing side of the greenhouse with a shading material to prevent excessive sunlight.
    Feed regularly with a high-potash tomato feed; use according to the instructions.

Dryness at the roots causes the skin to harden. The skin is then unable to swell when the rest of the fruit swells after heavy watering and so splitting occurs. Wide fluctuations in temperature and overfeeding following a dry spell can also cause it.
    Split fruits are often affected by grey mould or other rots.
Control Remove affected fruit.
Prevention Apply a mulch to borders to preserve moisture. Water frequently during hot spells, especially if plants are in pots or growing bags.

HOLLOW FRUITS
Inside of fruit hollow when ripe
There are several possible causes:
■ Hormone weedkiller damage (see page 124)
■ Lack of potash
■ Wide fluctuations in temperature and humidity when the fruit was pollinated.
Control None.
Prevention Feed regularly with a high-potash tomato feed. See also 'Preventing fruit problems' Box.

See Tables, pages 130–136 for guide to insecticides and fungicides

TOMATOES, PEPPERS, AUBERGINES: FRUIT

▨ BLOSSOM END ROT

Blackened patch at the flower end of the fruit

Very common on tomatoes and frequently peppers, too. It is caused by a deficiency of calcium in the fruit.

This in turn is caused by a shortage of water at a critical stage in the plant's development. Plants in growing bags seem particularly susceptible. Sturdy plants with healthy roots are less likely to suffer. Do not worry if the first fruits are affected, because it will not necessarily occur on later trusses provided the plants are fed and watered adequately.

Control When symptoms are seen it is too late to save affected fruits, though they can be eaten if the blackened area is cut out.

Prevention See 'Preventing fruit problems' (see page 127).

▨ GREENBACK

Yellow patches on the shoulders of the fruit

Greenback is generally thought to be a result of heat injury caused by direct sunlight, although high temperatures can sometimes affect shaded fruit, too. It is also likely to be a problem if plants have an insufficient supply of potash.

Control None, but greenback can be prevented on later ripening fruit.

Prevention Many modern tomato varieties are resistant to greenback (see right) but even these may suffer in very hot weather. See 'Preventing fruit problems' (page 127).

RESISTANT VARIETIES

The following varieties show some resistance to Tomato mosaic virus (T); Leaf mould (L); fusarium wilt (F) or verticillium wilt (V) (which both cause foot rot or wilt).

Aubergines
'Bonica' T

Peppers
'Bell Boy' T

Tomatoes
'Abunda' F,L,T,V
'Blizzard' F,L,T,V
'Counter' L,T
'Cumulus' F,L,T,V
'Danny' F,L,T
'Dumbito' F,T
'Estella' F,L,T,V
'Grenadier' F
'Piranto' F,L,T
'Roma VF' F,V
'Seville Cross' F,L,T
'Shirley' F,L,T

Greenback

GARDEN CHEMICALS GUIDE

It is illegal to use a pesticide against pests or diseases or on plants not listed on the label. The information in the Tables on the next five pages has been provided by the manufacturers and taken from the label instructions.

To help you to narrow down the choice we have picked out the garden chemicals that have done well in *Gardening from Which?* trials (on page 137).

USING THE GUIDE

The Tables tell you at a glance which of the garden fungicides and insecticides are recommended for each of the major pests and diseases, and which can be used on edible plants. All the products listed in the Guide should be widely available in DIY stores, shops and garden centres.

PESTICIDE TERMS

Systemic insecticides and fungicides are absorbed into the plant's sap. They kill fungi inside the plant and insects, such as aphids, that feed on the sap. Because they are transported around inside the plant, you do

not need to cover it completely. Some chemicals like pirimicarb are not truly systemic, but will permeate short distances – across leaves, for example.

Contact insecticides only kill insects that are actually hit by the spray or that eat sprayed leaves. It is important to spray or dust plants thoroughly when using contact insecticides, paying special attention to the undersides of leaves where pests congregate. Some chemicals are more persistent than others and will continue to kill pests that crawl across the leaves for a week or two.

Preventive fungicides form a protective layer on the surface of leaves, preventing fungal spores from penetrating. It is important to apply preventive

fungicides thoroughly, including the undersides of leaves, before a disease appears and to repeat the treatment according to the label instructions to keep diseases at bay. Systemic fungicides will also have some protective action.

Organic pesticides are derived from plants (such as pyrethrum or derris) or from naturally occurring chemicals like sulphur. They are quickly broken down into harmless substances and are acceptable to some organic gardeners, who will not use 'man-made' chemicals.

HARVEST INTERVAL

As a precaution you should leave the stated period of time between spraying fruit and vegetables and harvesting the edible parts.

USING GARDEN CHEMICALS
Always treat garden chemicals with respect. Read the instructions on the label and follow all the advice given. See also page 135 for general advice on using garden chemicals safely and page 137 for advice on application equipment.

NON-CHEMICAL ALTERNATIVES
Some gardeners prefer not to use pesticides at all. On page 139 we review briefly all the alternative methods available. Even if you are prepared to use pesticides to deal with any pests or diseases that occur, it is still worth using non-chemical preventive methods for the most troublesome pests. For more information see *The Gardening from Which? Guide to Gardening Without Chemicals* (£12.95, available from Consumers' Association, Gascoyne Way, Hertford X, SG14 1LH).

GARDEN INSECTICIDES

BRAND NAME	ACTIVE INGREDIENTS	TYPE [1]	FORM	KILLS [2] aphids	capsids	caterpillars	earwigs	flea beetles
Bio Crop Saver	permethrin, malathion	C	spray	O	O	O	O	O
Bio Friendly Insect Spray	derris, quassia	O	spray	O		O		
Bio Friendly Pest Pistol	fatty acids	O	ready to use	O				
Bio Friendly Pest & Disease Duster	derris, (sulphur)	O	dust	O		O		O
Bio Long-Last	dimethoate, permethrin	CS	spray	O	O	O	O	
Bio Multirose	permethrin, (sulphur, triforine)	C	spray	O		O		
Bio Sprayday	permethrin	C	spray	O				
Boots Caterpillar & Whitefly Killer	permethrin	C	spray			O	O	
Boots Garden Insect Powder	carbaryl, derris	C	dust	O		O	O	O
Boots Greenfly & Blackfly Killer	dimethoate	S	spray	O	O			
Boots Kill-a-Bug Spray Gun	permethrin, bioallethrin	C	ready to use	O		O		
Dipel	Bacillus thuringiensis	O	spray			O		
Doff Derris Dust	derris	O	dust	O		O		
Doff Fruit & Vegetable Insecticide Spray	pyrethrum	O	spray	O	O	O		
Doff Garden Insect Powder	fenitrothion	C	dust	O	O	O		
Doff Rose & Flower Insecticide Spray	pyrethrum	O	spray	O	O			
Doff Systemic Insecticide	dimethoate	S	spray	O	O			
Fellside Green Fruit & Vegetable Insect Spray	pyrethrum	O	spray	O	O	O		
Fellside Green Rose & Flower Insect Spray	pyrethrum	O	spray	O	O	O		
Fellside Green Vegetable Insecticide	derris	O	dust	O		O		
Fisons Nature's Answer to Insect Pests	pyrethrum	O	ready to use	O	O	O		
ICI Bug Gun for Fruit and Vegetables	pyrethrum	O	ready to use	O	O	O		
ICI Bug Gun for Roses and Flowers	pyrethrum	O	ready to use	O		O		
ICI Derris Dust	derris	O	dust			O		O
ICI Fumite General Purpose Greenhouse Insecticide	pirimiphos-methyl	S*	smoke	O				
ICI Fumite Whitefly Greenhouse Insecticide	permethrin	C	smoke					
ICI Picket	permethrin	C	spray	O	O	O	O	O
ICI Rapid Aerosol	pirimicarb	S*	aerosol	O				
ICI Rapid	pirimicarb	S*	spray	O				
ICI Roseclear	pirimicarb, (bupirimate, triforine)	S*	spray	O				
ICI Sybol Aerosol	pirimiphos-methyl	S*	aerosol	O	O	O	O	O
ICI Sybol	pirimiphos-methyl	S*	spray	O	O	O	O	O
Murphy Derris Dust	derris	O	dust			O		O
Murphy Liquid Malathion	malathion	C	spray	O	O			
Murphy Malathion Dust	malathion	C	dust	O	O			
Murphy Permethrin Whitefly Smokes	permethrin	C	smoke			O		
Murphy Pest & Disease Smokes	gamma-HCH, (tecnazene)	C	smoke	O	O			
Murphy Systemic Action Insecticide	heptenophos, permethrin	CS	spray	O	O			

[1] C=contact; O=organic; S=systemic; *=partially systemic
[2] Information based on manufacturers' instructions
[3] Also contains fungicide(s) (in brackets under 'Active ingredients'). See also Garden Fungicides Table
[4] See also Soil Insecticides Table
[5] 4 weeks for lettuce under glass

leaf hoppers	leaf miners	mealy bugs	raspberry beetle	sawfly	scale insects	spider mites	thrips	weevils	whitefly	other pests	EDIBLE PLANTS?	HARVEST INTERVAL
○	○						○		○		veg only	1 day
							○				yes	1 day
					○	○			○		yes	same day
					○	○				[3]	yes	1 day
○		○	○		○	○		○	○	beetles, maggots	yes	7 days
										[3]	no	n/a
○							○		○	ants	yes	1 day
		○							○	leatherjackets, pea maggot, cutworm	yes	1 day
○			○				○	○	○	[4]	yes	7 days
○		○				○				maggots	yes	7 days
									○		yes	1 day
											yes	same day
			○	○		○					yes	1 day
				○	○	○			○		yes	1 day
								○	○	codling moth	yes	14 days
				○	○	○			○		no	n/a
○		○			○	○	○		○	pear sucker	yes	7 days [5]
				○	○	○			○		yes	1 day
				○	○	○			○		no	n/a
			○	○		○					yes	1 day
				○	○	○			○		yes	1 day
									○	beetles, froghoppers	yes	1 day
○							○		○	froghoppers	no	n/a
				○							yes	1 day
○	○	○					○		○	sciarids	yes	same day
									○		yes	same day
○			○	○			○	○	○	codling, pea and tortrix moths	yes	same day
											yes	3 days
											yes	3 days
										[3]	no	n/a
○	○			○	○	○	○	○	○	sciarids	yes	7 days
○	○			○	○	○	○	○	○	codling, pea and tortrix moths, sciarids [4]	yes	7 days
				○							yes	1 day
○	○	○			○	○	○		○	pear sucker	yes	4 days
○						○	○		○	pear sucker, sciarids	yes	4 days
							○		○		yes	same day
○	○						○		○	woodlice, springtails, sciarids [3]	yes	2 days
		○		○			○		○	pear sucker	yes	1 day

GARDEN INSECTICIDES

BRAND NAME	ACTIVE INGREDIENTS	TYPE [1]	FORM	aphids	capsids	caterpillars	earwigs	flea beetles
Murphy Tumblebug	heptenophos, permethrin	CS	spray	O	O	O	O	
Murphy Zap Cap Combined Insecticide & Fungicide	permethrin, (fenarimol)	C	ready to use	O		O		
Murphy Zap Cap General Insecticide	permethrin	C	ready to use	O		O		
pbi Fenitrothion	fenitrothion	C	spray	O	O	O		
pbi Hexyl	gamma-HCH, derris, (thiram)	C	spray	O	O	O	O	
pbi Liquid Derris	derris	O	spray	O		O	O	
pbi Malathion Greenfly Killer	malathion	C	spray	O				
Phostrogen Safer's Fruit & Vegetable Insecticide	fatty acids	O	ready to use	O				
Phostrogen Safer's Rose & Flower Insecticide	fatty acids	O	ready to use	O				
Rentokil Blackfly & Greenfly Killer	pyrethroid, pyrethrins	C	aerosol	O				
Rentokil Greenhouse & Garden Insect Killer	pyrethrum, resmethrin	C	aerosol	O		O		
Secto Garden Powder	dimethoate, gamma-HCH, (thiram)	CS	dust	O		O		
Secto Greenfly and Garden Insect Spray	pyrethrins, gamma-HCH	C	ready to use	O		O		
Secto Rose and Flower Spray	dimethoate, gamma-HCH, (thiram)	CS	ready to use	O		O		
Spraydex Greenfly Killer	permethrin, bioallethrin	C	ready to use	O		O	O	
Vitax Derris Dust [7]	derris	O	dust			O		O
Vitax Py Garden and Household Insect Killer [7]	pyrethrum, piperonyl butoxide	O	dust	O	O	O		O
Vitax Py Garden Insecticide [7]	pyrethrins, piperonyl butoxide	O	aerosol	O	O	O		
Vitax Py Spray Insect Killer [7]	pyrethrum	O	ready to use	O	O	O		
Vitax Py Spray Garden Insect Killer [7]	pyrethrum, piperonyl butoxide	O	spray	O	O	O		O

[1] C=contact; O=organic; S=systemic; *=partially systemic
[2] Information based on manufacturers' instructions
[3] Also contains fungicide(s) (in brackets under 'Active ingredients'). See also Garden Fungicides Table
[4] See also Soil Insecticides Table
[5] 4 weeks for lettuce under glass
[6] Chemicals are in separate 'caps': 1 day for insecticide only; 14 days for combined insecticide and fungicide
[7] May also be available under 'Synchemicals' brand name

SOIL INSECTICIDES

BRAND NAME	ACTIVE INGREDIENTS	FORM	cabbage root fly	carrot fly	chafer grubs	cutworms	leatherjackets	millipedes	wireworms
Boots Garden Insect Powder	carbaryl, derris	dust	O		O	O			
Fisons Soil Pests Killer	phoxim	granules	O	O	O	O		O	O
ICI Sybol Dust	pirimiphos-methyl	dust	O	O					O
ICI Sybol	pirimiphos-methyl	spray	O	O		O	O		O
Murphy Gamma-BHC Dust	gamma-HCH	dust	O	O			O	O	O
Murphy Combined Seed Dressing	gamma-HCH, (captan)	dust	O					O	O
Murphy Lawn Pest Killer	carbaryl	spray			O	O			
pbi Bromophos	bromophos	granules	O	O	O	O			O

[1] Information based on manufacturer's instructions
[2] Follow label instructions
[3] Also contains a fungicide (in brackets under 'Active ingredients'):
    prevents damping off and foot and root rots

leaf hoppers	leaf miners	mealy bugs	raspberry beetle	sawfly	scale insects	spider mites	thrips	weevils	whitefly	other pests	EDIBLE PLANTS?	HARVEST INTERVAL
○	○	○	○	○			○	○	○	pea moth, pear midge	yes	1 day
							○		○	[3]	yes	[6]
							○		○		yes	same day
			○	○						pea moth, codling moth	yes	14 days
○	○	○	○		○					ants [3]	yes	14 days
		○	○			○					yes	1 day
	○	○			○	○			○		yes	1 day
○			○						○	pear sucker, soft scale	yes	same day
○							○	○		soft scale	no	n/a
											yes	9 hours
			○						○	beetles	yes	9 hours
○		○	○		○	○			○	[3]	yes	14 days
○	○						○		○	ants, woodlice	yes	2 days
		○	○		○	○			○	[3]	no	n/a
							○	○	○		yes	1 day
											yes	1 day
○		○				○	○		○		yes	1 day
○							○		○		yes	1 day
○							○		○		yes	1 day
○		○				○	○		○		yes	1 day

woodlice	other pests	EDIBLE PLANTS?	HARVEST INTERVAL
○		yes	7 days
	springtails	yes	[2]
	caterpillars, flea beetles, onion fly	yes	7 days
○		yes	7 days
○	ants, earwigs	yes	14 days
	flea beetles [3]	seeds only	n/a
	earthworms, ants	no	n/a
	onion fly	yes	7 days

CONTROL OF PESTICIDES REGULATIONS

Everyone who uses pesticides, even in gardens, must abide by these regulations. In particular you must:

■ Only use products approved for amateur use

■ Not make your own pesticides; this includes making your own lawnsand to kill moss or using washing up liquid to kill aphids for example

■ Take reasonable precautions to safeguard the health of other people, pets, wildlife, plants and the environment – and particularly to avoid water pollution.

GARDEN FUNGICIDES

BRAND NAME	ACTIVE INGREDIENTS	TYPE [1]	FORM	DISEASES CONTROLLED[2]	
				blackspot	blight
Armillatox	cresylic acid	P	spray	○	
Bio Friendly Pest & Disease Duster	sulphur, (derris)	P	dust		
Bio Multirose	triforine, sulphur, (permethrin)	PS	spray	○	
Boots Garden Fungicide	carbendazim	S	spray	○	
ICI Benlate	benomyl	S	spray	○	
ICI Nimrod-T	bupirimate, triforine	S	spray	○	
ICI Roseclear	bupirimate, triforine, (pirimicarb)	S	spray	○	
May & Baker Systemic Fungicide Liquid	thiophanate-methyl	S	spray	○	
Murphy Pest & Disease Smoke	tecnazene, (gamma-HCH)	P	smoke		
Murphy Systemic Action Fungicide	carbendazim	S	spray	○	
Murphy Traditional Copper Fungicide	copper oxychloride	P	spray		○
Murphy Tumbleblite	propiconazole	S	spray	○	
Murphy Zap Cap Combined Insecticide & Fungicide	fenarimol, (permethrin)	PS	ready to use	○	
Murphy Zap Cap Systemic Fungicide	carbendazim	S	ready to use		
pbi Dithane 945	mancozeb	P	spray	○	○
pbi Hexyl	thiram, (gamma-HCH, derris)	P	spray	○	
pbi Supercarb	carbendazim, activator	S	spray	○	
pbi Systhane	myclobutanil	S	spray	○	
Phostrogen Safer's Garden Fungicide	sulphur, fatty acids	P	ready to use	○	
Secto Rose and Flower Spray	thiram (dimethoate, gamma-HCH)	P	ready to use	○	○
Spraydex General Purpose Fungicide	copper sulphate, ammonium hydroxide	P	ready to use	○	○
Vitax Bordeaux Mixture [7]	copper sulphate	P	powder		○
Vitax Green Sulphur [7]	yellow sulphur	P	dust		
Vitax Yellow Sulphur [7]	sulphur	P	dust		

[1] P=preventive; S=systemic
[2] Information based on manufacturer's instructions. Do not use garden fungicides for purposes other than those stated on the label
[3] Also contains insecticide(s) (in brackets under 'Active ingredients'). See Garden Insecticides Table
[4] Roses only   [5] 14 days for lettuce

WEEDKILLERS

WEED PREVENTERS

Arable & Bulb No Weed (propachlor) will prevent weeds amongst vegetables or ornamentals for up to eight weeks. Vitax Casoron G4 (dichlobenil) will prevent weed seeds from germinating for up to a year and at a high application rate will also prevent perennials from emerging. Murphy Weedex (simazine) will prevent annual weeds germinating for a year.

TOTAL WEEDKILLERS

ICI Weedol (paraquat, diquat) will burn off the top growth of all weeds but will not kill the roots. Murphy Tumbleweed (glyphosate) and Monsanto Greenscape (glyphosate) will kill the roots of most perennial weeds, including grasses. Areas treated with these weedkillers can be sown or planted within weeks. If you need to tame a wilderness other options include sodium chlorate (many different brands) and Dax Root Out (ammonium sulphamate), but you must wait at least six months or six to eight weeks respectively before sowing or planting.

PROBLEM WEEDKILLERS

These contain hormone weedkillers and will kill broadleaved weeds, but not grasses. Some also claim to control tough or woody weeds, like brambles. They can be used for clearing overgrown areas, maintaining a weed-free strip along a fence or hedge or for spot treating difficult weeds. Read the label before buying to make sure they are suitable. Choose from:
■ Boots Nettle and Bramble Killer (dicamba, dichlorprop, MCPA)
■ May & Baker Ground Clear (dicamba, dichlorprop, MCPA)
■ Murphy Problem Weeds Killer (amitrole, MCPA)
■ Vitax (Synchemicals) New Formula SBK Brushwood Killer (2,4-D, dichlorprop, MCPA).

PATH AND LAWN WEEDKILLERS

We have not listed these – there are many brands, but all make similar claims. See Best Buys on page 137.

GRASS KILLERS

These will kill couch and some other grasses but not broadleaved weeds. Use May & Baker Weedout (alloxydim-sodium) for couch amongst garden plants, Vitax (Synchemicals) Couch and Grass Killer (dalapon) for couch and grasses on vacant land or amongst perennial vegetables or soft fruit.

SPOT WEEDERS

These are either wiped or sprayed on to individual weeds on paths, or amongst garden plants. Choose from:
■ Bio Weed Pencil (2,4-D, mecoprop)
■ Boots Kill a Weed Spot Weeder (2,4-D, dichlorprop, mecoprop)
■ Elliot Pocket Touchweeder (2,4-D, 2,3,6-TBA)
■ Monsanto Greenscape Ready to Use (glyphosate)
■ Murphy Tumbleweed Gel (glyphosate)
■ Murphy Tumbleweed Ready to Use Spray (glyphosate)

									EDIBLE PLANTS?	HARVEST INTERVAL
downy mildew	lawn diseases	leaf spots	grey mould	peach leaf curl	powdery mildew	rust	scab	other diseases		
								clubroot, honey fungus	no	n/a
					○			storage rots [3]	yes	1 day
					○[4]			[3]	no	n/a
○	○	○			○		○	raspberry cane spot, spur blight	yes	7 days [5]
○	○	○			○		○	blossom wilt, seedling diseases [6]	yes	same day
					○	○	○		fruit only	7 days
					○[4]	○[4]		[3]	no	n/a
○	○	○			○		○	anthracnose, clubroot [6]	yes [7]	same day
			○					[3]	yes	2 days
		○	○		○		○	cane spot, leaf mould	yes [7]	same day
			○	○	○			bacterial canker, cane spot, damping off, foot rot	yes [7]	same day
			○	○					no	n/a
					○			[3]	fruit only	14 days
	○	○	○						yes	same day
○	○		○			○	○	leaf mould	yes [7]	7 days [8]
○						○	○	leaf mould [3]	yes	14 days
○	○	○			○			anthracnose, big bud, canker, clubroot [6]	yes	same day [5]
					○[4]	○[4]			roses only	n/a
	○				○	○			yes	1 day
					○			[3]	no	n/a
					○		○	cane spot	yes	1 day
	○		○		○			leaf mould, bacterial canker	yes	same day
					○				yes	same day
					○				yes	same day

[6] Cane spot and spur blight on cane fruit; leaf mould, stem rot and wilt on tomatoes; storage diseases of bulbs, corms and tubers
[7] Fruit and vegetables as specified on leaflet inside packet
[8] Lettuces 21 days
[9] May also be available under 'Synchemicals' brand name

USING GARDEN CHEMICALS SAFELY

■ Read the label *before* you buy a pesticide and make sure it is suitable. Is it recommended for the pest or disease you want to control and in the part of the garden in which you want to use it? Are any of your plants likely to be damaged by it?

■ Read the label every time you use a pesticide. Make sure that you make up the correct quantity of a spray and apply it to the correct area. Note any other precautions.

■ When treating edible plants, observe the harvest interval stated on the label.

■ Store the pesticide in its original container. Keep it out of reach of children, preferably in a locked garden shed or garage, not in the house.

■ Wash watering cans and sprayers thoroughly after use, since even small residues of weedkillers can harm sensitive garden plants.

■ Wash your hands after using garden chemicals. It is also a good idea to wear rubber gloves when handling the concentrates.

■ Wash your hands and face immediately if you accidentally splash concentrated pesticides on them. Take particular care with products bearing the black cross and the words 'Harmful' or 'Irritant'.

■ If you make up too much, dispose of it by spraying it on to an unused part of the garden to allow it to disperse safely. Do not empty it into drains or near ponds and water courses.

OLD GARDEN CHEMICALS

Do not keep old chemicals year after year. Apart from becoming less effective once they have been opened, their use may now be illegal. A few chemicals have been withdrawn – weedkillers containing ioxynil and chlordane wormkillers, for example. The labels on others have been changed, so the uses and precautions may be out of date.

Do not use pesticides if the labels have been lost or have become illegible.

DISPOSING OF OLD CHEMICALS

Small quantities of pesticides should be put in the dustbin. Close the lid firmly and wrap glass bottles in newspaper. If you have larger quantities contact the Waste Disposal Department of your local council. They may be able to arrange collection of large quantities or advise you where to take chemicals.

GARDEN INSECTICIDES AND FUNGICIDES – GUIDE TO INGREDIENTS

INSECTICIDES

ACTIVE INGREDIENT	BRAND NAMES
bacillus thuringiensis	Dipel
bioallethrin	Boots Kill-a-Bug Spray Gun, Spraydex Greenfly Killer
bromophos	pbi Bromophos
carbaryl	Boots Garden Insect Powder, Murphy Lawn Pest Killer
derris	Bio Friendly Insect Spray, Bio Friendly Pest & Disease Duster, Boots Garden Insect Powder, Doff Derris Dust, Fellside Green Vegetable Insecticide, ICI Derris Dust, Murphy Derris Dust, pbi Hexyl, pbi Liquid Derris, Vitax Derris Dust
dimethoate	Bio Long-Last, Boots Greenfly & Blackfly Killer, Doff Systemic Insecticide, Secto Garden Powder, Secto Rose and Flower Spray
fatty acids	Bio Friendly Pest Pistol, Phostrogen Safer's Fruit & Vegetable Insecticide, Phostrogen Safer's Rose & Flower Insecticide
fenitrothion	Doff Garden Insect Powder, pbi Fenitrothion
gamma-HCH	Murphy Combined Seed Dressing, Murphy Gamma-BHC Dust, Murphy Pest & Disease Smokes, pbi Hexyl, Secto Greenfly & Garden Insect Spray, Secto Garden Powder, Secto Rose & Flower Spray
heptenophos	Murphy Tumblebug, Murphy Systemic Action Insecticide
malathion	Bio Crop Saver, Murphy Liquid Malathion, Murphy Malathion Dust, pbi Malathion Greenfly Killer
permethrin	Bio Crop Saver, Bio Long-Last, Bio Multirose, Bio Sprayday, Boots Caterpillar & Whitefly Killer, Boots Kill-a-Bug Spray Gun, ICI Fumite Whitefly Greenhouse Insecticide, ICI Picket, Murphy Permethrin Whitefly Smokes, Murphy Systemic Action Insecticide, Murphy Tumblebug, Murphy Zap Cap Combined Insecticide & Fungicide, Murphy Zap Cap General Insecticide, Spraydex Greenfly Killer
phoxim	Fisons Soil Pest Killer
pirimicarb	ICI Rapid Aerosol, ICI Rapid Greenfly Killer, ICI Roseclear
pirimiphos-methyl	ICI Fumite General Purpose Greenhouse Insecticide, ICI Sybol Aerosol, ICI Sybol Soil Pest Killer, ICI Sybol
pyrethrins	Rentokil Blackfly & Greenfly Killer, Secto Greenhouse & Garden Insect Spray
pyrethrum	Doff Fruit & Vegetable Insecticide Spray, Doff Rose & Flower Insecticide Spray, Fellside Green Fruit & Vegetable Insecticide Spray, Fellside Green Rose & Flower Insect Spray, Fisons Natures Answer to Insect Pests, ICI Bug Gun for Fruit & Vegetables, ICI Bug Gun for Roses & Flowers, Rentokil Greenhouse & Garden Insect Killer, Spraydex Greenfly Killer, Vitax Py Garden & Household Insect Killer, Vitax Py Garden Insecticide, Vitax Py Spray Garden Insecticide, Vitax Py Spray Garden Insect Killer
quassia	Bio Friendly Insect Spray
resmethrin	Rentokil Greenhouse & Garden Insect Killer

FUNGICIDES

ACTIVE INGREDIENT	BRAND NAMES
benomyl	ICI Benlate
bupirimate	ICI Nimrod-T, ICI Roseclear
captan	Murphy Combined Seed Dressing
carbendazim	Boots Garden Fungicide, Murphy Systemic Action Fungicide, Murphy Zap Cap Systemic Fungicide, pbi Supercarb
copper	Murphy Traditional Copper Fungicide, Spraydex General Purpose Fungicide, Vitax Bordeaux Mixture
cresylic acid	Armillatox
fenarimol	Murphy Zap Cap Combined Insecticide & Fungicide
mancozeb	pbi Dithane 945
myclobutanil	pbi Systhane
propiconazole	Murphy Tumbleblite
sulphur	Bio Friendly Pest & Disease Duster, Phostrogen Safer's Garden Fungicide, Bio Multirose, Vitax Green Sulphur, Vitax Yellow Sulphur
tecnazine	Murphy Pest & Disease Smokes
thiophanate-methyl	May & Baker Systemic Fungicide Liquid
thiram	pbi Hexyl, Secto Garden Powder, Secto Rose & Flower Spray
triforine	Bio Multirose, ICI Nimrod-T, ICI Roseclear

BEST BUYS

The following garden chemicals have done well in *Gardening from Which?* trials.

INSECTICIDES

Aphids ICI Rapid Greenfly Killer (kills aphids but spares bees, ladybirds and lacewings); Bio Long-Last. None of the organic insecticides performed as well, but Vitax Py Garden Insecticide was the best of these.

Caterpillars ICI Picket; ICI Sybol; Murphy Tumblebug.

Spider mites ICI Sybol; Bio Long-Last.

Whitefly ICI Bug Gun (expensive but ready to use); ICI Picket; Murphy Tumblebug.

Soil Pests Fisons Soil Pests Killer.

FUNGICIDES

Damping off Murphy Traditional Copper Fungicide.

Blackspot only pbi Dithane 945.

Blackspot and mildew ICI Nimrod-T.

Rust on roses only pbi Systhane.

Rust on other ornamentals Murphy Tumbleblite.

SLUG KILLERS

ICI Mini Slug Pellets; pbi Slug Mini Pellets. Fertosan is worth considering as an alternative to pellets.

WEEDKILLERS

Lawn weeds Boots Lawn Weedkiller (from larger Boots stores); **(with fertiliser)** Boots Lawn Weed and Feed (from larger Boots stores); May & Baker Supergreen and Weed.

Lawn weeds and moss May & Baker Supergreen Weed, Feed and Mosskiller (small lawns); Fisons Evergreen Extra (for large lawns); ICI Grasshopper (expensive but convenient on small lawns).

Lawn spot weeders Elliot Pocket Touchweeder (large rosette weeds); Spraydex Lawn Spot Weeder (small creeping weeds).

Mosskillers Fisons Mosskil Extra; J Arthur Bowers Mosskiller.

Path weeds Boots Long-Lasting Weedkiller (from larger Boots stores); Arable & Bulb Deeweed.

Problem weeds Murphy Tumbleweed; Vitax New Formula SBK Brushwood Killer is worth considering for woody weeds.

Weed preventers Vitax Casoron G4; Murphy Weedex for established shrubs and fruit bushes.

GARDENING FROM WHICH?

Gardening from Which? regularly carries out impartial trials of garden products and gardening techniques. To keep right up to date with the best information, take out a subscription. For three months' free trial, write to *Gardening from Which?*, Consumers' Association, Freepost, Hertford X, SG14 1YB for an application form.

SAFEGUARDING PETS AND WILDLIFE

■ Many garden chemicals can harm fish and other pond creatures. Keep them well away from ponds if this is advised on the label.

■ Keep pets like rabbits, guinea pigs and tortoises off treated lawns for a day or two, or at least until the weedkiller has dried.

■ Spray insecticides in the evening when bees are not active and try not to spray plants in flower.

■ Choose a still day so that pesticides do not drift on to other garden plants.

■ Slug pellets are coloured blue and contain an animal repellent, but as a further precaution do not leave packets or large heaps of pellets where pets or wild animals have access to them. Scatter them thinly.

■ Do not use soil insecticides indiscriminately – they can harm beneficial insects.

THE FIRST LINE OF DEFENCE

Although you can wait until problems occur before going out to buy the appropriate pesticide, fungicide or weedkiller, it is a good idea to keep a few chemicals to hand, to tackle common problems. Aim to buy just enough to last one season and replace next year. Do not accumulate lots of old chemicals. We suggest the following:

General Insecticide Bio Long-Last or Murphy Tumblebug.
Aphid Killer ICI Rapid Greenfly Killer.
Fungicide Choose either pbi Dithane 945 (for fruit, vegetables and ornamentals) or Murphy Tumbleblite (for ornamentals only). If you have a lot of roses you could include pbi Systhane for rust and ICI Nimrod-T for blackspot and mildew prevention.
Spot weedkiller Elliot Pocket Touchweeder or Spraydex Lawn Spot Weeder (for lawns); Murphy Tumbleweed (elsewhere in garden).
Slug killer ICI Mini Slug Pellets.

APPLICATION EQUIPMENT

INSECTICIDES AND FUNGICIDES

If you want to treat only small plants in a greenhouse, for example, a ready-to-use spray will be the most convenient (but expensive) option. A small hand pump sprayer that you refill by diluting the concentrated chemical will work out cheaper.

For spraying large areas, or large plants, a garden sprayer is indispensable. In *Gardening from Which?* trials, the Best Buy proved to be Hozelock Killaspray Courier 8. Hozelock Killaspray 8 which has an external pump, making it more convenient for taller gardeners, is worth considering.

WEEDKILLERS

For lawns Use a watering can, fitted with a fine rose rather than a sprayer or, better still, an ICI Dribble Bar or a Plysu Spray Head. If possible keep a watering can specifically for weedkillers. Otherwise wash the can out very thoroughly after applying a weedkiller and again before using it to water garden plants.

For treating larger lawns, consider the Walkover sprayer for liquid treatments or a lawn spreader such as the Wolf Multichange Lawn Spreader WE-M for applying lawnsand or granular lawn fertilisers and weedkillers.

For weeding between plants
Use a watering can fitted with a dribble bar (ICI Dribble Bar, for example) so that weedkiller is not splashed on to garden plants. Alternatively, use a garden sprayer fitted with a spray hood (Hozelock Weedkiller Kit, for example). It is important to set the spray nozzle to produce a coarse spray to prevent fine droplets drifting on to garden plants and to place the hood over the weeds to be killed before pressing the trigger.

APPLYING WEEDKILLERS

When using weedkillers on lawns, paths or when clearing ground, it is important to use the correct application rate. Make up the amount of solution in a watering can or sprayer. This will treat a given area of ground. Use string or garden canes to mark out strips within this area and apply the weedkiller as evenly as you can. The best method is to apply half the amount walking in one direction and the rest by walking at right-angles to the original direction. Practice first using a can of plain water to help you judge walking speed.

With granular weedkillers, divide the area into strips one metre (or one yard wide). Mark out each strip into squares. Weigh the recommended dose per square metre (or sq yd) into a plastic cup. Mark the level in the cap and use this to measure the dose for each square metre (or sq yd). Walk along each strip applying the measured dose evenly to each square as you go.

Always choose a still day when rain is not forecast for at least 24 hours.

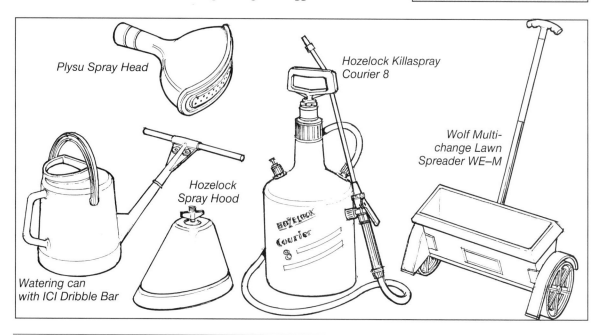

Plysu Spray Head

Hozelock Killaspray Courier 8

Wolf Multi-change Lawn Spreader WE–M

Hozelock Spray Hood

Watering can with ICI Dribble Bar

NON-CHEMICAL PEST CONTROLS

CROP COVERS

If put in place well before flying pests appear, crop covers should prevent or greatly reduce damage. Several different materials are available:
■ non-woven polypropylene 'fleece' (Agryl P.17, for example)
■ perforated polythene (Gro-Cover, for example)
■ fine netting (Enviromesh or Papronet, for example)
Suppliers Fleece from garden centres; Agriframes; Hydrocut; and several other mail order suppliers. Gro-Cover from Newbrook. Netting from Agralan (Enviromesh); Direct Wire Ties (Papronet).

YELLOW STICKY TRAPS

These will trap greenhouse pests like whitefly, fungus flies and other flying pests. But they may also trap some beneficial insects. They should last one season unless large numbers of whitefly are present.
Suppliers Bio Friendly from garden centres; Agralan; Oecos.

GREASE BANDS

These prevent winter moths climbing fruit trees.
Suppliers Vitax Fruit Tree Grease, pbi Boltac Grease Bands from garden centres.

CABBAGE COLLARS

These protect brassica plants from attacks by cabbage root fly.
Suppliers Fyba from garden centres.

CODLING MOTH TRAPS

Male moths are attracted by a pheromone to a sticky trap. One trap should protect up to five trees for a season.
Suppliers Agralan; Oecos.

BIOLOGICAL CONTROLS

Parasites or predators that control greenhouse pests.

Suppliers Aphid and mealy bug controls from Applied Horticulture; English Woodlands; Natural Pest Control. Spider mite and whitefly controls from Applied Horticulture; Bio Bugs; Chase; English Woodlands; HDRA; Natural Pest Control.

BACILLUS THURINGIENSIS

A bacterium that kills only caterpillars. Sold as Dipel.
Suppliers Chase; Dig 'n' Delve; English Woodlands; HDRA.

NON-DRYING GLUE

For vine weevil protection. Not yet tested by *Gardening from Which?*
Suppliers Agralan; Oecos.

SUPPLIERS' ADDRESSES

You may be able to obtain some of the non-chemical controls from DIY stores and garden centres, but most are available only by mail order.

GENERAL SUPPLIERS

These list many of the non-chemical controls in their catalogues:

Chase Organics (GB) Ltd, Coombelands House, Coombelands Lane, Addlestone, Surrey KT15 1HY
Tel: Chertsey (0932) 858511

Dig 'n' Delve Organics, Fen Road, Blo' Norton, Diss, Norfolk IP22 2JH.
Tel: Diss (0379) 898377

(HDRA) Henry Doubleday Research Association, National Centre for Organic Gardening, Ryton-on-Dunsmore, Coventry, West Midlands CV8 3LG
Tel: Coventry (0203) 303517

SPECIALIST SUPPLIERS

Agralan, The Old Brick Yard, Ashton Keynes, Swindon, Wiltshire SN6 6QR
Tel: Cirencester (0285) 860015

Agriframes Ltd, Charlwoods Road, East Grinstead, West Sussex RH19 2HG
Tel: East Grinstead (0342) 328644

Applied Horticulture, Toddington Lane, Littlehampton, West Sussex BN17 7PP
Tel: Littlehampton (0903) 721591

BCP Ltd, Bio Bugs, Acorn Nurseries, Chapel Lane, West Wittering, Chichester, West Sussex PO20 8QG

Direct Wire Ties Ltd, Wyke Works, Hedon Road, Hull, Humberside HU9 5NL
Tel: Hull (0482) 712630

English Woodlands Ltd. Hoyle Depot, Graffham, Petworth, West Sussex GU28 0LR
Tel: Graffham (07986) 574

Hydrocut Ltd, Burkitts Lane, Sudbury, Suffolk CO10 6HB
Tel: Sudbury (0787) 71171

Natural Pest Control Ltd, Yapton Road, Barnham, Bognor Regis, West Sussex PO22 0BQ
Tel: Yapton (0243) 553250

Newbrook Agricultural Products Ltd, Hillside Mill, Swaffham Bulbeck, Cambridge CB5 0LU
Tel: Cambridge (0223) 811215

Oecos, Daisy Distribution, PO Box 595, Adstock, Buckinghamshire MK18 2RE
Tel: 029-671 3838

INDEX

Page references for main entries are set in **bold**; entries with illustrations are indicated in *italics*.